The Freedom Of Being

Forget the opinions of others and release your authentic self.

By Steven Sisler

The Freedom of Being; Forget the opinions of others and release your authentic self.

Published by: Focus Media Group, a division of Sisler Solutions, LLC.
Focusbooks.org

ISBN 978-1506090825

Written by: Steven M. Sisler

"Change the way you look at things, and the things you look at change." —Wayne Dyer

Acknowledgments

My dear friend Michael Hodge: thank you for your unconventional clarity and your most precious friendship. Your insights and contribution to this work has been invaluable. Thank you for your tireless help with the flow although I take full responsibility for any errors all my highly compliant friends may soon find.

It seems impossible to catch them all even after six books. It's our humanness that makes us all feel the need to hide our flaws in order to feel acceptable in their world. Mike, you are a rare find, the best friend one could ever hope to have, and my life is better for knowing you.

Thank you Ravindra B. for your painstaking edit. Your part in the overall manuscript has been inestimable.

Just wow.

Contents

1. The Essential Need to Be 1
2. The Eros Prison of Expectation 27
3. Measuring Down Within the Eros Prison 38
4. Heart Moves and the Self 55
5. Religious Validation and its Effect on Performance and the Self 69
6. Our Need for Self-Validation 93
7. The Power of Thought Reform and the Self 124
8. Everyone Loved Jesus 135
9. Lateral Thinking 155
10. The Five Ethical Platforms and the Self 183
11. The Rules of Disgust and Contamination Psychology 191
12. The Power of Parenting, Personality, and the Self 206
13. Our Insatiable Need for a Satan 216
14. Satan and the Old Testament 236
15. Satan and the New Testament 248
16. The Power of Self-Worth 258
17. The Shame Game 269
18. Our Preoccupation with Shadows 286
19. Living Without Wax 293
20. What Do We Do Now? 297

About Steven Sisler 303

1

The Essential Need to Be

Oscar Fingal O'Flahertie Wills Wilde was an Irish playwright, author, and poet. Known for his satirical wit and a variety of adages, he became one of the most successful playwrights of the late Victorian era in London, and one of the greatest celebrities of his day.

Wilde once said, "Be yourself, because everyone else is already taken."[1] This phrase probably speaks to all of us on some level. If you take a moment to think about it, you'll come away wishing it were that easy, but we all know it isn't. It is our *differences* that drive us.

I want to begin this chapter with a few questions, and then I would like to explore some possible answers. The questions are simple, yet profound. The first question I want to propose is how comfortable are you with yourself? And second, do you see yourself as a human-being content with who you are right now, or are you more like a human-doing attempting to reestablish yourself in the your current world?

You might be pondering the difference between the two or maybe why I am asking the questions at all.

It's a simple answer really, and although it carries with it some profound implications, I believe the differences between *doing* and *being* in relationship to our *being* can be summed up in one word: contentment.

The dissimilarity between a human-*being* and a human-*doing* is, literally, an intense personal satisfaction that reaches a level of serenity. I like to say it this way: human beings are content—sat-

1) Although often attributed to Wilde, most authorities do not believe he was the author of this.

isfied with *who* they are, *as* they are. Human-beings have no illusions about whether or not they are loved by God—if one exists.

Human-doings, on the other hand, are not in this same position—they can only *long* for it.

Usually unsatisfied with the way they *feel* about themselves inside, they live a life of constant self-help and radical insecurity masked by the walls of an Eros prison of performance.

Thought Invader: Human-doings are performers whereas human-beings are explorers.

Human-beings are distinctive in that they are free to *explore* their talents, their spirituality, their intelligence, and many other areas of their *being*—they're fluid. They unfold over time without the unreasonably hard lines and inconvenient boundaries we sometimes place on ourselves through religious tradition, insecurity, and need-based relationship experiments.

On the other hand, human-doings are fastened to life's stage as static performers—overly concerned about others opinions about who they are, what they do, or their fear of displeasing the gods. They lack the fluidity and freedom to explore the boundaries of who they are in their *present* condition because they don't see themselves as good enough.[2] They're in a prison—the Eros prison.[3]

Before we discover the nuances surrounding the Eros prison, I want to define contentment in a way that might surprise you. Contentment is when one is completely comfortable to *know nothing*, *do nothing*, and to be *known for* absolutely *nothing*.

It's what I call the death that counts. I learned this idea from an old friend and mentor Doug[4] in the nineties—he probably doesn't know the extent his words impacted my *being* or how right

2) Many who struggle with being are performance-based doers who rely on others' praises and strokes in order to gain personal or career momentum. Theirs is a static universe held together by particular rules and expectations.

3) The Eros prison is a personal prison designed to preserve what we believe about ourselves, no matter if it is right or wrong or true or false. Fundamentally fueled by religion and religious mindsets, the Eros prison keeps people captive to rules, rituals, rites, and false expectations associated with gods and supposed goodness, which in turn produce more performance rituals.

4) Doug Dyke is a man that greatly influenced my life in the mid-90s. His philosophies were instrumental in rearranging the way I looked at the fundamentals of religion and main line biblical concepts. Some ideas have changed and been redeveloped since that time, but my love for Doug always remains the same.

he was when he spoke them.

It's when we finally have that long awaited funeral for everything that once defined us (or *presently* defines us) and made us feel important, useful, or worthy of existence or being loved. It's an intentional *suicide* of the soul-self that wore out its welcome for the last time. Suicides, homicides, pesticides, and genocides, all have one thing in common—they're all associated with killing and death.

The common thread in all these terms is what I call the "cide" effect. This is why decision-making is really about *deciding* (de-*cide-ing*) or *killing off* the objects and stuffs in our lives that are harmful, hateful, hideous, and hindering. Decisions are meant to *do away with* the harmful belongings while harnessing the health.

The death that counts is a decision. It's when we de-cide (undoing what causes potentially deadly outcomes) to *stop* the madness that accompanies competitive living, trumping, and both public and private performance initiatives aimed at others, ourselves and our perception of God. It's a surrendering to the world at large and a "giving up" on having to *prove* we matter.

Thought Invader: When one dies *the death that counts*, no longer do the distinctive characteristics of our performances within the arenas of work, family, or our religious community indicate our value or our right to be.

It's when we sit up and say our final goodbyes to our self-image and the illusions we've created around this image in an attempt to impress others and ourselves and be okay with ourselves. Whether it is our job or the college degree we worked so hard to get or our new exciting girlfriend or boyfriend, whatever worth we've been attaching to these personal trophies is now and forever deceased—intentionally buried by the safe-self overseeing the death that counts.

It's when we finally close the chapter on everything that once shaped our identity and brought definition, meaning, and clarity to our lives: what we do, what we imagine others think about what we do, our titles, our gifts, our talents—all of it. All is buried beneath the need to appear whole and sophisticated (from sophist)[5] among our peers.

Contentment is all about letting go of the need to perform or to be recognized *for* that performance. It's taking the Nest-Tea plunge into the beauty of *who* we are *as* we are in this present moment while nobody is paying attention to it and then caring less if they do.

That's all it is. I know it's a tall order. But being utterly content with *who* we are, *where* we are, *as* we are, and *why* we are, with no need to perform for God or others or to extrapolate other people's opinions about something we might have accomplished, is life altering.

That's what being content is all about. No longer are we *running* the race, but rather we are *watching* it and enjoying it—it's when we are wise observers rather than needy performers. It's about not having to win or prove anything to anyone ever again. And this includes not having to prove things to ourselves.

Thought Invader: The death that counts allows us to live peaceably with others rather than arduously living *for* others and their accolades or in competition with others.

For instance, when we share our life *with* our partners, our coworkers, or our friends rather than *receiving* our life *from* these relationships, amazing things happen. A sense of absolute satisfaction is created between *us* and our true *authentic*-self. No facades. No masks. No competition. It's the beauty of *being* and it has no strings attached to it—none. Does this sound like you? I didn't think so.

This personal place of satisfaction does not in any way mean we are lazy or without a sense of personal responsibility or urgency; it's more like believing we are *good* enough—*worthy* enough—*as we are* instead of focusing our attention on what we believe we *should be* based upon the things we are convinced others expect.

Contentment is about being comfortable with ourselves in the

5) According to Robert A. Krupp in his book "Golden Tongue and Iron Will," the teachers of rhetoric were considered the pride of every major city in the Roman Empire. After the religious specialists began to take root within the Roman culture and its systems, the philosophers and leaders of the early Christian movement, known today as The Early Church Fathers, began to regulate and professionalize the movement into an established system with all its parts and perks (Not to be confused with Paul's idea of body parts and human worth).

sight of whatever we call God—in high spirits in relationship to our present-*self* and our associations. Although many times our present circumstances can be grueling or out of our control, we do not believe these environments are a direct expression or a reflection of who we are as a living soul. They are nothing more than conditional steps to a greater plateau of being.

Living in this most beautiful place means we understand the distinction between *who* we are as an individual entity and *where* we are in the space-time continuum. We understand the fluidity of movement between our surroundings and us—we recognize and appreciate that circumstances are always changing.

In other words, I know I'm worthy and wonderful even though I'm *not* currently working the job I initially wanted. Or I still believe in myself even though you don't believe in me. And because I understand the difference between the two, I can afford to wait until the better job opens up or until an opportunity arises that I can boldly take hold of in faith that it will work out for me. I can also wait until you figure out what you want in regards to a relationship—you not believing in me is your issue.

It's this mindset that enables me to make better and lasting decisions about my own work, relationships, destiny, and purpose. It's the reason why I will better understand my purpose as opposed to a life of searching for it in comparative ways.

Thought Invader: When you live in contentment, your purpose finds you.

You might be tempted to think I'm anti self-improvement at this point, but that would be a mistake. It's not really a question of *if* we want to make improvements; the question is more about *why* we believe we *need* to make them—why we feel desperate to make them. Sure, we all make steady improvements of one kind or another throughout our life; that's normal as it's a part of living and growing.

But I'm talking about impulsive, irrepressible, and unnecessary improvements; when we believe the lie that says we're not good enough and we secretly preoccupy ourselves with thoughts of how we can modify ourselves to better fit the opinions of others or the god we think we're displeasing—when we have an unhealthy interest in who we are *not* and feel we must change it right now or suffer the supposed consequences.

For instance, let's say I want to make a few improvements to my physical body because I want to be in better health, or I want to be more conscientious regarding my food intake or have more energy to do the things I really enjoy, then by all means we should go for it! But if our innate desire to improve our *self* is because we don't believe we are *lovable* or *worthy* as we are—as our true-self, we will only be rearranging the deck chairs on our emotional Titanic.

Unfortunately, this manner of thinking doesn't fix what's wrong with us. It fundamentally ends up being another stay of emotional execution—a short-term drug that lasts only until I'm reminded of how off the mark I am. Whether it's our human relationships or our religion, both will inadvertently produce the need to *perform* if we don't harness our true worth and believe in *it* first.

Thought Invader: When our happiness merely depends on favorable circumstances, our results are short lived.

It's for this reason that we must make a clear distinction between what we believe we *want* and what we believe we *need*. Needs are instinctively insatiable—they're a black hole in our space-time that eventually extorts all our natural ambition and self-respect by sucking it into itself.

An Insatiable Need Machine

Beliefs such as "I need to be recognized," or "I need to be promoted," or "I need to be seen driving a nicer car," or "I need to lead a home group at my church," etc., are all products of the Eros prison belief system. There's a huge difference between *want* and *need*, and it's about five million miles wide.

For instance, if I *want* a great wife to share life with, I may put appropriate energy into making sure I look in the right places, do my homework, or make suitable choices for myself. I may find a great wife, in due time, because I've been appropriately cautious, optimistic, and authentic in my approach to women.

I'm respectful, helpful, careful, and delightful as I am at peace with who I am in general and how I believe they view and understand me. I'm not suspicious or convoluted. I'm not overly concerned about my appearance, talents, or my place in the universe. I can be altogether open and honest about myself without fear of rejection or ridicule. I embrace my perceived weaknesses and meet them with a kiss.

Conversely, if I believe I *need* a wife, I may settle for regrettable short cuts or pretend I'm someone or something I'm not and end up making incompetent decisions that reflect my *unworthiness* and fear of failure. Eventually, my *inability* to acquire the partner I likely deserve will play into my belief that I am not worthy of such a relationship, and I will settle for less.

This cycle will continue until I stumble upon the realization, or perhaps a faithful friend brings it to my attention. More often than not, many never come to these personal conclusions and thus will continue to suffer the high costs of low expectations throughout most their life.

It is for this reason that need-based relationships can turn out to be a mirage—an illusion. And if you're not prudent or self-correcting, a poorly placed decision made out of *need* can throw you over the event horizon[6] of the black hole of low expectation and unworthiness you created. It will stretch your insides for a million miles until you collapse in on yourself.

Furthermore, it's important to note that wants and needs are part of being human. But we must open the package and separate the socks from the underwear. We have to make clear distinctions between the two in an effort to match the mechanics of our emotional framework.

For instance, sometimes we need a job or perhaps we may be in need of a glass of water—that's different. Natural needs must be met and we all have to work. But needing to change my appearance—again, could be problematic seeing I have had four different hairstyles in the last six months.

Understanding where needs and wants *fit* properly within our lives is generally an *essential* part of personal well-being and satisfaction. Misunderstanding it can be confusing at best and emo-

---

6) Within the theory of general relativity, an event horizon is a boundary in space-time beyond which events cannot affect an outside observer. In layman's terms, it is defined as "the point of no return," i.e., the point at which the gravitational pull becomes so great as to make escape impossible.

tionally terminal at worst. In other words, it's not really an option. Needs and wants are so closely associated with *being* and *doing* that it can be difficult to separate them.

In other words, it's possible to *need* a job while presently experiencing the joy of *being*. On the other hand, if one is busy *doing* instead of simply being, then looking for work can be a full time job in itself and tantamount to eating glass. If you're experiencing excessive turnover within your occupational life, it could be a sign of low self-worth or a dysfunctional approach to being.

Some don't know who they are. They haven't landed their plane in regards to a career. This isn't out of line between the ages of eighteen and thirty, but if you are experiencing poor outcomes and feel like you are not "doing" your passion after age thirty, it could be a sign that you're not tapped into your authentic-self.

If you're not enjoying your humanness in whatever you do and not apologizing for it to those around you who threaten you by appearing nobler or worthier, you may be living within the *need* machine. Because these needs are insatiable, *employment enjoyment* is hard to come by when in this frame of mind.

Living *outside* of the need machine is all about joyfully experiencing the world around you and *within* you without the burden of misplaced expectations on yourself or the need to meet the unreasonable expectations of other people in work and life, especially if their expectations are unwarranted or unreasonable or based upon the misplaced ideas of others.

When we live in this place of contentment of *being*, we no longer need constant affirmation from other people or from the gods we are told we have to serve. We don't need the acceptance of others or quick credit for our accomplishments. Our emotional stomach is full of fine foodstuff. We're well fed, and therefore, we're no longer begging for attention like a starving person in need of a food fix. A good way to measure where you are in regards to wholeheartedness is to do a little experiment.

Next time you are engaged in conversation with a group or a single person, watch yourself. Step out of yourself and watch and see whether you feel threatened by their accomplishments or whether you are tempted to one-up their story or circumstance. Watch and see how you compare what they are wearing to what you are wearing or the words they use in comparison to your own words.

Look to see if you are in a quiet competition with them. Check to see if you're competing for the applause or the blue ribbon that says "#1 smart person," which you mentally award yourself with after the exchange. These are signs of insecurity, low self-worth, and misappropriation of the ego-self.

Experiencing the comfortableness of *Being* while interacting with others is therefore a fundamental part of wholeheartedness—it's the authentic sign that we are wholehearted.[7] This includes being self-aware and comfortable with our true-self through the cultivation of those things that bolster our self-worth.

It includes personal *enlightenment*, which the Buddha described in simple terms as being "*the end of suffering*." It's when we enjoy our life "as is" instead of suffering through it in hopes of a better one. It's enjoying your story rather than opting for a better one (although some stories need to be changed).

Thought Invader: There's nothing supernatural or superhuman about being comfortable with yourself. It may take some time to get there, but once you arrive, you will never leave.

Wisdom from a Skin Horse

In the classic children's book "*The Velveteen Rabbit*," Margery Williams writes profoundly about what she calls *being real*. William Nicholson beautifully illustrates this classic story published in 1922 by Double Day and Company, Inc. (I recommend reading it).

Williams tackles the identity struggles of a few small toys including a stuffed toy rabbit and his search for *real* self-worth. In a short time the rabbit encounters an old skin horse, a patriarchal figure who has lived his best years in the little boy's nursery observing the lives of all the other toys in their own personal identity struggles.

While the little rabbit struggles to find purpose, he eventually

7) At the start of the book Daring Greatly: How the Courage to be Vulnerable Transforms the Way We Live, Love, Parent, and Lead by Dr. Brené Brown, she refers to ten guideposts to wholehearted living. These ten guideposts are cultivating authenticity, cultivating self-compassion, cultivating a resilient spirit, cultivating gratitude and joy, cultivating creativity, cultivating play and rest, cultivating calm and still, cultivating meaningful work, and cultivating laughter, song, and dance.

asks the skin horse if he understands what the term *real* actually means.

The Velveteen rabbit's question is insightful seeing that most people find their worth in what they *do* as opposed to who they *are*. In this beautiful story, we find the same dynamics taking place within a small group of nursery toys and discover how the wisdom of the skin horse helps guide the little rabbit into a place of self-acceptance and then ultimately into becoming a *real* rabbit.

Early in the story the rabbit encounters two toys that attempt to find fault with him in somewhat indirect ways. Williams' insight into this human phenomenon is profoundly accurate. Although their issues stem from their own low self-worth, they are experts at projecting it on others.

For instance, the more mechanical toys find hope and worth in their superiority and what they believe to be superior internal modernistic ways, while the toy boat boasts of his exterior rigging apparatus in an attempt to belittle what he believes to be the rabbit's *plain* exterior, out of fear it might be better than his.

I ran into this myself when I was a child; in an effort to wow a friend with a Christmas or birthday gift, I would be inadvertently thrust into a competitive gift-race where I would ultimately lose.

The weaker toys (toys with low self-esteem) discover new ways to stifle the potential threats to their own personal worth by pointing out hypothetical setbacks in the rabbit. Timothy the jointed wooden lion doesn't miss out on the competition and boasts about his being made by the local disabled soldiers, in his pathetic attempt at self-importance and therefore claims significant connections with the local governments.

In light of these superficial traits exhibited by the group of unwelcoming toys, the rabbit then begins a process of in-looking and self-sabotage while searching for his own significance now grossly misplaced by the insatiable needs in the other toys. This instilling of uncertainties by those with low self-worth concerning the *worthiness* of the rabbit causes him to question his own *being*, thus creating an unsafe-self.

Like Timothy the jointed wooden lion, we also may lay claim to make-believe notions of grandeur in an attempt to mask what we believe to be a more or less plain self. Our significance, therefore, does not rest on who we are, but on what others *think* we are. More importantly, it may rest on what we believe others *expect* us to be. Either way, when our unhealthy interest in what others think we think persists, it works against us in significant ways.

Like the mechanical toys, we too have the potential to delve into performance-driven behaviors, modernistic ideologies, or the hyper focus on certain accomplishments in an attempt to shed the shell of our perceived boring human condition. This is a most unwise and destructible path. When we focus on our exteriors we miss the most important place of all . . . the interior *self*.

The Interior Self

The value of anything is always internal, not external. This is the reason why we paint particleboard and varnish oak. When we believe we lack importance on the inside, we prop up our exterior self in an attempt to mask what we believe to be an unimportant reality *internally*. This affects the people around us in significant yet unnoticeable ways because they're always the target market for our poor self-worth experiments—measuring rods if you will.

Take furniture, for instance. If the internal construct is particleboard, manufacturers will coat it with high gloss black paint in order to mask the crude realties beneath—the heavier the furniture the lesser its quality. Some people have paid a significant amount of money for something akin to cardboard. People are the same way.

A prostitute will pile on the makeup and eye-catching clothing in an effort to mask the distortion and havoc they may be experiencing within their inner-self. The soul-self tricks them into believing they aren't worth anything or that they don't deserve anything of real merit, and therefore, they *settle* for whatever they can get by going with the lowest bidder—they choose abuse over abundance.

Their beauty ends up only skin deep. Inside are chaos and confusion, hopelessness and despair. Death has a pretty dress. They self-sabotage in ways that would shock them if only they could see themselves from another perspective.

Poor self-imaging blinds us. It masks the realities we live in and turns them into literal fantasies. Our brains will actually reconfigure in an attempt to protect the self. A 90-pound woman full of uniqueness and potential can gaze into a mirror and see a 190-pound failure.

Many professional people experience this at work too. You may have come into contact with people using terms like vision, authenticity, or gravitas in order to appear engaged, smart, or leadership-like. Leaders that lead from their authentic-self never draw attention to their functional ability; they simply lead without thinking about it.

As a matter of observation, the best leaders are likely not aware of how well functioning they really are. They don't have to *do* because they already *are*. It's more a product and less a goal.

The Intra-personal Gap

The intra-personal gap happens when there's a wide gap between where we *are* and where we believe we *need to be*. The size of this gap becomes the size of the quandary it creates. In the example of the toy boat in the story of the Velveteen Rabbit, his living through two seasons in the nursery, along with his semi-worn out condition, fashions a gap between his perceived wounded-self and what he fears the rabbit's perceptions might be about him.

This perceived gap causes the model boat to change his external view of self much like the prostitute example. Therefore, the toy boat *must* invent new methods of presenting himself to others in order to fill the growing gap between its authentic-self and its perceived self, much like the pretty dress on the prostitute.

The new and improved presentation is fueled by the model boat's inability to see itself as worthy in its current condition. Instead the toy boat tells itself rational lies (rationalizing) about what its capabilities truly are in an effort to feel better about its internal self.

These lies become self-evidentiary truths, and therefore, the toy boat never misses an opportunity to lay claim to its newfound image that has been brought on by the perceived intra-personal *gap* between itself and the new toy rabbit. The boat reinvents itself and believes the new invention is real. The problem is that *none* of these toys are *real.*

The model boat has a poor self-image and its actions are proof of its low self-worth. Timothy the jointed lion also gets in on the act of dissimulation. The lion uses an entirely different approach to the same problem. The lion uses the process of *association.* He looks for an opportunity to associate with what he perceives to be a respectable party and then attempts to align himself with the character of his newfound associates; in this case it's the government. Not the best choice of friends.

When people incorrectly sense they have no quality of their own, they typically identify with those whom they believe have the acceptable qualities through a process of identification. Name-dropping and referencing other people and their outstanding accomplishments, much like photos on Facebook with important people, allows them to take on the merits of the more impressive individual[s] through personification.

People do this at work—"I had lunch with so-and-so" or "last night when I was meeting with the vice president of the company," . . . blah. We scheme and jockey for position in an attempt to look important. Perhaps we arrange to have lunch with the individual we think *others* think is important.

Work becomes nothing more than the self-esteem Olympics.

We pull strings and seek personal relationships for the sole purpose of advancing our current position, grossly unsatisfied with the one we already have.

We do this in our religious communities as well. We seek position power or an audience with those deemed important by the majority of the community. I've spoken at churches across America for nearly thirty-five years and many times I'm forced to feel like a Hollywood personality at a red carpet event.

Some people clamber for a minute of your time in hopes of identifying with you. They want to feel important for five minutes because during the rest of the day they don't. They want to be touched or simply acknowledged.

Unfortunately, the more insecure you are the more important you might be *tempted* to believe you are when others are attempting to make you more important than *they* are for all the wrong reasons. For many it's easier to make others important and associate with them than it is to feel just as important and simply appreciate them.

Healthy outcomes hinge on whether or not we are a human-being or a human-doing when offering any kind of service to others. How many religious leaders are leading for the wrong reasons? Unfortunately, much of leadership is simply a poor attempt at being someone they don't believe they actually are. April Fool's Day is every day for many in influential positions.

> "Let someone else praise you, and not your own mouth; an outsider, and not your own lips." –Solomon[8]

Achieving vs. Receiving

Relationships should not be *achieved* through these performance-orientated behaviors (such as speaking to a live audience or any other performance strategy); they should be *received* through a process of automation by simply *being* yourself and making informal contributions to the world around you. Relationships should not be driven by unreasonable efforts; they should be a result of who you *are*.

---

8) Proverbs 27:2 NIV.

In the case of the Velveteen Rabbit, notice how the skin horse never instigates a knee-jerk reaction that causes the rabbit to labor for the relationship *or* his special wisdom. When engaging with the skin horse the rabbit is at ease. However, the other toys create *dis*ease in everyone they meet.

The other toys make him jump through emotional hoops and then reward him with doubt and guilt for not jumping well enough. By referring to their exterior rigging, mechanical prowess, or government ties, the toys cause the rabbit to feel *small* and less fortunate. Their magnification of their own positions, contacts, and government associations creates intimidation within the small toy.

If the rabbit is going to fit within their relationship circle, he's going to have to *achieve* the same level of governmental or technical prowess they claim to have.

This behavioral dynamic is everywhere today, and it's exhausting for most people to keep up with, but we never seem to get enough of it. They may offer their services or advice on how to be like them. Religious leaders are famous for this behavior, which is why people are placed in rows facing the leader while the leader stands on a platform in a raised position of perceived authority.

I've seen these leaders sit atop the platform on a chair that looks like a throne next to a gold table with water in crystal glasses while awaiting the show. We take this for granted; however, it's nothing but a huge sign of insignificance that inadvertently produces "us and them" paradigms.

The skin horse on the other hand, reflects on his *brokenness* and longevity as it relates to his authentic-self—he's vulnerable. Vulnerability is more valuable than gold. He remembers when he was the new toy on the block and how important it made him feel, but he also has the wisdom to know those days are past.

Thought Invader: Our vulnerability is where our value is both seen and understood by others.

The skin horse makes room for the rabbit without respect to his own self because he's secure in his non-wounded-*self* rather than challenged or threatened by the newness of the rabbit and the boy's love for him. He is comfortable with who he is *not* in light of the boy's affection. He respects the boy's need for a new friend.

This vulnerable stability attracts the rabbit to the skin horse like a velvet magnet. The horses truthfulness and his ability to be *real* about who he is *not* without pretense or exaggerated claims makes the rabbit feel safe. This is usually the result when associating with secure people—they make you feel comfortable and valuable, not uncomfortable, worthless, or stupid.

Let's look at a simple conversation between the Velveteen Rabbit and the skin horse as outlined in this spectacular children's story:

> "What is REAL?" asked the Rabbit one day, when they were lying side by side near the nursery fender, before Nana came to tidy the room. "Does it mean having things that buzz inside you and a stick-out handle?"
>
> "Real isn't how you are made," said the Skin Horse. "It's a thing that happens to you. When a child loves you for a long, long time, not just to play with, but REALLY loves you, then you become Real."
>
> "Does it hurt?" asked the Rabbit.
>
> "Sometimes," said the Skin Horse, for he was always truthful. "When you are Real you don't mind being hurt."
>
> "Does it happen all at once, like being wound up," he asked, "or bit by bit?"
>
> "It doesn't happen all at once," said the Skin Horse. "You *become*. It takes a long time. That's why it doesn't happen often to people who break easily, or have sharp edges, or who have to be carefully kept. Generally, by the time you are Real, most of your hair has been loved off, and your eyes drop out and you get loose in the joints and very shabby. But these things don't matter at all, because once you are Real you can't be ugly, except to people who don't understand."
>
> "I suppose you are real?" said the Rabbit. And then he wished he had not said it, for he thought the Skin Horse might be sensitive. But the Skin Horse only smiled.

The skin horse in his wisdom breaks the relationship down to its simplest form. Like a fraction becoming simplified, he subtracts all the unnecessary elements from the equation and presents the Velveteen Rabbit with his answer. *To be real is to be loved for who you are.*

Thought Invader: Being real is when you can love yourself for who you once were.

When we project pretend images to those around us, we end up with pretend relationships, pretend friendships, and pretend marriages. We also end up with pretend religion. Love and faithfulness becomes a fictitious movie or a fairytale reserved for bedside reading.

We spend the rest of our lives trying to hold onto the make believe relationships we've created through a process of continued scheming and relentless pretending in hopes of establishing a reality we don't really believe is possible.

This is the process of the achiever. Achievement is only warranted when the motives are in alignment with a healthy goal; otherwise, it becomes a *need-oriented* goal fueled by exaggerated or unreasonable accomplishments. This can cause relationships to become instrumental in meeting our *personal* needs rather than meeting the needs of those around us. It becomes an unhealthy, most lonely pit of self-interest at the expense of others.

What to Expect in the Coming Chapters

In the coming chapters I'll be using some spiritual terms. Terms like "*spirit*" or "*God*" will be used, but I want to encourage you to let go of your own partisan definitions and perhaps imagine these ideas through another lens. Wayne Dyer said, "Change the way you look at things, and the things you look at change." He is onto something.

None of us really knows what God is, but many of us *believe* we know, which is okay. I personally don't want to be arrogant about what God is or isn't, but I want to focus on *you* and your divine nature—your own mysterious miracle-being: that part of *you* that resides within your body and is untouched by religion and the pretenses produced by believing we know anything at all. This is your raw authentic-self.

I will speak of Jesus as well. But again, I want to encourage you to imagine Jesus as a person and *not* a deity. I therefore won't be speaking about him in the sense that he *is* a God, but rather that he was in essence an embodiment of what we all imagine God likely represents.

He was both *conscious* of his mission and *comfortable* with his true authentic-*self*. He was a sage and a revolutionary with unconventional wisdom, intelligence, and insight who treated others with respect and dignity while calling out those who lived in contrast to what they proclaimed.

His essence was felt by those who came into contact with him or felt the power of his words in ways that have stood the test of time. He stood up for the disenfranchised and the downtrodden while denying the elite and the pious center stage. I want to extrapolate the profound essence of what he stood for—justice, mercy, sacrifice, faithfulness, forgiveness, and personal worthiness.

My goal is not to debate, *who* God is or *what* God is—that may be another book. Whatever one believes about the Gods they choose is one's personal business. I'm not about to disparage one's belief in God, nor am I going to encourage it. My goal is to investigate the affect our beliefs have on our performances as well as our self-worth.

Our beliefs are frequently fused through our experiences and upbringings, and grounded in our emotional *needs* or lack of needs. Albeit, religion might possibly be the greatest and most profound act of placebo the world has ever known, it works for most of us. I understand this, but if we all understand both religion's *impacts* and *drawbacks* we can proceed with an open mind and eliminate any setbacks.

If your belief is working for you then I applaud your belief, but if it isn't working, it may be worth an investigation as to why. Sure, we've all had experiences and some of these occurrences we might even call supernatural for a lack of a better term, but many of us tend to wait for an opportunity to correlate our experiences[9] with *proof* of the existence of the ethereal or a possibly religious idea we have made heavy investments in. The greater the degree that

9) Experiences as defined in this book are personal "encounters" within everyday life that we tend to twist into subjective notions in support of beliefs we need to have. This could be a bad dream, an image in the mind's eye, or some other anomaly that could be explained if we only tried.

our relationships are connected to our beliefs, the more difficult it becomes to separate them later on when we have questions.

Experiences are simply experiences—we can both learn and grow from them. We can *receive* from our experiences or we can *misuse* them to *achieve* and separate ourselves from others for fear of having less value or impact by creating competitive frameworks that only divide. Healthy people don't need to do this.

Healthy people don't need to exaggerate or be dogmatic in their beliefs. They don't twist their experiences in support of some grand celestial scheme. They don't get angry or upset when they don't know *all* about something or if someone doesn't buy into their beliefs. Nothing becomes *fighting* words.

Many times people will use extraordinary *experiences* to bring definition to themselves and through a process of exaggerated claims or mysticism. It may appear that they are in support of their favorite deity, but underneath it is only a means to be seen as smart or important.

The experiences thus become an idol they worship in place of simply being authentic. Like the toys in Williams' nursery, they lay hold of so-called supernatural *activity* in a feeble attempt to associate with the divine and deflect from the pain they live with every day.

Many defend their experiences at all costs as if by doing so they prove their position of worthiness in the world or their association with a God or some powerful deity with a big following. An excessive *need* to be important can cast an unsuspecting spell on people, which can get them locked in the Eros prison for a long, long time.

Or maybe, they believe they must keep their God alive by defending his majesty or by over-promotion here on earth. Many times this is nothing more than a sign of our desperate need to belong to something larger than ourselves. It can also be a sign that we're afraid of being alone. If an all-powerful God really does exist, surely it doesn't need our protection, performance, or promotion to sustain itself.

If our God cannot promote itself then we may need to reevaluate what we are both doing and believing about our idea of god. If we have to unpack his bags *for* him and prop him up in our church or place of worship's window and invite others to "come and see," then maybe, just maybe, we are the creators of the carnival we're selling tickets to—it's certainly a possibility worth looking into.

Using our personal experiences as mechanisms to feel important can not only cheapen our experiences, leaving them impure and substandard in the eyes of others whom we attempt to impress. Moreover, they can quickly become an obstacle that separates us from others if we are not happy with who we are when apart from it.

That being said, placing any experience above reality can delude reasoning, thus making it difficult for others to make sense of our claims *and* us as a person worth investing in or associating with. After all, relationships, especially within the spheres of belief and religious affiliation, provide the greatest opportunity for self-promotion and performance strategies.

The Journey

Let's undertake a journey. We'll begin in a prison—the Eros prison. From here we'll explore the power of performance and the ill effects it can have on our being in relationship to love and life. My goal, through this process, is to uncover, discover, and recover our true authentic-selves, but before this can be done, we must endeavor to better understand why we do the things we do and what may be driving us to any particular end.

We will also look heavily at the frameworks and fundamentals of faith, religion, and spirituality as they merge with behavior and human performance needs in hopes of bringing clarity and distinction to you the reader. Like it or not, faith and religion, and even the lack of it, are the strongest foundations of separation, isolation, and anxiety between people groups. These ideals may be the most explosive and compulsive frameworks associated with performance living and emotional in-grouping there ever are.

I hope we will also encounter more clarity in regards to identifying behavioral patterns found within communities of faith strictly associated with being human. I hope to help us find distinction in regards to identifying the *real* reasons why we compete and behave the way we do as a species and explore a few healthy alternatives.

I also hope to dismantle the illusions we position in place of reality in order to feel better about ourselves in relation to others within communities of faith, family, and work. I want to uncover the differing tendencies associated with the six levels of decision-making, which I will call the six decision multipliers.[10]

A Definition of Terms

Before moving on, I want to do a recap and define for you a few important terms for better understanding. This way you will be able to reference the terms if you forget what they mean in the coming chapters. These terms will be used throughout although the latter terms listed are merely to help you better grasp the concept of the self.

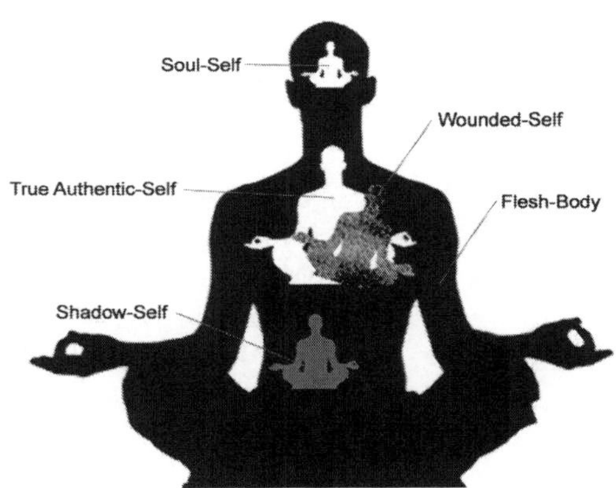

The wounded-self: The wounded-self is the self that has been wounded through negative reinforcement during the formative years and even beyond, including pre-adolescence and sometimes adulthood. It's the soulish-self or the mind. It comes from the Greek term *psyxḗ*, which is the root of the English words "psyche" or "psychology" meaning *individual personality*. Soul-mind, soul, soul-self, and soulish are all interchangeable terms.

The true- (authentic-) self: The authentic-self is the divine nature within us. Our divine-self that remains untouched and un-

10) The six decision multipliers involve how we see and understand the exterior world around our interior self and us. These multipliers consist of empathy, practical thinking, system judgment, self-esteem, role awareness, and self-direction.

able to be marred or improved upon. It is the *light* within which no other person can put out. This is the genuine self; the *perfect* light of being which we all possess, but often times neglect.

It's what moves on uninterrupted when we transition out of this natural realm. It is the god-self that reflects the beauty of being. The true-self, the true authentic-self, the self, the spirit, and the spirit-self are all interchangeable terms.

The shadow-self: The shadow-self is the counterpart of the authentic-self. It's intermingled with the soul-self which reasons through the mind and feelings, and is inseparable from the true authentic-self. In other words, it cannot be divided into two distinct selfs but only distinguished.

The shadow-self is our nemesis (darkness) that we must endeavor to subjugate through the power of the authentic-self driven by the *light* of our divine being or else be controlled by it. It is the Hebrew *ha-Satan* in the books of Job and Zechariah translated diabolos in the Greek Septuagint meaning slanderer.

It's the *adversary* of our true authentic-self—the opposing side. Up and down, light and darkness, good and bad, it's the contradiction or the contrast of the authentic-self. The negative-self, the shadow-self, and the *ha satan* (devil) are all more or less interchangeable.

"The sinful nature [shadow-self] wants to do evil, which is just the opposite of what the Spirit [God and the authentic-self] wants. And the Spirit gives *us* [our authentic-self or divine nature] desires that are the opposite of what the sinful nature [shadow-self] desires.

"These two forces are constantly fighting each other, so you are not free to carry out your good intentions [that come from within our authentic selves]" –Galatians 5:17 (italics mine).

The soul-self: The soul-self is the mind and the seat of the emotions; the brain or soul; Greek, psyxḗ from psykhe, to breathe or to blow, which is the root of the English words *psyche*, *psychology*-soul (psyche); a person's distinct identity and its neural and electrical components. This is many times controlled by the shadow-self and can lead to self-destruction, self-hatred, or even suicide.

It's where drama and insecurity are produced. The soul-self or soul-mind can cooperate with the shadow-self as a tag-team and antagonize the authentic-self, but it cannot change, touch, or harm it in any way.

The soul-self is irresponsible, wishy-washy, need-based, intellectually based, logic-based, emotion-based, or limbic driven. The unauthentic-self, the soul-self, the mind, and the wounded-self, are all interchangeable.

The flesh-body: The flesh-body is our physiological structure containing the vital organs, including the brain and its electrical impulses.

The ego-self: The part of the mind that mediates between the conscious and the unconscious and is responsible for reality testing and a sense of personal identity and affirmation. It's what longs for popularity, position, and power.

The safe-self: The safe-self is the authentic-self being allowed to pervade and influence the whole person without the fear of failure, ridicule (by the shadow-self), or rational lies. It's living beyond *the death that counts* as Jesus did. It's a well-adjusted state of being that does not require permission to be.

The unsafe-self: The unsafe-self is a limited authentic-self in reaction to the intimidations and assaults of the shadow-self and the soul-self. This disallows the true authentic-self to *be* safe and flourish. Although not harmed or marred by these other selfs, the authentic-self can often be discouraged by them. Thus the authentic-self does not blossom or encourage the person into a present state of beautifulness of being.

The unsafe-self may trigger the soul-self to *feel* anxiety, fear, intimidation, insecurity, depression, and many other soulish qualities that can stunt personal growth. This creates what I call psuché soufflé. Interestingly enough, Psyche or Psykhe was the wife of Eros, and is referred to as the Goddess of the soul in Greek mythology.

In-group: In the field of social psychology, an in-group is a social group with which a person psychologically identifies as being a member. In contrast, an out-group is a social group with which an individual does not identify. The need for excessive identification is prevalent within our individualistic society.

Many people are, more or less, need machines searching for the next victim to be better than. All these battles take place within our *middle* (center of being), or our soul-mind while we mask its reality through poise and positive attempts at appearing normal and productive. This is the Eros prison, and it's a very dreadful place to live.

Self-categorization theory: This is a social psychological theory that describes the circumstances under which a person will perceive collections of people (including themselves) as a group, as well as the consequences of perceiving people in group terms.

Although the theory is often introduced as an explanation of psychological group formation (which was one of its early goals), it is more accurately thought of as general analysis of the functioning of categorization processes in social perception and interaction that addresses issues of individual identity as much as natural group phenomena.

Why do people arrange themselves into groups? Why do we draw lines and create us-against-them scenarios that hurt others? And why do we justify religious groups as apart from all others by saying "it's because we *love* them?" Is that what love is? Could loving others really be more about a God complex?

Like God, do we have pity on others? Do we offer them a solution as if we're in a position to give one? It's hard to look at ourselves and uncover our real motives rooted in insecurity, self-hatred, or shame. Maybe believing we are at God's right hand is one way to help us cure it.

Categorization: This is the process in which ideas and objects are recognized, differentiated, and understood. Categorization implies that objects are grouped into categories, usually for some specific purpose. Ideally, a category illuminates a relationship between the subjects and objects of knowledge.

Therefore, categorization is fundamental in language, prediction, inference, decision making, and in all kinds of environmental interaction. It is also indicated that categorization plays a major role in computer programming, but this won't help us here.

The fact is that people need *definition* and *recognition* can be unsettling when you really think about it. Our current times indicate this notion, especially when we see religious and political in-grouping taking place on the news every evening. But why do we do this? Why do we have to draw such distinct lines between people, thoughts, beliefs, and ideas? I ask myself this question daily and have a few ideas around which I'd like to discuss. One possibility is one's self-concept.

The self concept: This primarily deals with self-perspectives, self-identities, and self-construction. These ideas evolve into beliefs, thus creating a worldview about one's self and can include elements such as gender identity, racial identity, religious identity, and so on.

This is not self-awareness, but rather what one does once they are aware of where they stand in relationship to other people and their ideas (and others' perception of them) within a society. Unfortunately, it really matters what other people think, and for many of us it's paramount.

According to social psychologists, the self-concept is made up of one's self-representation and how this self interacts with self-esteem, self-knowledge, role satisfaction, self-direction, and the social-self to form the self as a whole person. It includes the past, present, and future selves—where future selves (or possible selves) represent individuals' ideas of what they *might* become, what they would like to become, or what they are afraid of becoming.

Possible selves (what one could become) may function as incentives for certain behaviors, but are they authentic actions? The perceptions people have about their past or future selves are directly related to their current self and their perceptions of how that plays out in social groups.

Temporal self-appraisal theory: This theory argues that people have a tendency to maintain a positive self-evaluation by distancing themselves from a perceived poor or broken self, which may include supposed negative traits about oneself. Interestingly enough, it's mainly religion that informs an individual of the poor-self, thus kick starting a general awareness of where one is lacking and perpetuating the likely entrance into the Eros prison of performance in an attempt to get the much-needed nod from the gods.

2

The Eros Prison of Expectation

This is where it all begins. It begins with a question. Do you find yourself wondering what *other* people are thinking about you when in social settings or in a decision-making position at work or within your religious community or affiliation? I don't mean our natural wondering, but rather a gnawing, an unhealthy need to know what others are thinking about what we are thinking. This can include an unhealthy *need* to make an adjustment in order to align ourselves with whatever others expect.

Do you find *their* definition of who you are to be more important than your own definition of *self*—more accurate maybe? This is common among people within the performance prison, and it's common among people in general. Although a few no longer find themselves controlled by what others think, many more still do.[1]

When under the spell of others' expectations, we find ourselves living in the shadows created by the light of what others expect or what others believe to be best for us. This is the *normal* setting for many people, but it unfortunately produces *abnormal* results.

These shadows can also be produced by a well-lit emotionally driven filament that fuels misunderstanding—when we believe fantastic things about others that aren't entirely true or when we believe that they believe untruths about us. The difficulty with this kind of external projection is twofold.

First, by nature we tend to place higher expectations on ourselves on the behalf of others when it comes to our own performance much like the toys in Margery Williams' nursery. In other

1) There are two groups of people: those who live in relationship to what others think of what they are doing and thinking, and those who do so no longer.

words, we assume and consequently *believe* the expectations placed upon our perceived talents by others to be *higher* than our own—more valid because we have a *lower* view of self.

For this reason, we (again by nature, which means it can be an automatic impulse) place ourselves in a *lower* position in comparison to others and spend the rest of our lives attempting to live up to the imagined expectations this emotional maneuvering creates.

This mindset multiplies performance for all the wrong reasons. It fogs our windshield thus making it difficult to navigate relationships and realities much like driving in heavy rain without wipers.

Thought Invader: If we are not careful, need-oriented relationships can easily become nothing more than personal "clamoring for self-worth" sessions masked as camaraderie.

This behavior brought about by this type reasoning can backfire and lead to the dumbing down of our personal worth. For instance our attempts at not feeling bad about ourselves fail in light of someone else's ability or exceptional performance and, therefore, turn into unexpected deathtraps.

Sure, this sort of behavioral choreography appears harmless, but is it really? Is it not affecting our outcomes or lack of outcomes in our relationships or our life-work? Does it even matter? I'm going to introduce the idea that it does matter and that it matters a whole lot more than we want to believe it does.

The Wounded-Self

There is a *self* that I'm going to refer to as the *wounded-self.* It's our authentic-self that has been wounded through negative reinforcement during the formative years and even beyond, including pre-adolescence and in some cases adulthood.

Additionally, our authentic-self can also be wounded through emotional or physical trauma, shame, social disruptions, poor parenting, social outcasting, body violations, betrayals, unforgiveness, physical handicaps, bullying, emotional wounding, etc. The list goes on and on.

The self can also be wounded through very simple or small things like being called stupid or being corrected publicly—what you might consider little or so-called harmless things. The impact will differ based upon the fragility of the persons involved. The wounded-self may stay in a childlike state for many years if the experiences have been more difficult or with lasting effects.

I can only share aspects of my own story in order to help you understand how the wounded-self can come into being and how it can be healed of its pain. My story is unique to me as your story is unique to you. All our stories are equally important so please don't succumb to the temptation to compare the size of your fish to mine.

Healing can sometimes happen in a moment although it can take many years to rid ourselves of the accompanying "phantom pain" as in the phantom pain we associate with the loss of a limb. [2] All of us have a wounded-self at some level, which is why faith and religion many times become increasingly attractive instruments to billions of people—especially the critically wounded. About 84% of faithful followers to any faith (especially Christianity) will convert through a personal crisis including tragedy, loss, or some extreme difficulty.

Faith is a favorite refuge for wounded-selfs.[3] Faith becomes our treatment—oftentimes it is our therapy—or our friend much like a new puppy to a sick child. It acts as a prescription for the treatment of the wounded-self although it nearly always treats the symptoms associated with a far deeper need.

By and large, we can ultimately end up dependent upon its medicinally enchanted effects on our psyche. Faith can be *had* and it can be adequate for less harmful wounding's, but it's not sufficient when *it has you* and when it holds your brain captive to less sensible thoughts. If it fails to address the grim realities within, it nearly always becomes just another pretty dress to cover our imperfections and those "private" parts that we like to keep under wraps.

I grew up a social outcast—granted, I looked like a more frag-

2) Phantom pain sensations are described as "perceptions" that an individual experiences relating to a limb or an organ that is no longer physically part of the body. The phantom sensations associated with limb loss are a result of either removal by amputation or congenital limb deficiency. We can experience emotional "phantom pain' even though the circumstances that created the original pain no longer exist.

3) The majority of conversions (after pre-adolescence) to any faith system are associated with crisis, tragedy, or hopelessness. It is rare that very healthy people turn to subjective mysteries for support and self-assurance.

ile being. Diagnosed with *Hyper Kinetic* Behavior in the second grade, I was placed on a regimen of Ritalin at a very young age. I was thin, goofy, loud, and uncoordinated. I was quick with my mouth, but not as quick with my mind, which seemed to work against me on all occasions.

I was a target for bullying in the early years before it became uncool. Truth be told, in the 1970s we were expected to work things out on our own. This worked better for those of a more sturdy nature. But it worked against those of us who lacked the social poise for navigating these war-ridden playgrounds effectively.

I'm reminded of poor "buzzy" Siemen, an unfortunate child I attended school with in the early years. He wore diapers to school in the fourth grade. He was relentlessly bullied beyond belief. As a child I would weep for him. The cratorial impact his personal trauma had on my own life spawned the children's stories I used to tell my own children before bedtime.[4]

In those days I was not just a target; I was an *easy* target—a flaming target with big red lights on it. And this was not your run-of-the-mill bullying; it was often intense, pointed, constant, and extremely alarming. It has become a part of the fabric that has since defined me.

Unfortunately, I lost my left eye because of an injury at the age of ten. Ten was too young an age to deal with the challenges that accompanied this type of physical trauma. This was the beginning

4) 'Buzzy and the Gang' were made up stories I told my kids before bed. They consisted of a small group of characters involved in adventures surrounding innocence and personal discovery.

of my social sorrows as I related to the exterior world around me as a young boy. I can still remember going to school and being laughed at and called a pirate after the injury.

Several boys punched me directly on the eye-patch that I had to wear (for a year) when the teachers weren't around. It was shocking to my system, my person-hood, my soul, and my authentic-self.

The wounding experience resulting from the constant ridicule and scorn during the formative years became a "normal' setting within my soul-self. I was beat up and confronted by girls and boys as well as larger groups of boys and girls weekly, beginning in the sixth grade.

I can remember a number of specific occasions when I was circled by at least ten children on the playground. They were all engrossed in kicking me in the head and face until a teacher finally saw it and stopped it.

I have a vivid memory of my sister watching the drama unfold in horror through my fingers as my hands covered my face in shame. She wept aloud as they pummeled me on the ground. I remember shouldering the pain of her having to witness it more than my own pain of having to bear it in my feeble attempt to withstand it.

Looking back, I am dumbfounded when I think of the amount of bullying I endured during those years. It's no wonder that faith and the comfort of knowing *God loved me* created a refuge for such an innocent little boy seeking social recognition and acceptance.

The altar at the church I grew up in was more of a therapeutic couch where I lay before God, the celestial sociologist who listened to my cries of anguish. I also found solace in the comforting words of my mother who always went to bat faithfully for me whenever she was aware of the sordid occurrences, but I never told all.

In the seventh grade, I was beaten unconscious and left outside in the grass on the school grounds. I feared pressing charges when the local police became involved, so my parents (at my pleading) decided to let it go lest something worse happen down the road. I would be thrashed in the school bus and many times would be covered in blood from my bloody lips and nose, throughout the school years.

Teachers would have to drive me home from school, from time to time, when word got out that I was the target on the bus or at school that day. It was humiliating to ask them for a ride, but the circumstances far outweighed the humiliation.

In 1977 my reading teacher (Mr. Egan) kicked me in the rear end after he picked me up by my hair and yelled at me in front of the whole class. He called my parents in front of everyone telling them how terrible I was, using a red rotary phone he kept on his desk. I wept in my seat as the children laughed and scorned. Looking back it seems imaginary—surreal. Impossible.

That was also the year when I was stripped down to my underwear by several kids and thrust into a six-inch gym locker. They locked it with a combination lock somebody had donated to the cause and left me there. I was too afraid to speak up. I don't remember how long I stayed in that locker, but it was longer than I wanted to be there.

I received no sympathy from the gym teacher, who eventually let me out. I remember feeling like it was somehow my fault for allowing such a tragedy. I was made fun of and groped in the shower by the bigger kids while everyone laughed. I remember asking to get out of it, but was always told "no." It was apparently against the school policy to avoid the group bath.

I broke my nose in the ninth grade and the gym teacher nicknamed me 'Gonzo," a tribute to the furry blue Muppet character with a hooked nose because my nose was swollen as scar tissue had accumulated over the bridge. Kids called me gay, fagot, and other disparaging words, as I was always the last one picked for games or teams.

I knew nobody wanted me on his or her team, which played deep into my wounded-self. This fighting for my life went on for eight years, beginning in the second grade and continuing until we moved out of state after I was a sophomore at high school. That was the year I was repeatedly stabbed in the back with a safety pin, between classes, by one of the school kingpins. There was nothing I could do about it. He would run it right through my shirt deep into my flesh as I walked the halls in between classes.

This created in me a huge wounded-self that would many years later experience a *spiritual* rebirth of exceptional quality although I didn't quite understand it. Of course, these experiences made me a superb candidate for Jesus who said, "Come to me all ye who are *burdened* and heavy laden and I will give you rest." But until that time, it was necessary that I remain the victim of social circumstance—hell is home.

An Island of Misfit Toys

The fact that I was a social misfit had long-lasting effects on my life, even up to the age of about 39. But around the time I turned 40, an amazing transformation occurred. I'm going to take the next few paragraphs to describe for you in detail what I consider one of the most powerful watershed events that I have ever witnessed. Very few people know this story, and fewer still will ever understand it.

I was asked to work with the youth group at the local church which I attended in 2002, but I openly wanted little to do with teenagers, as you can well imagine. At that time, many valuable people saw me as one who could bring some fresh ideas into an already thriving group of 30 to 40 teens.

They didn't need my help, but they thought I could possibly bring another angle of looking at life and its challenges. This is common within youth groups, as we have to change things up with kids so they don't become bored to tears. Several people in voluntary leadership positions asked if I would share some of my story with the thriving group.

When I was first asked about sharing my experiences with the kids, I flatly declined. I told them that I couldn't deal with teenagers and that they wouldn't care to listen to me anyway, even if I tried. Truth be told, I was afraid of failure and ridicule. Fortunately, they continued pursuing me, and I finally gave in—maybe just to quell their asking. But what happened next was not only totally unexpected, but also life altering for me.

After completing three one-hour weekly discussions on my *then*[5] view of God and the world around me with these kids, I re-

5) My view of God has since changed dramatically. Rather than seeing God through the eyes of a Christian worldview in association with biblical claims of literalism, I have since undergone another metamorphosis that has enabled me to be far more inclusive and less rigid. I no longer view the Bible as God's Word to man, but rather man's words about God, as he understands it within a Jewish framework and worldview.

ceived an unexpected applause from both the youth and the leaders that attended. My eyes flooded with tears and I wasn't sure why. This specific occasion, fortunately, led me to embark on a quest that I didn't know I was on for quite some time.

I ultimately ended up joining the group of teens as a volunteer leader, as I found solace and acceptance by the thriving group—I was somebody. I also discovered some great support people and worked with that particular group for the following three years as former leaders took a break and did other things—it was a full time job.

One winter in 2002, I attended a youth retreat along with several other youth groups in New England at a retreat center situated in the mountains of New Hampshire. After arriving I was asked to fill in for a workshop speaker who was unable to fulfill their obligation for some reason. I wasn't assigned a speaking role originally, but this unexpected opportunity happened along so I took it.

To my surprise, the room was standing-room only, after word got out of the first workshop I had done a few hours earlier. There was literally no place in that room for anyone else to stand, so some were on the floor in awkward positions.

Those meetings brought life to my wounded-self as I performed like an actor on the stage, and I believe, prepared me to receive what followed a few months later. That being said, this was a *performance*-driven opportunity, an opportunity to receive praise and strokes for a job well done, a must for wounded souls. Most of us with a wounded-self long for such opportunities and feel better about ourselves when people respond positively to them. I was in acceptance heaven.

I studied the Bible for years before this opportunity arose. Having attended a small seminary in the mid-1980s, I had spent thousands of hours within the pages of the ancient text. Memorizing the information defined me and brought purpose and personal satisfaction to everything I did.

I unleashed my years of accumulated knowledge of the holy book on those teens like a bursting dam in unique and unordinary ways. I have since discovered that if you have something to say and you have a unique way of saying it and it solves somebody's problem, you will be in demand.

Denis and the Divine Message

Several months later, a thirteen-year-old boy named Denis said he had something to tell me after a Monday night gathering. I was together with about ten young adults having a simple discussion about current affairs, God, spirituality, school, biblical concepts, and cultural trends; it was a question and answer night—I miss those nights.

I loved those times with the kids, and even as I write this paragraph, I can feel the warm memories floating to the surface of my being like a soft mitten around my heart.

Denis claimed he had a message from *God* for me, and he was the one scheduled to deliver it. Denis was a boy that the gods obviously drafted—it appears that the entity[s] on the other *side* of awareness don't take volunteers to do the crazy things that Denis did so easily.

Denis was a real gem. He didn't know all the spiritual lingo or have the hallmark tone and false humility that many religious folks tend to mask themselves with in an attempt to feel or be *real*—he was obviously connected with his authentic-*self* as well as his true *divine* nature. He was a velveteen rabbit with skin horse quality.

He was unassuming in that he likely lived out of his true authentic-self. In other words, he was unaware of his impact in the truest sense. He looked down towards the floor and claimed he was *seeing* a toymaker in his mind's eye—like an open vision as he described it.

In his *vision* (within his mind's eye), an unnamed toymaker was picking up and examining a few selected toys as they slowly moved by on a conveyer belt, making sure each one was in perfect working order. The toymaker was old and sage-like—likely a figure of God.

As he continued speaking slowly in low tones and without drama, Denis' eyes squinted with eager anticipation of the next image to deliver. It was as if he needed to get the story exactly the way he saw it lest it lose its impact and importance. Denis said the toymaker was waiting for the *special* toys to arrive, those that needed *special* attention unlike many of the other toys that needed less attention. I listened intently as Denis drew me into his spiritual vortex.

When one of the *special* toys made its way past on the moving conveyor belt, the toymaker stopped the conveyor altogether and picked up the *special* toy and worked on it *extra specially* for several moments before gently setting the toy down and restarting the machinery. This only happened about once in every five hundred toys, according to Denis' mental vision.

That's when it happened. After a few minutes, Denis suddenly looked up and gazed me in the face as if coming to a startling revelation. Without flinching he said in a tone that resembled someone who had just struck gold, "*Mr. Sisler, you're one of those special toys*!"

Boom. The dam broke. I was supernaturally waylaid right there in front of those kids. I wept. I didn't know what I was feeling, as the feelings took me by surprise. I grasped for composure, but found none. It was at that moment I heard my own small voice deep in my wounded-self. As I struggled to pay close attention to its sound, my own inner voice began to speak to me. The voice informed me that for the first time in my life a *peer* had affirmed me.

My *own* inner voice, that part of my divine nature that typically remains locked away deep inside, told me that I had never emotionally matured beyond the age of 13. The voice was as a gentle teacher. I later realized I didn't have the correct tools or a viable experience that I could depend upon to properly and confidently engage any social circle at the time.

In 1978 my own youth group experience was telling. Although the kids would associate with me in the youth group, unfortunately they avoided me like the plague in public school. I sign of the disingenuous framework within them.

Denis was thirteen the year he unlocked my prison and apparently *so was I.* When I was physiologically thirteen in 1976-1977, it was unarguably the worst year I can remember. That was the year when I had been kicked by my reading teacher, beaten up by a girl, knocked unconscious by eleven kids, had my ears smashed in the school hallway, and locked in the gym locker in my underwear and left for dead—and that was just some of it.

My true-self—my *wounded* emotional-self apparently never matured past the age of thirteen because of these unfortunate circumstances. And it took a thirteen-year-old boy, nearly thirty years later, to open the door and let me out. My outer-self, my emotional *soul*-self was also deeply wounded—stunted really.

That part of me that feels and dreams, longs and desires for security—that part that thinks thoughts and assembles information brought in by the senses—and that part that feels pain and torment and tries to make sense of not being liked or popular in school was locked away.

But when a small boy obeyed his authentic-self and shared with me his thoughts about what he was *seeing* through his own inner eyes—even though he could not make sense of it himself—both my emotional-self and wounded-self were seemingly restored in an instant. Before this encounter, I couldn't bring myself to look teenagers in the eye.

Up to that point in my life, I would become stricken with fear even as a grown man when confronted by teenage emotional grandstanding—when they stare you down in a public place as you walk by. I was living in the halls of shame and ridicule from the early years of being the odd person out and never the acceptable person in.

Thought Invader: Ridicule can be the pivotal point between ruin and restoration in the life of a child.

The very next day, I was ruminating over the episode that had so profoundly impacted my life the day before. That's when I *saw* it—perceived it, perhaps. In my mind's eye, I could *see* a surgeon's hand. The hand had no protective glove, but somehow I knew it didn't need one. It was sewing up a flesh heart split down the middle as if torn by some tragic event. It was *my* heart—my wounded emotional-self.

After welcoming the much needed surgery, I have since never been the same. While opportunities abound to return to the Eros prison of shame, I refuse to let myself go there any longer. Once I had experienced the freedom of self-love and rested in the hands of a loving doctor, the prison no longer called my name.

3

Measuring Down Within the Eros Prison

When the self suffers a wounding through social trauma, as I suffered, or by some another means more or less challenging, in an effort to protect the wounded-self we may *bend* reality in order to make it more palatable. In other words, it's like favoring an ankle that was sprained or another body part that was hurt through some injurious event.

This can and does involve many kinds of emotional placebos that act as salve to our wounded souls. I certainly do not want to disparage these keen and cunning tools, but I most clearly would like to define them. It's only fair. After their definition we can make better choices about our continued involvement with them minus the masks.

The way we favor our circumstance, or the emotions created by them, is to inevitably invent an *alternative* world-view that allows us to cope with the realities that work against our potential worthiness and our authentic-self. One of the ways we do this is to measure ourselves *down* rather than measure ourselves *up*.

It's an automatic behavioral positioning that allows for a sense of being without challenging the self or identifying the weak link responsible for the flaw within our emotional framework. It's simply a way to cope with a poor or mistaken belief in ourselves.

This downward positioning whether associated with personal relationships, workplace relationships, religious relationships or anywhere we find people leads not only to performance-based living, but also we will quit trying—we will easily give up where we would normally try harder.

Because we lower our expectations on the self, some of us

won't make an effort to take calculated-risks or endeavor to explore new options, when faced with normal difficulty. Not only is this a slippery slope, but also the slope is exceedingly steep and points in the direction of nowhere.

This process of positioning one's self lower can easily develop into a chronic lifestyle of measuring down. When we live *down* to mediocrity or the status quo rather than living *up* to more exceptional ideals worth taking risks for, we lessen our chances of reaching our full potential.

This process is a bottomless pit of performance that plays out in the Eros prison. There are no winners in this prison, only losers and those too weak to escape its shame and torment—its familiarity no longer unwittingly breeds contempt, it demands it.

If we engage this lower mindset, we may quit going to school or quit believing we are worthy of a raise at work. We may quit a long-term relationship or quit pursuing a meaningful one. We can also live an *exaggerated* life where we exaggerate outcomes for better affect in order to solicit a positive reaction from those on the listening end.

This process of giving up or exaggeration is birthed through the wounded-self in all of us. Expecting these overextended potentials from ourselves comes from favoring the wounded-self (much like the ankle example) and the feelings of inferiority these wounds produce.

The wounded-self can also invent a preemptive need to strike ourselves before others strike us—a kill or be killed state of affairs. It's a knee-jerk reaction to low self-worth brought on by believing the lies we create in our low self-esteem laboratories. We have seen this scenario in the movies.

An individual gets wounded by an enemy and takes himself or herself out of the running: "You guys go ahead; I'll stay back and hold them off as long as I can. You save yourselves; I'll never make it up that hill." We do this to ourselves while no *real* enemies are present—we invent them in order to keep the cycle of insecurity and victimization going.

Thought Invader: Ideas that spawn surrender are not only unhealthy, but also they will produce a guaranteed ticket to the island of misfit toys.

When we don't measure up to the overextended images that we create for ourselves because of our distorted view through the wounded-self and project wrong assumptions born out of this distorted view on others (by believing people are thinking we should be capable of more than we are), it's not only easier to measure down to our inaccurate expectations of self as we discussed, but also we will measure down to false ideas we imagine others are thinking about us.

We will measure down to ideas we simply make up in order to support our false notions. This serves as justification for the distorted view of our wounded-self brought about by the loss of social recognition or whatever else we have experienced.

I know that was a mouthful. To make this simpler, we simply misjudge the warped expectations of self and the false expectations of others. Someone may rightfully expect more from us, but rather than rise to the occasion, we quit for fear of not meeting their expectations completely—especially if we believe those expectations are more than they actually are. This is a reflection that mirrors our low expectation of self brought on by the wounded-self.

The false, but common, cure for this conundrum seems to be the same for all who experience this. Unfortunately we believe lowering the bar in relationship to other people's standards is the answer.

We may look for people far worse off than we are and measure ourselves by their broken standard rather than seeking out the successful and attempting to measure up to their level. We're proud we're not Jeffery Dahmer rather than trying to be like Jesus. This takes no personal strength or keen insight to do, which is why so many do it so often.

We'll say things such as "At least I'm not like so and so," or "You should see the way my dad acts. I'm not nearly as bad as he is." This deceitful rationalization robs us of the courage to live *up* to a better ideal while giving us a free ticket to the island of misfit toys. If we desire, we can drive towards something far more productive, but many of us don't because we're afraid of failing or we don't know where to begin. We spilled coffee on our roadmap and it has become unreadable.

Jesus shares an insightful parable with his close devotees about a man who was about to go to war with another man—his enemy. And because his enemy had more soldiers than he did, Jesus explains how the man sent a delegation ahead to secure terms for peace before the expected war began because he was *afraid* of getting pillaged or worse.

He increases his chances of not losing everything, through a truce *with his enemy* out of fear and low self-worth. In other words, he attempts to make a deal with his fears instead of planning an escape or confidently fighting for what he believes in. He's content to lose *something* instead of the possibility of losing *everything* out of fear of not super succeeding—a must in a war.

His terms for peace might have been something like "just take the women, but leave the kids," or maybe he said, "we'll give you six months worth of our food and half of our cattle if you just leave us alone and don't hurt us." We've all done similar things—made truces or unintended sacrifices with our poor assessment of self, but like rabid hamsters the ramifications end up eating through our soul while we're sleeping.

We might say things like "at least I don't do *that*" and then we describe something with worse consequences than what were produced by our own poor decisions of the past. This again is measuring *down* instead of measuring *up*. Instead of trying to live up to a better superlative, we think about how we're not nearly as weird as some other people or as bad as a serial killer or a kidnapper or someone who eats people and puts the leftovers in the freezer.

We believe those scenarios make our own situation look pretty good, so we inadvertently remove the desire to change or become better, in the light of scenarios much worse than our own. We feel pretty good about ourselves in light of someone who murders people. We thus surrender to mediocrity as if it's the brightest idea we've had all year for the simple reason that it isn't a total failure.

Unfortunately, this ensures zero productivity and plays into the vicious cycle of poor self-worth—it essentially confirms it. We measure ourselves using the ruler of differing levels of failure instead of a ruler that reflects both failure *and* success. We are afraid of success. I'm afraid of success—I'm still susceptible to this unwarranted fear if I take the time to stop all the noise and think deeply about it.

Being a victim can be a drug of choice for thousands of people across all walks of life. The cure? Never let that friend into your emotional house. Let that friend cry as long as it wants to on the curb outside of yourself.

When we remove the pacifier from the baby, we know that the tears won't last forever. Never justify your love for inadequacy with the sentiment you set aside for the victim it makes you.

The Shadow-Self

The enemy of self always lies—always. This enemy of the authentic-self is likely not some elusive devil or supernatural Satan outside ourselves with a forked tail and horns. It's doubtful that it's an invisible demon or the same universal "tempter" that religion conveniently provides in order to help us cope with the inescapable realities that we all hate to face.

I'll introduce the enemy in more simple terms. The adversary of self is the negative energy we produce all by ourselves and allow others (motivated by their own shadow-self) to put on us. It is the shadow-self that is responsible for all our self-doubt and personal misgivings which acts as a veneer of shame many times masked as self-confidence.

This shadow-self can generate inner desires to serve self at the expense of others when we feel weak, alone, afraid, unworthy, and unimportant. People who understand and reject the shadow-self (because they have figured this out) no longer have any need for devils and demons.

They realize that the lack of attention towards these assumed entities neither elevates nor lowers problematic occurrences in their life—stuff consistently happens regardless of the belief or lack of belief in an author of evil. I suspect that those who are brutally honest with themselves don't feel the need to blame their behaviors or unfortunate circumstances on an external enemy who's out to get them simply because they identify with a higher ideal.

They understand that the rain falls on the just and the unjust alike—bad things happen to everyone, not just a select few special people who are allegedly a threat to the dark side.

Many have convinced themselves that they're a danger to the dark side through subtle self-importance masked in religion. It brings unimaginable self-worth when we believe we are the "target" of an all-powerful entity and arch enemy of the God of the universe.

This dynamic can bring an injudicious form of encouragement to a wounded-self in need of special attention. How often I have heard people virtually brag about their heroic bouts with the dark side—nobody wants these bouts with the *enemy*, but I fear many *need* them. Some of us simply cannot think outside this archetype and therefore cannot believe there are any alternative explanations for positive and negative aspects of human life.

The complete failure to take personal responsibility for self was the first behavioral blunder brought about by this shadow-self in the garden myth found in the Hebrew book of Genesis. "The woman made me eat it" or "the serpent beguiled me and so I ate it" become the standard trademarks of behavior and decision-making influenced by the shadow-self attempting to serve itself while placing the blame on another invisible entity or person—classic redirection in ancient form.

It is actually an ingenious decision made by our soul-mind, masquerading as an invisible devil, that *makes* us "do it" or suggests we try. Unfortunately, the ill-fated satanic being has no way of defending itself against our sleight-of-hand behavioral magic. In the business world this is not seen as a devil, but rather it's simply called passing the buck. It's hard for many of us to admit that we like unhealthy things.

Thought Invader: The sins we habitually date are the sins we have fallen in love with.

Nobody thought to say, "I screwed up." Unfortunately, nobody had the wherewithal to take personal responsibility for a wrong decision within the garden story. It's an admission nobody ever wants to make. Taking personal responsibility is hard and humiliating—it screams "I failed." The garden myth reflects the pain of honesty and our fight to appear good and clean while balancing a need for frolicking in the mud of earth life.

Life is muddy. If we're not careful, we will become covered in the muddy shame that accompanies the unavoidable engagements with poor decision-making surrounding our need to satisfy the wounded-self. Many of us create imaginary gods in an effort to regulate our shortcomings.

Unfortunately, these gods end up standing by with arms folded, waiting to condemn us for our inevitable failures. Therefore, we painstakingly create religious frameworks designed to mask the ugly realities of human interaction and self-deception.

The beginning of our journey in life must always begin with the taking of personal responsibility for *all* of our actions and outcomes. It's what separates the winners from the losers in the game of personal honesty.

Taking personal inventory and lying on the excel sheet is a personal killer for personal productivity and the power of *being*. The Eros prison is filled to the brim with irresponsible people claiming their innocence while pointing their finger at the devil or some other culprit allegedly responsible for their poor outcomes.

In the Hebrew story of Ahaz[1] found in the Old Testament of the Bible, the writer exposes the *power* of the shadow-self motivated by fear and its effect on our decision-making capacity. Ahaz, the ancient Hebrew king of Judah, was so apprehensive and intimidated by one of the other Israeli kings that he ended up giving away all the beaten gold in the Holy Temple to an Assyrian king.

Not only did he give away the temple gold, Ahaz also gave up the gold from his own personal wealth chest to this Assyrian king as a gift for personal protection. He believed the low opinion of his shadow-self and thus allowed himself and his entire kingdom to be overwhelmed by his shadow reality.

Ahaz gave away all the precious gold the community had amassed over many years because he allowed another king to re-

---

1) Ahaz's reign commenced at age 20 in the 17th year of the reign of Pekah, king of Israel. Immediately upon his accession to the throne, Ahaz had to meet a combination formed by northern Israel, under Pekah, and Damascus, under Rezin. These kings wished to compel him to join them in opposing the Assyrians, who were arming a force against Syria and Palestine under Tiglath-Pileser III.

Out of fear and to protect himself, Ahaz called in the aid of the Assyrians at great financial cost. Tiglath-Pileser sacked Damascus and annexed Aram. According to 2 Kings 16:9, the population of Aram was deported and Rezin executed. Tiglath-Pileser then attacked Israel and took Ijon, Abel Beth Maacah, Janoah, Kedesh and Hazor.

He overtook Gilead and Galilee, including all the land of Naphtali, and deported the people to Assyria. Tiglath-Pileser also records this act in one of his inscriptions… blah.

define his capacity for keeping it. The shadow-self will make you feel inferior and incapable of accomplishments, thus creating "performance anxiety" which leads to a very *poor* decision-making capacity.

> "So Ahaz sent messengers to Tiglath-pileser king of Assyria, saying, "I am your servant and your son; come up and deliver me from the hand of the king of Aram and from the hand of the king of Israel, who are rising up against me."
>
> "Ahaz took the silver and the gold that was found in the house of the Lord and in the treasuries of the king's house, and sent a present to the king of Assyria. So the king of Assyria listened to him; and the king of Assyria went up against Damascus and captured it, and carried the people of it away into exile to Kir, and put Rezin to death."—2 Kings 16:7-9

Don't settle for the high cost of low self-worth brought on by your shadow-self. Its costs can be higher than you initially expect. If you don't, you'll end up giving away most of what you have amassed emotionally and end up locked away in the Eros prison for life, without any hope of getting out. We are experts at denying that we have any intention or *need* to do erroneous things.

When we measure ourselves among those that surround us, we inevitably become the performer while those watching become the observers capable of rating our performances with the all too familiar thumbs down. As long as we place ourselves on an altar of performance, we will nearly always end up becoming the sacrifice for others to gawk at when things don't turn out right.

Thought Invader: Inferiority is a thief that continually steals all that we work for and leaves us with less than what we started with.

Self-worth has a huge effect on our decision-making capacity. It can cloud our view or create overconfidence, both of which can derail a decision at its core. Our decision-making process is a fundamental aspect of our capacity for success and continued self-worth, but it can also be responsible for our failing to reach our full potential.

Understanding the decision-making process will be helpful in identifying your own processes. I will begin by identifying the science that surrounds human decision-making theory.

The 6 Levels of Decision-Making

Axiology is the science of value, but few know anything about it. The word "axiology," is derived from two Greek roots, which are *axios* (worth or value) and *logos* (logic or theory), and represents the theory of value. The development of the science behind value theory makes possible the unprejudiced measurement of value as accurately as a tape measure measures any length.

The search for a science of value originated with early Greek philosophers and ultimately concluded with the work of Dr. Robert S. Hartman. Facing the brutality and uncivilized outcomes accompanying Hitler's rise to power in prewar Germany, Hartman envisaged a science which could categorize "good" as successfully as the Nazis categorized "evil." "Dr. Hartman dedicated his life to the realization of this vision, and after many years of research, created a new mathematical system which successfully orders the values of our everyday experiences."[2]

Axiology has countless advantages. It generates new knowledge about the everyday world and creates a frame of reference, which provides a new way of looking at our environment and *our authentic-selves*. Moreover the knowledge axiology provides is objective and autonomous of any one onlooker. We are a product of our decision-making capacity.

According to Axiological expert Harvey Schoof's definition of Hartman's work, "Realizing that the primary difference between natural order and moral disorder lay in the mathematics which orders the natural world, Dr. Hartman set out to discover a value mathematics."

According to Schoof, "In a stroke of genius comparable to the discoveries of Galileo, Newton, and Einstein, he discovered the principles which order and structure not only our moral decisions but also all value judgments. From these principles, Dr. Hartman

2) Valueinsights.com's Axiology page.

constructed value mathematics which can and does bring order to our value world."[3]

The six integrated dimensions of decision-making can be summed up below. This specific combination of our outer-world and inner-world valuation framework provides two unique perspectives. Because decisions or "choices" precede action and because action translates into results, this decision-making measurement allows us to predict a person's probable performance with a great deal of precision when measured through an appropriate algorithm.

2 Worlds in 3 Dimensions

Outer Intrinsic: or better known as Empathy: understands other persons as *unique* individuals; the spiritual, irreplaceable worth of others, the value of a "thing" as it exists in itself. The ability to see and appreciate the inner worth of others; to see and accept others as they *are* without placing any further stipulations or expectations on them; "the ability to place oneself in another person's shoes without judging them."

Inner Intrinsic: or better known as Self-Esteem: understands the inner *self* as infinitely valuable; the unique individuality of each person; the understanding of "who" one is and accepting *actual* strengths and limitations. The ability to see and appreciate one's inner *worth* and unique individuality; to be authentic, honest and sincere; to see clearly and pragmatically appreciate one's strengths and limitations as they are.

Outer Extrinsic: or better known as Practical Judgment in regards to thinking: understands and sees comparative choices in relationship to material value, things, classes or groups of things; other things as they serve useful roles or have functional value; comparison of things, people or situations; concrete, functional value in general, practical concrete thinking and organization.

The ability to see and *appreciate* practical, common sense thinking, concrete functional and material values; concrete organization; comparative thinking; the ability to see the worth of social

3) Quoting Harvey Schoof, President of Insight Consulting. Insight Consulting, Inc. was founded in 1987 by Harvey Schoof. Harvey has over thirty years of experience in personal and organizational consulting with business, government and non-profit agencies. Axiology is defined well at valueinsights.com if you are interested in more information.

organization and expectations and norms; street sense.

Inner Extrinsic: or better known as an inner understanding of personal Role Awareness: understands what one is; the role function one plays; the sense of using time in a useful, functional way; career thinking; satisfaction or dissatisfaction with what one is doing in the world.

The ability to see and appreciate one's place and function in society; to feel that one is serving a useful function, is contributing; to feel confident either that one can or is performing; to feel a sense of satisfaction with one's actions.

Outer Systemic: or better known within Axiological circles as Systems Judgment: understands the analytical or structured thinking necessary for structure, order or consistency in thinking; theoretical or conceptual organization and planning; valuing what ought to be.

This is the ability to see and *appreciate* system, order, structure, conformity, and authority; conceptual, analytical, or structured thinking, organizing and planning; rules, regulations, organizational principles, and guidelines.

Inner Systemic: or better known as Self-Direction: when one understands where one is going or ought to be going; self direction; persistence; drive motivated from commitment to inner principles and goals; self concept; ideal self image.

These dimensions translate into value capacities which can be measured. The ability to see and appreciate inner ideas and inner thought; to feel a sense of duty, loyalty, and commitment to what one believes is right; to have a clear sense of self direction; to be persistent.

The ability to emotionally maneuver these six levels of the human decision-making pattern is critical for making good choices around important decisions that will affect your life in meaningful ways. Making the wrong decision can set one back, stall, or confuse legitimate outcomes. Not only are we able to measure the level of clarity one has within these six dimensions, but also we can measure the level of importance one places on it.

Clarity & Bias

The human mind evaluates *everything* via six separate but

integrated views. Three are workplace or *outer* focused (empathy, practical thinking, and systems judgment) and three are *internally* focused (self-esteem, role awareness, and self-direction) as seen above.[4]

Each view has an element of *clarity or understanding* and an element of *Bias or Importance* assigned to it. These 12 *bimodal* views (6 dimensions x 2 views each) combine to form the strength, that is, clarity and bias/attention that form a person's critical thinking ability and their evaluative judgment capacity.

An individual either understands on a level that is *Crystal Clear* (about 98%), Clear (about 83%), *Unconventionally Clear*, which indicates an ability to see outside of the box (what others do not see), *Visibly Clear*, which indicates an absence of *some* of the aspects associated with any decision subjecting the person to some errors in judgment, or finally, *Transitionally Clear*, meaning they will generally have a *poor* understanding with many questions and confusion relating to the problems, challenges, and opportunities they face.

Regarding the levels of *importance* we place on whatever level of understanding (above) we have relating to the decisions we all must make in regards to any problems, challenges, or opportunities we face, there are four:

1. Inattentive Double Negative: indicates it is of little importance.

2. Cautious Single Negative: indicates little reliance upon their clarity level as a strength when making decisions.

3. Attentive Single Positive: indicates importance without losing the balanced perspective necessary for making a good decision.

4. Over Attentive Double Positive: which means one is likely to pay too much attention to this view as it becomes overly important.

4) Borrowed from Greg Smith of the Maui Analysis, Maui, Hawaii at mauianalysis.com.

To translate what a common *clarity* (understanding) and bias (importance) leveled decision might look like, consider this: let's say you have a *Crystal Clear* level of understanding concerning how your particular decision *will* (future) affect those around you.

This would be the Outer World Empathy category, which deals with the *intrinsic* value one places on others—their uniqueness if you will. This would mean the individual would see 98% of the impact that the potential decision they are *about* to make will have on another person directly or indirectly affected by it.

If the level of Bias/Attention or *importance* is an *Inattentive Double negative* level Bias, then this individual will not care how those on the receiving end fare after the decision is made nor the *impact* the decision has upon them. For example, an individual fires an employee over some work offense.

The employee is distraught and begs for mercy claiming that she is a single mom. If the Bias is *Inattentive* and *double negative*, one may say, "That's not my problem. You should have thought more about your position before you made that poor decision. See where it has gotten you?"

Of course attitudes, behaviors, emotions, and worldviews all come into play in these scenarios, but you understand what this can create. Those who care too much about what others think because of low self-worth or any other potential handicap that can or may have unfortunate implications on decision-making may adjust their decisions to incorporate what everyone else is thinking, thus allowing others to be the framers of their worlds and not themselves.

Allowing Others to Frame Your World

Second, by placing higher expectations on our authentic-self (on behalf of others concerning our performance), we no longer live a life of self-acceptance. Instead, we live for others' acceptance. This is meaningless, harmful, and unauthentic. It's another ingenious trick of the shadow-self to keep you from taking a chance lest you make a huge mistake, or better yet, a first class fool out of yourself—it's defensive at its root. We've been taught since the beginning that mistakes are bad. This happens when our view of others' ideas about us are overly important.

When I was in grade school in the 1970s, if your answer was wrong, it was marked boldly with red ink. When the teacher passed out the students' papers everyone could see it before you could tuck it away in your desk or coat pocket for your wounded-self to feast on later when you were alone and feeling stupid.

Rather than viewing mistakes as a proven process of discovery or a natural means to learning new things, they become identifiers revealing an absence of aptitude or perfection. Our world becomes defined by red ink rather than the divine check mark that shouts uniqueness, creativity, and physical wonder.

Who marks up a new baby with red ink because it fell while trying to walk? Who puts a giant red X across a baby's chest because it failed to dress itself? These are simple strategies by those in charge to separate right from wrong, at the expense of those who are trying desperately to learn. I had the privilege of teaching a group of home-educated students for several years when I lived in Massachusetts.

I taught art, science, communication, and logic for about five years. I believed that the goal was to inspire new thought, expand their worldview, and assist them in being creative. I always looked for effort and creativity. I looked for ways to give them the grades they deserved rather than the grades they *made* through their own personal processes of trial and error. Never see mistakes as failures. And never allow others to call your mistakes failures.

When we allow others to judge our mistakes as failures, we willingly permit others to frame our world *for* us. When we grant others consent to frame our world *for* us, we become subject to *their* expectations not our own—we become slaves to a world we are not acclimated to, or associated with, in any real way. We develop into performers in hopes of winning their affirmations or sidestepping the red pen.

Allowing others to frame our world means others will always frame our world according to their *own* dimensions and *their* best interests and not *our* basic needs—needs we deserve. Regardless of the size of their world, by nature it will be smaller than ours because they have no stake in our world.

Many teachers under the cover of the Teachers Union allow the need for financial funding to frame the world of their students thus neglecting their intrinsic value.

Thought Invader: In psychoanalytic theory, Eros represents the sum of all instincts for self-preservation.

People have their own worlds. Living while allowing others framing our world strips us of all the instinctive enthusiasm that accompanies hope and courage in a world that needs us. This also is a prison—this is an Eros prison.

Eros

Typically, Eros is used within sexual contexts, but in this sense it runs much deeper than that. It burrows deep down into the emotional regions where our subconscious middle makes the real rules we all live by.

Just as sexuality in its rudimentary sense is about procreation and the prolonged and preserved existence of a given species, so also the Eros nature is really about the preservation of the self and our ability to exist in harmony *with* our self for prolonged periods of time.

Self-preservation is one of the strongest drives within humankind next to procreation and it resides deep within all our human *middles* (the Greek word *kardia* or the *heart* in the Bible—"the middle"). When imprisoned in this very deep and elusive place, it's easy to misplace or intentionally throw away the only key that can get us out—belief and trust in our safe-self created and divine in nature.

We are good "*as we are*" and not as we are "*told to be*" by the overlords of any Eros prison of performance. But make no mistake: this does not *excuse* actions that resemble anything less than "good" in regards to others and ourselves.

The actions do not determine the inner worth of a person although they may reflect how it is perceived. The Eros prison will always be the result of actions empowered by the shadow-self bent on disputing the authentic-self.

This is a place where our true rights and abilities can be stripped away like the gold in the temple by the demands and expectations of a wounded-self or others in competition with us.

Many remain chained to the walls within this once attractive place now converted to a lowly dungeon of low expectation created by the shadow-self, when forming our poor self-image, or by others who sit idly by, desperately waiting to feed upon it.

No longer are we pleased with our own outcomes or excited about potential opportunities—all must pass under the rod of impossible expectation by the shadow-self and the acceptance of others or the super-low expectations of the wounded-self.

No longer can we plot our own path or experience the joy of trying something new. The fear of failure, the fear of social rejection, or the ridicule by others imprisons us within our own self-made prison of solitary self-confinement.

This is when our emotions wreak havoc on our authentic-self and beat us into *doing* rather than *being*. It's like breaking rocks in the quarry of incompetence while the shadow-self stands with arms folded in rude observation and in a disenchanted disposition.

We end up at the lowest level within the Eros prison of performance fueled by others expectations or the lower expectations brought on by our own wounded- or shadow-self.

A Purposeful Journey

Lets embark on the journey into the self and how we depend on the greatest tool for behavioral modification ever invented—religion. Faith and religion have become the two most useful tools to define our being and bring purpose and meaning to our lives while on the physical plane.

The next several chapters will endeavor to break down all the parts and pieces within every religious framework associated with feeling worthy to love, live, and let others live the lives they choose—or not.

Our goal is to expose religion's real face and the behavioral gymnastics it creates to cover it up. It is to expose the power of the mind and emotions as we rationalize our way through the cosmos in a feeble attempt to understand why we are here at all. I'm inviting you to drop all your weapons and surrender your mind and understanding to a most unconventional view of the world.

May you be bold enough to read on and imagine that you are not the manager of the universe, but rather a speck of stardust lying open and willing to be whatever the cosmos needs you to be, in order to bring some semblance of order, appreciation, and divine love to the part you live in.

4

Heart Moves and the Self

The fundamental need in all of us to *be* can only be satisfied when we believe with our mind and spirit that we already *are*. We *must* believe we are already "good enough"—worthy enough. For instance, statistically speaking 84% of American workers are waiting for their *dream job* within the Eros prison of performance.

This is very telling because it shows us that most people are settling for what they currently *do* rather than making a concerted effort to become what they believe (possibly without wholeheartedness) they could or should possibly *become*. Either that or they are just sitting around waiting for the dream job to show up in their driveway.

This is an outgrowth of not being up to par within the authentic-self. When our personal view of God and the cosmos communicates our need for re-creation then everything must therefore lack or be substandard until whatever happens actually happens to make things otherwise. This will ultimately play out in our work, our relationships, and our faith—we will *settle* for less while quite possibly disguised as more.

Have we learned to settle for less than what we actually are? Is it because our desires are not important? Is it because we are content with the life position we're already in? Or is that we just aren't good enough or talented enough to deserve anything else. According to statistical data, the answer is no.

We are most definitely *not* content because many of us long for that which we don't yet possess even though we have lost the energy and enthusiasm to do anything about it.

Thought Invader: Many of us have settled for satisfactory simply because we do not believe in our authentic-self.

At first glance you may be tempted to think this violates *the death that counts* in that one might desire specific employment, enjoyment, or relationships that simply work, but this would be a misrepresentation of the idea. We should love what we do, and we should experience satisfaction when we do it and with whom we do it. If not, we are not doing what we love.

There's a healthy satisfaction that accompanies personal alignment when it's actually aligned. But dissatisfaction reins when our abilities are misaligned with our work, when our self is misaligned with another self, or when our performances are misaligned with the gods who rate them.

Settling for where we are in any of these areas and being happy and fulfilled as a result is one thing, but settling and complaining about what we do, who we do it with, or the gods who are watching it is another thing altogether—it's really not being settled at all: it's denial.

This is why many become consumers of material things such as food, clothes, electronics, or people and religion in order to fill the need to *be* better than we believe we *are*. Some turn to substance abuse or self-destructive behaviors in a feeble attempt to fill the holes left by surrendering our personal emotional management to the wounded-self or someone outside ourselves less interested in our personal welfare and proper alignment.

Some turn to religious obligation, the dos, and don'ts in an attempt to appease the angry gods. We grope for things that are easy to capture through simple monetary means rather than making the personal adjustments in our thinking or taking the necessary risks associated with better returns or maybe just believing in ourselves.

We may settle for less when it comes to more difficult tasks, but this lowers our walls of protection. The feelings of inadequacy that accompany settling for less spark the need for fillers such as drugs, sex, religion or some other flesh-body experience that tricks us into thinking we're all good—loved or important.

All this is crazy if you think about it long enough. We look at our internal gas gauge and it's consistently on empty. Within this Eros prison, much of our happiness is based *only* upon the favorable circumstances that never seem to come our way. And because we are preoccupied with performance nonsense, we don't really see it.

Thought Invader: Rather than great risk for return, some of us relax into no risk for rubbish.

Yet within, we long to be accepted for who we are regardless of what we have or don't have in relationship to others. We long to be accepted no matter what we settle for. Many of us are over focused on what *will be* as opposed to what already *is* because we don't like the way things are in the present. We find in-groups and loyalties that reflect our lower level of living and join forces with other prisoners and then together rage against the machine that devours us.

If only we understood that authentically *being* in the present—living and breathing in the beautiful present state of being—*the now*—is the place of true fulfillment. Once we believe it's possible and once we have accepted, cherished, and embraced its opportunity, its benefits become self-evident.

When we experience a personal planetary alignment,[1] which involves the alignment of things like our self-life, domestic-life, love-life, or work-life, everything works in tandem.

Self Sabotage

The authentic-self functions in a perpetual positive state of being free of personal assault, but few know it. Like a car transmission, it operates best in drive, which is where it stays. The soul, on the other hand, is always in neutral. It has the ability to take sides depending on the perceived emotion or understood logic before it or what *feels* good.

If decisions are made from an emotional or *limbic* perspective (fight or flight emotional decision making), then those decisions will be in accordance with what one *feels*, but if decisions are made in relationship to the frontal lobe of the brain, it will act on the facts based on reasoning and not intuitive insights. Either way, the soul will rest in one of these two available camps, depending on

1) Personal alignment involves our gifts, talents, education, family, and workplace although not limited to these altogether. It's when all pistons are firing and even those things left to chance fall into place. This alignment begins with attitude and ends with gratitude.

the individual's personal bent, training, and life experience.

The flesh-body, on the other hand, functions principally in reverse and according to natural human organic instinct. Its root is in the ground and according to dirt, stardust, and the quantum matter from whence it came. For example, the physiological flesh-body may require nicotine or some other drug, even though it may be harmful to the flesh-body—it doesn't seem to care either way. The flesh-body is by itself without reason ability.

Or it may require alcohol or some other foreign substance because it has become acclimated to its affects through habitual use. These negative infusions do not necessarily speak negatively to the flesh-body, but rather they might fulfill its needs apart from sensibility. The reverse often seems good to the flesh-body if left to itself.

Thought Invader: When the flesh-body and the soul-mind take sides against the authentic-self, the authentic-self always loses.

Only when the authentic-self and the soul-mind (whether limbic or frontal) take sides against the flesh-body does discipline and self-direction bring a positive result to living. This is why St. Paul speaks often about renewing the soul-mind and subjugating the flesh-body that fancies the reverse. The epistle of St. Peter also speaks of the torment associated with this war of the internal worlds in this wise:

> "Yes, Lot was a righteous man who was *tormented* in his soul by the wickedness he saw and heard day after day." –2 Peter 2:8.

You may remember the story of ancient Sodom and Gomorrah in the Old Testament of the Bible. The Bible is probably the best book on the subject of human behavior ever written. Each story tells a tale that reveals the inner struggles all humans face, along with anecdotes and strategies for potential freedom.

If one takes these stories too literally, one will miss the intent of the story which spells out the entanglements every human faces along with the possible paths to personal independence.

The Bible is not as much a book of solutions as it is a book of struggles. Answers are hard fought through much deliberation and intuitive insight, beyond the veil of what we think we understand. It takes a solid belief in who we are before embarking on such a complicated journey—self-assurance and personal freedom from the Eros prison are a must. A disregard for the opinions of those around us is necessary, not withstanding an ability to discern what is worth taking into personal consideration.

In the story of Sodom, Abraham's nephew Lot decides to move his tents towards the city of Sodom. Because he was physically "exposed" to the religion of Sodom, which was rooted in sexual reproduction and everything associated with physical pleasure, it affected him negatively—it cut crosswise against his traditional grain rooted in purity metaphors. Overexposure to their religious festivals and rituals "vexed" his *soul* according to the ancient text.

Because their religious practices involved sexual intercourse, something all humans are attracted to and in *need* of, he became *torn* between what he was instructed to do through his own religious upbringing and what his flesh-body *wanted* to do in relationship to the religion of Sodom and his own *natural* human desires. Even what is considered reasonable becomes corrupted when interrupted by the power of religion's influence.

Lot was accustomed to a purity ethic entrenched in dos and don'ts while Sodom had no such rules to live by in relation to sexuality. The experience with Sodom became the familiar "wet paint" sign.

His authentic-self was thus overcome by the tag teaming of his soul-mind and flesh-body because of the constant wearing down of his senses and the ideas surrounding his authentic-self and its divine intentions, saturated with purity rules and a god that punished their violated order.

As a result, his actions ruled his intentions birthed by rigid instructions. This is known as self-sabotage. Self-sabotaging takes place when we allow ourselves to contradict our deepest intentions, regardless of what they are or where they come from. We become a kingdom divided against itself. For Lot, it was likely *wrong* to desire naturally the opposite sex even if he failed to violate the purity rules his religion created.

This isn't about right and wrong as much as it's about abandoning your greatest intention and substituting it for the quick fixes designed to meet a false temporary need created by the soul-mind and the flesh-body. It's about disallowing what is right for your authentic-self and giving way to things that do not support your better perceived future, physiology, or total framework in regards to the self and others. This type of reasoning leads to living in the *instant* instead of living in the *constant* without perfect *presence* of mind.

Regardless of where one stands in light of what one believes about procreation, it is a poor decision to live against it in secret while publicly appearing to be for it no matter what *it* is. It's not only the religious who suffer this dis-ease; but also the nonreligious.

That is why it's so important to live out your own personal convictions without passing judgment on those who differ in personal preference. Our convictions must remain *ours* alone and not become the standards we hold others accountable to.

Every person has his or her own roadmap. Invading the personal convictions and intentions of others makes about as much sense as making a resident of Barcelona follow a map of St. Louis, Missouri. The map is worthless unless one intentionally moves there.

We must endeavor to stick to our own maps rather than making our maps trump the maps of someone else who doesn't want to live in the same district. This is religion's largest fault—the uninvited imposition on others living satisfied lives.

The Beautiful Present State of Being

Jesus was a man who may or may not have lived according to some, but for this book we will assume he did live and that what was written about him is likely true. Jesus undoubtedly lived in the present with total presence of mind as noted in this memorable statement, "I tell you the truth, before Abraham was *I Am*."[2]

Jesus' reference to being the *I Am* is a telling position of *being*. When we unravel the ancient texts that help us see the life of Jesus, we can see that he refused to focus on the *past*. The profoundness

2) John 8:58

of the present is only seen in relationship to the past and future states. The past typically tends towards shame and regret—things already happened.

Similarly, the future, which can create fear of failure or anxiety of what might or might not *yet* happen, can be equally daunting. Their juxtaposition has been a problem since space-time began.

It is for this reason that Jesus focused on the *present* reality as he understood it, which disallows shame, regret, and anxiety altogether as it rests sandwiched between them both. This is where he *lived* all the time, and it's where he expected everyone to live—I am the *way*—it's the *way* he lived and experienced his idea of God. Jesus was saying to the religious Jews, "I am the Torah." More on this later.

Thought Invader: "Take no thought for tomorrow, for tomorrow will take care of itself." –Matthew 6:34

This statement by Jesus, as read in the Gospel of Matthew, is another indicator that he lived in the present and was not emotionally needful of what he did not have or caught between the walls of the Eros prison filled with *coulda*, *shoulda*, and *woulda*'s.

Where do we live? Are we able to live in current circumstance and find contentment within present difficulties that might surround us? Do we know the *secret* of being content in whatever state we find ourselves[3] as one first-century teacher once said?

Or do we allow the flesh-body and the soul-mind to concoct a strategy not in our best interest when things are not moving as fast as we'd like or when the conditions of our life change without warning. I find I've had to make bold declarations to be present over the years—even when I didn't want others to know I wasn't in the best state of mind to believe it.

For example, I remember one time about fifteen years ago when I stood up in front of a large crowd of people and declared, "I love my job!" I was feeling the tension created by where I *was* in relationship to where I wanted *to be* and I was longing for personal freedom and contentment beyond my existing place of *being*

3) St. Paul claimed he learned the secret to contentment. He described it as the "joy of the Lord" being the source of his strength and not favorable circumstances. Anyone who relies on a fixed position of strength can do this within a fluid circumstance if they believe it wholeheartedly.

within my work-life.

I knew that if I could say it with my mouth loud enough, I might set in motion the process of fulfillment within my current work condition. So I did the only reasonable thing I could do; I professed it aloud with an audience that could hold me accountable to the desired outcome.

My soul and my flesh-body were desperately attempting to strategize a way out of the risks associated with moving forward without the due respect to my authentic-self that deserved it. If not for the intervention of my wife who had as much respect for my authentic-self as anyone, I may have been tempted to disregard the obvious in an effort to gain the quick fix my soul-mind was trying to convince me as necessary.

The powers associated with my positive words were in direct contradiction to the warped desires of my soul-mind which was bent on illogical shortcuts out of fear of failure. I was being set up by my soul-mind for impatient knee-jerk implementations that were driven by emotional fatigue and fear.

I decided upon this course of action because as people we are more *committed* to what we *confess* than we are to what we think. This is why spoken vows are so important both in marriage and in court. The great King Solomon said, "*Better not to vow at all then to make a vow and later break it.*" He knew the power of words *after* they had been spoken into being.

Sometimes we have to override *with our mouth* our present *feelings* and *thoughts* of dissatisfaction within the soul-mind as a declaration of hope and courage that challenges the present circumstances and creates new ones. Words have creative force. As Solomon says, the power of life and death resides within the tongue.

Many times our ego, the part of the mind that mediates between the conscious and the unconscious and is responsible for reality testing and a sense of personal identity, keeps us locked away in the Eros prison because we fear realities that others may interpret as negative.

Unfortunately, pride and the ego-self are notorious for promising freedom, but delivering only Eros enslavement and domination by the wounded-self who struggles to accept as true, all things are possible to him who *believes*. Belief is the *key* that unlocks every attempt to change and gives it legs.

Thought Invader: Courage is not the absence of fear; it's the absence of the ego-self.

It wasn't long after speaking those affirming words that my career in consulting launched and changed my and many others' lives forever. When I embraced where I *was* at *present* as opposed to where I wanted to *be* in *future* while disallowing the ego-self to govern my actions, it set in motion the *results* that sprout from the process of *being* fully content in your present authentic state. It made belief in what *could be* a reality for me and caused *what was* to cease and desist.

This was the day I truly died the *death that counts*—when I no longer *needed* to know everything, *needed* to do everything, or *needed* to be known for anything in exhausting, exaggerated, or unimaginable ways in order to satisfy the ego-self who was afraid of failure and not being liked.

Not only was I willing, but also I *was learning* to be content to be where I did not desire to be, and I sealed it with a confession of faith. I was willing to be not only content in the circumstance, but also happy while I waited[4] for the *better* place of being in relationship to my occupation in this case. This conscious decision opened the doors to new possibilities formerly locked behind previously closed doors of trepidation.

I lived in that present condition for years and have done so for twelve years now. Since then I have traveled around the world helping, mentoring, and assisting people in understanding themselves in meaningful and momentous ways.

I assist them in understanding *what* they are capable of and *how* they're wired in relationship to their emotions, attitudes, blockers (interferer's of their strengths and potentials), and values so they can embrace their safe-self and capitalize on it.

Before this career shift, I ran the DreamKote Company, a custom painting firm I started many years before. I painted houses for eighteen years while at the same time yearning for a more definitive purpose in my work—more depth and meaning in what I did

4) My wife Anita says patience is "being happy while you wait."

in exchange for money. It all changed at the age of forty.

Thought Invader: Being present invites the future; it doesn't feel threatened by it.

When I embraced the good in what I did presently within my work environment (customer relations for instance) and my capacity for the mundane and simple (the act of painting), the greater part of who I was showed up in response to being *present in my work*. The power to embrace your present will ignite the opportunity to secure your future.

Mastering Heart Moves

When you're living in "present" you'll likely be generating more *heart* moves and less *smart* moves. Smart moves are rendered through the logic and reason parts of the soul-mind whereas heart moves are made through *intuitive* impulses that come from a more *secure* authentic-self. Over time these insights can be trusted.

This doesn't mean we neglect intelligence and throw our brains away; it means we balance intelligence with intuitive movements within the self. Some call this being *led by the spirit* within. Others might call it being lucky, but all in all its benefits are without number.

Thought Invader: Trusting heart moves signifies we are living in balance between our intuition and our intelligence.

It takes years to develop this intuitive trust, but over time, like an old friend, the self-directed intuitive decision-making process can be heavily counted upon. Once one has mastered this way of being, it's amazing how these intuitive *knowings* become more and more frequent and reliable.

It's a level of *unconscious competence* few people ever experience—when we are not even aware that we are aware. This doesn't mean we are rich in material wealth, but rather we are rich in intuitive decisions that benefit us and those around us in significant ways.

Thought Invader: Money follows the authentic-self; it doesn't precede it.

Smart moves are not completely absent within this way of life. But heart moves become more frequent and without premeditation. In time you may feel as if you're simply *flowing* in the spirit-self. This is what many first-century followers of *The Way* meant when they said things like "*The spirit said . . .*" This happens when we connect with our divine nature and partner for a greater purpose and destiny.

These individuals were relying on *intuitive* impulses from *within* for navigating present realities without. The process of mastering these intuitions is simple: they're developed through practice—by exercising them over and over again. Through the years one becomes part of them. The author of the Hebrew letter in the New Testament speaks of this when the writer says:

> "For everyone who partakes only of milk is not accustomed to the word of righteousness, for he is an infant. But solid food is for the mature, who because of *practice* have their *senses trained to discern* good and evil." –Hebrews 5:13-14.

When this process is in place, our words, actions, and thoughts are all running in the same stream of consciousness—there are no traffic jams. Worry, fear, and anxiety drift away and make way for peace and contentment. This is when Monday is Friday. Life is like one continuous day filled with hope and expectation only separated by sleep.

Thought Invader: When we experience heart moves, our senses are spiritually aware rather than mentally alert.

This is when we *step over* and realize we've been living in the matrix. No longer do we measure ourselves by unreasonable standards or expectations set up by others or the undependable inventions of the shadow-self. We measure ourselves by our true worth as seen by God—the divine nature.

This is when we finally believe we are good enough—without having to be reminded or prodded to reluctantly embrace it through forceful means or religious obligations. Stepping over means we are connected to everything around us through a divine invisible connection called *life* much as what was depicted in Disney's *Lion King*.

It's a *flowing* in the spirit. This is when you *sense* more than you know and you intuitively *feel* more than you think. Reasoning and intuition are married and bright ideas are its child. This is where sages and prophets like Jesus lived. It's where we can live, breathe, and have our being.

The three Enemies of Being

Unfortunately, there are three main enemies to this intuitive lifestyle: the fear of failure (losing), the fear of not being liked, and the fear of being misunderstood (or misrepresented). These are the three enemies of *being* and they are the unmerciful wardens within the Eros prison of self-doubt. These three amigos will stifle intuition and creative thought, thus leaving us to depend only on that which we can taste, see, touch, smell, and hear.

Unfortunately, these three concepts are what make up the mechanism behind many people's behavior, especially those attracted to the limelight. Although masked by optimism and enthusiasm, the gregarious outgoing behavior exhibited by many lime-lit leaders is nothing more than the outgrowth of a deep longing to be noticed, accepted, and loved. It's hard to imagine this as true, but if truth be told, some of the truest things sit right under our nose.

This is a most deceptive place to be in. And we're unaware that we are actually there—in the prison. It easily deceives the self and others equally, and it does this without prejudice. Preferring not to be alone in this place, our excessive need for social affiliation, interaction, recognition, and the acceptance of others are all fueled by our fear of failure—the fear we don't or won't measure up to exterior expectations or the lies of the shadow-self.

Many are tricked into believing that their goal is winning—when the real goal, unknown to the soul-self, is actually *not losing*. This is very subtle. Many are tricked into believing their successes have something to do with their personal drive or extraordinary ability.

It tricks them into believing they're some sort of super hero or maybe some fantastic entrepreneur. Many are tricked by the response of others to their perceived prowess. You've seen it: celebrities who you believe have it all, abruptly ending their life in a pool of despair nobody knew existed.

Masked by all the right moves, the fear of failure masquerades as the pursuit of success and popularity, which it seems to be by all appearances. Unfortunately, this is hardly ever true. Sometimes it is, but usually it's not. Religion promotes it, the shadow-self controls it, and life exposes it.

This fear of the loss of social recognition or the favor of the gods is an enemy to the authentic-self because it creates reactive behaviors built upon ideas that are completely untrue at worst and speculative at best. The fear of failure or the loss of social acknowledgment or the loss of the favor of the gods is an emotional killer.

Fear of failure is never your friend when it determines your every move. Fear of not being liked by others is an enemy to your soul—to your gifts and abilities—it cheapens them because in the shadow of these fears your gifts become gaffs.

Thought Invader: When we succumb to the enemies of being, we criticize our lack rather than allow ourselves the freedom to enjoy our outcomes.

Self-improvement as well as religious rituals becomes our number one quest. Our bookshelves become littered with books filled with techniques and tricks to become better people, only we never get any better.

We fear speaking about the things we're not good at and avoid others we believe to be more successful than ourselves in any particular area until we rival their competence. Churches become platforms of performance in hopes of getting the all-familiar nod of the gods.

Sure, this makes us a better candidate for help, but it cannot be self-help if it's a reliable means to self-love. Many attach themselves to a social group where they can act and interact in order to keep morale moving forward. Many times this is a religious affiliation where constant validation and praise and strokes abound—where a supreme deity loves us regardless of what we have done because of some mysterious treaty or act of courage by another deity. Either way, it's *never* because we deserve it.

But what kind of effect does this have on the real self? What does it do for the self if our self is a wounded-self and unfit for eternal life? On the surface, faith can appear to be the answer to self-doubt and the quest for real meaning in this world—for love.

In the next chapter, I want to break this down into its many pieces and parts, and help you understand that although faith and religious affiliations are helpful in many cases, they are not fool-proof for creating self-love or an authentic safe-self; they can only pacify it until one violates the rules that support it.

And although the wonderful ideas of redemption, purpose, and faith sound like terrific opportunities for self-growth, there's a deeper truth that eludes us—their true effect on the wounded-self is not all that it seems. The fact that we are not acceptable as we are damages the true authentic-self on the deepest level.

It makes us feel second rate and insecure. Whether it's Jesus pleading before his father not to hurt us or throw us into the abyss or our begging Allah not to kill us, we stand naked and ashamed before deities (we believe are angry, fed up or displeased with our root self) and in need of saviors to sacrifice themselves in order to rid us of the shame brought upon us by the failures of others that have gone before us. Can we change this seemingly impossible dilemma?

5

Religious Validation and its Effect on Performance and the Self

Although religion is designed to encourage the unsafe-self through communal activities, tribalism, solidarity, and conversion processes that hopefully unites us with the gods and ensures our safe passage into eternal life, it has a fundamental flaw at its root.

And although religion acts as a seemingly necessary framework for positive self-maintenance, self-esteem, role-awareness, self-direction, and communal benevolence, it tends to create the very thing it's designed to destroy—performance initiatives.

Granted, many religions support a positive-self and generally bring better self-awareness and self-esteem to most people who might lack it, but the process typically begins on a negative, as it must in order to warrant its imposition.

The idea of a negative-self was likely birthed through the theory of the *fall* within the garden myth, which speaks of the "disobedience of *all* mankind" early on in the Hebrew Genesis account. This is an astounding Hebrew attempt at understanding the *duality* within us all through the power of story.

Religion thus provides a framework for people to live within that allows for distinctions between what many see as a positive and a negative-self or an *authentic-* and *wounded*-self or a saved and lost self.

In other words, the role of religion is to create a cosmic standard for mankind to fall short of while ensuring a roadmap for living up to it along with boundaries upheld by rewards and punishments to guarantee one stays within it. At first glance, it appears to be somewhat successful, but is it really?

In an attempt to help you understand the meaning and the possible motive behind most religious traditions and what people expect, assume, and believe about themselves when living out these ideological frameworks, I want to break down a few ideas and thought streams behind one of the most popular religious communities in America known as modern day Christianity.

Please understand that this is not an assault on the faith or a personal axe to grind against experiences—although my experiences are fundamental and instrumental in coming to all my conclusions.

This is my ongoing attempt at deciphering one of the largest strongholds on the modern mind and the social/tribal group phenomenon. And although Christianity, Mormonism, Judaism, and many other religious affiliations bring hope and governance to many who are in desperate need of self-direction, these sects do not solve the pervading problems all humans face, but rather they enable us to *better* cope with them.

You might be asking the question is religion bad? Certainly not. Is it effective? Yes. Most of the time it is effective at behavioral modification. Are all it claims emphatically true? Probably not, which is why I feel the need to concentrate on some of the fallout it creates.

Although I affiliate with this in-group, I don't rely upon its dogma and traditional interpretations of the Holy Scripture for personal sustainability and acceptance, at least not anymore. Although I formerly would consider myself the archetypal Bible-thumper, I have since become an adult within my *own* universe and have moved beyond the crude mindset I once embraced.

This is not at all meant to portray any other person who is fluent in the scriptures and traditional-minded as crude or immature, but I say this in order to define my *own* experience and my progressive path to authenticity away from the Eros prison of performance I once lived in. Albeit, this is to define my *own* universe and my *own* path to freedom. You can choose yours as I have. And if it works, I'll be your biggest fan.

I also want to insist that I know many people within my faith circle (tribe) who are wonderful and amazing. These are people I personally long to emulate in both action and thought, but at the same time I wish to remain honest and fair in considering the realities about ourselves and our differences in belief. We are not all of the same mind and we are at differing levels of consciousness within the cosmos. It's extremely important that you do not define *different* to mean *better*.

Formerly, my faith was a way to feel important. It was something I was categorically good at and was able to capitalize on rather well. My natural talents and temperament certainly fit comfortably within this social order.

Furthermore, the thousands of hours of study and dedication to the sacred Scriptures over the last thirty years has allowed me to move into a greater dimension of understanding and personal enlightenment, both within *and* without the community, as well as provided me a platform for instruction and leadership—all good in my estimation.

Again, this is not to say that others are unenlightened where they stand, but rather to say that *I* am further enlightened when compared to where *I* was many years ago. This is about *me*, not *you*, although I'm sharing my experiences *with* you in the hope that you can come to terms with your own beliefs if you so desire.

People shouldn't compare *personal* enlightenment with others on another journey—we all drive different vehicles and our level of knowledge concerning the engines within our own vehicles differ greatly.

I want to use this *illumination* in the hope that it will give us a deeper understanding of why people do the things they do in order to feel better about themselves, and more importantly, why faith-based living hasn't completely fixed the inconsistencies within the wounded-self or the outer-world around us.

Many questions remain unanswered such as why, after all these decades, haven't the communities of the faithful been able to overcome the inconsistencies within their own wounded lives. Is it because we cannot make humans stop being human? Are our tribal based rituals, revelations, and rites nothing more than spiritual nicotine-patches designed to numb us to our humanness and create the hope that it will all be over soon?

These questions are difficult to answer, but an understanding of what motivates people's behaviors will be helpful. I want to say from the start that I call myself a Christian in that I both emulate and appreciate the teachings of Jesus, but that is all.

Where I depart from the traditional *norm* is when it comes to my interpretation of the Bible; I see the scriptures as the *word of man* about God as opposed to the *Word of God* about man, to borrow a statement from bishop Carlton Pearson.[1] After all, people wrote it, not God. And we all know what it is to be a human.

Although I see the scriptures as highly valuable and insightful, I do not see them as categorically *literal*, supernaturally imposed, or transcendentally binding upon anyone's life. My desire is not to defend my position or to dismantle another's, but rather the goal is love and a healthy process of personal discovery that can make good sense of the irrefutable issues religion creates for all of us.

Mankind has always been on a search for meaning and origins, but the best we can do with this age-old mystery, in my opinion, is hypothesize. I learned in the ninth grade that a hypothesis was a general principle based upon considerable data, which is then proposed as an explanation for what is observed.

I've had a incredibly open mind for the past fifteen years and see myself as a broadminded progressive thinker. As I get older and hopefully wiser, I have discovered that past beliefs and traditionally/tribally driven ideas formerly unnoticed and largely accepted, no longer work for me. Neither are they in my best interest.

If I may borrow a phrase I heard from bishop Carlton Pearson, I've realized that I haven't really changed my mind in regards to these former ideas as much as my mind has changed me. I trust you'll take no offense at my reasoning, but I want to encourage you to think carefully about the following concepts and musings as I present them and to greet them with the same amount of love and respect they are given—after that you can do

1) Bishop Carlton D'Metrius Pearson, DD (born March 19, 1953 in San Diego, California) is an American minister. At one time, he was the pastor of the Higher Dimensions Evangelistic Center, later named it Higher Dimensions Family Church which was one of the largest churches in Tulsa, Oklahoma. During the 1990s, it grew to an average attendance of over 5,000. Due to his stated belief in universal reconciliation, Pearson rapidly began to lose his influence in ministry with the Joint College of African-American Pentecostal Bishops and was eventually declared a heretic by his peers in 2004.

whatever you want with them.

A Reference Point outside Ourselves

While observing these concepts over the many years that I have been studying them, I have come to a startling realization: most people need an external reference point in order to make the many distinctions regarding their authentic-self. This, I suggest, is a phenomenon.

But there's a fundamental difficulty; people's perceptions differ widely based upon cultural norms, individual knowledge bases, life experiences, upbringing, and geographies—not all people feel the same way, nor do all have the same mind.

Unfortunately, there's a guaranteed singularity that seems to persist among all humans; it's never enough to simply believe something for yourself and enjoy that belief in private—we must create a solicitous in-group forcing everyone else to believe it *with* us if it's going to have any real meaning or evidential merit. Almost like, the larger our in-group, the truer its beliefs become.

Religion appears to do for us what we cannot *allow* ourselves to do *for* ourselves. In other words, if God says I'm good then I'm most definitely good, but if I alone say I'm good apart from what God might think (if God does exist), there will inevitably be another person somewhere in space-time who could announce that I'm *not* as good as I originally thought and influence others to believe it.

As a matter of fact, if I say I am good without any gods saying so, then those within the traditional Eros system will deny my claim altogether. This concept of God declaring we are good not only trumps our behaviors in regards to thought (how we *think* about our behaviors in light of what we *believe* God and people think about us behaving badly), but also it literally *modifies* our behaviors.

Thinking does not have to be the enemy of belief; it can also help support or discourage a belief. Thinking mustn't always be subject to belief as if the belief has more enormity. Both thinking *and* believing are done within the same mind—they cannot be separated so easily.

People's beliefs differ in that people are fundamentally different just as our fingerprints differ. Thinking is an essential part of being human—we have the capacity to think for a very good reason—it keeps us safe.

For example, one male mindset "believes" it is a good thing to physically and brutally *beat* a woman into submission because of cultural standards, religious fundamentalism, and acceptances within their personal religious frameset; however, another male mindset believes it is good to *support* the "weaker" vessel because he believes it was the woman who was first deceived and not the man as the Genesis narrative suggests and St. Paul allegedly affirms.

One believes a woman to be completely inferior, while another believes many women to be *silly*[2] or gullible (weaker) as St. Paul again believed. We must always approach the Hebrew mindset knowing that Judaism is a shame-based culture with a patriarchal frame of mind—men are in charge.

Good is therefore subject to an individuals perception, which can differ enormously between people and is based upon one's personal interests, worldview, culture, or upbringing. In other words, without an outside (of this physical world system or planet) influence establishing a standard rule of conduct, people tend towards what appears to be right in their own eyes.

In other words, while one believes it's okay to have a glass of wine, another believes it to be a sin. Both should respect their own belief without passing judgment on the other. Unfortunately many with strict regulatory driven mindsets cannot allow others to participate in whatever they themselves believe to be wrongdoing.

This can be harmful to a society if those who are at the top administer in harmful ways through ego-driven behaviors, encouraged by the shadow-self and supported through a religious effort. Otherwise we settle for doing what seems right based upon worldviews, community norms, education, or perhaps natural instinct.

This imposed *outside* rule is a phenomenon and is prevalent in not just a few religious communities. The Torah, the Koran, the Bible, the Book of Mormon, the Apocrypha, and other works of standard rules and conduct, allegedly designed *outside* this world

2) 2 Timothy 3:6: "They are the kind who worm their way into homes and gain control over gullible women, who are loaded down with sins and are swayed by all kinds of evil desires" NIV.

system and penned by wounded and broken people, provide a peripheral scaffold for reliance and behavioral modification.

But if these rules are to be followed, there must, unfortunately, be introduced into the system a process of rewards and punishments to ensure its celestial weight and enforcement by the people that preside over it.

Thought Invader: Hell by definition is the naughty step—forever.

All religions offer rules of conduct (typically from *above* less they not be followed) that if violated spell dread and punishment in some form for all offenders. Christianity, for example, offers hell for those in rebellion to the guidelines of conduct or to the *unbeliever*, whom they believe to be *lost*.

Hell is where the unbeliever will reside for all eternity after transition. Flames of fire, torture, and screaming regret and pain are a few descriptors that are designed to thwart unwanted behaviors or to lure nonbelievers into following the religious orders.

Those perceived to be living *outside* the standard operating procedures can be harmful to the religious community and so are typically expelled. It is these distinguishing trademarks within all religious institutions that perpetuate the Eros prison of performance and enable us to follow hard after the correct behaviors acceptable to both the community as a whole and the god who smiles upon us when we properly perform.

People must understand this fundamental truth; behavior is modified best by what we believe to be the best reason for its correction. The claim that behavioral modification is the authentic sign that one has found the true faith or the one true God is both irrational and ridiculous.

For example, obnoxious persons will alter their behavior for the simple reason that they are in a library. A suitor will alter his behavior in order to get the girl, and so on. Any religious in-group will be filled with converts who have aligned behaviorally with what is expected by the code of conduct handed down in order to ensure membership within the coveted tribe.

Figure 1. Pavlov's dog with saliva tube.

My daughter was vegan for many years simply because of her beliefs about cruelty to animals. My own faith in traditional norms was never powerful enough to make me modify my eating habits like my daughters belief in the treatment of animals did for her.

So what is it that accounts for the fundamental changes we make if it isn't the fact that we *believe* we need to make them or we believe we are *supposed* to make them? And what about those who don't make the behavioral transition well?

The answer might surprise you. The fact that the scriptures are riddled with efforts, letters, and pleas to curb human behavior should be the biggest clue imaginable, but for many this glaring opportunity is altogether missed.

It's definitely not automatic; it's a trained response like Pavlov's dog in Figure 1. Depending upon the personality and temperament of each individual, both lasting or limited outcomes will be determined.

Fairness and Equality

What's good for the goose is good for the gander. This is how humans think. Studies have shown that even before the age of one, children notice when one child doesn't receive the same reward as another. This train of thought persists throughout an individual's life. Religion compounds these ideas by setting a cosmic standard of operation for all to follow.

This inadvertently creates in-groups and loyalties toward the cosmic standard. In other words, if I'm going to go to hell because I do such and such then so will you if you do it. It's unfair that you get to cheat on your mate and I don't get to cheat on mine. This is known as the traditional or *regulatory* driven mindset.

Thought Invader: If my traditional mind believes God doesn't want me to kick my dog, then you cannot kick your dog either.

I grew up listening to religious peers who were constantly talking about the behaviors of those outside the in-group. "They shouldn't be smoking" or "I cannot believe they are unmarried and living together." This phenomenon is common among people within the Eros prison of performance.

Living within the prison causes us to take unhealthy interests in what other people do in relationship to what we are doing—we become comparing machines.

It's nearly impossible to let people do what they want and leave them alone from within the Eros prison. If those within the Eros prison cannot change the behavior of outsiders, they will determine the eternal destiny of those outside their tribe in silence. This is another phenomenon: the idea that religious people are somehow *charged* with the mission of determining other people's destiny by determining their behavior *and* motives. Since when did this job fall on us?

Unfortunately, we cannot hold those *outside* our in-group to standards created *within* our in-group anymore than I can hold my neighbor's child accountable to the rules I hold my own children to. This is known as the "right of possession." I have a right to manipulate only the things I possess. I cannot name my neighbor's child; only my neighbor can name his or her own child. My wife heard a child speaking with her friend outside the rod-iron fence that encompasses our backyard and our two beagle's, "You cannot name someone else's dog," she said. It was quite funny.

Unfortunately, because of this internal struggle to both make paradise and please the gods, we must by necessity, hold others accountable to our cosmic standard of operation lest it appear that another is getting away with something we are disallowed to do. These accountability checks that we tirelessly run on others become *markers* that bring clarification to where *we* are, and perhaps where we are not, in the eyes of any given deity.

Without them, we won't know for sure where we stand in the cosmic order. Without comparison, it all falls apart—including the nod from above when we fair better than others in life's sack race. Therefore, those around us both in and outside of our tribal groups become the method of measurement used to establish the goodness of our own deeds.

Without other people to *save*, we would not have an accurate measurement of our role-awareness within communities of belief. Role-awareness thus becomes imperative for sustaining belief and performance initiatives.

This is why evangelism is so important to communities of faith. It creates a standard of performance we can measure up to and feel good about. Ironically, and according to the scriptures, not many who believe it take it seriously enough. And it appears to get more lax as time goes on.

Of course, it's rather difficult to allow others to live however they want to, especially when one believes the standard to be *cosmically* true and binding for *all* peoples. This is the underlying foundation that fuels the ideas of ruling the world. Many people groups have had their chance at power in the times past, including the Babylonians, Persians, Greeks, Romans, and the Americans, and each one determined the ruling religious operation that created subjugation to its machine.

All these nations have both had their day in the sun and lost it (or losing it as in our case). And all those groups who have not ruled it *believe* they eventually will. Christians believe that they will ultimately rule the world for a thousand years with Jesus sitting at the helm from downtown Jerusalem.

Foundational Christian doctrine claims that the nations will bring all their wealth to the Christians who will take it and heap it upon themselves like cosmic winners of an enormous lottery—payday for holding out until the end.

The punishment of those who refuse to believe, therefore, becomes a necessary element that many who believes they have mastered the rules of the game unfortunately *welcome* although would likely never admit it. This has happened in large part with the ISIS movement and Hamas in-groups who are now enforcing their cosmic standard on those *outside* their in-group with severe consequences if resisted.

Evangelicals who condemn it simply and nonthreateningly warn others of the *coming wrath* and use practical persuasive techniques such as *Evangelism*, which are organized acts of proclamation, many times without strings attached, designed to drop people's guard and pique their interest in what they believe.

This is specifically and eloquently designed to influence outsiders to join the in-group before the apocalypse that will melt every individual outside their in-group with fervent heat.

But times have indeed changed and are further changing. Most evangelicals no longer use abusive tactics to convince the gainsayers as they did in the past. No longer are the tactics of the Crusades welcomed in our civilized society. Most have settled for light invitations although it seems odd when you stop to think about what they believe they are inviting people *to* and allegedly rescuing them *from*.

It seems to me that the idea of eternal torture would require a little more enthusiasm. We have Mormon groups and Jehovah's Witnesses who still rely upon door knocking and pamphlets to warn people of the coming doom. Just last night a Christian stopped me at Home Depot in order to introduce me to his savior.

It was not that important to him though—he quickly scurried away when I refused his gesture as if relieved. He did consequently shout, "He loves you!" over his shoulder on his way to his car. It was pretty sad really. I felt bad for the uncomfortable conundrum his need to behave this way had created.[3] His personal imprisonment was revealed.

Thought Invader: People outside the Eros prison mind their own business rather than making everyone else's business their own.

---

3) Solomon said in his proverbs, "He that wins souls is wise." This is a great modifier for those who claim indoctrination under the guise of the 'Great Commission' is necessary to please the gods. Nobody wants to appear stupid.

Needing others to walk the same path we walk is a behavior driven by a perceived celestial mandate that both supports and is common among most faiths. Christian's rely upon what is known as the "*Great Commission*" found in the gospel narratives.

Although contextually this call to action was focused on seventy direct disciples of Jesus during the first century, many use this as a modern day mandate to grow the church and measure both performance and the degree of loyalty to the cause.

> "When you are persecuted in one place, flee to another. Truly I tell you, you will not finish going through the towns of Israel before the Son of Man comes." –Matthew 10:23

This above passage is believed to be Jesus speaking to his disciples who were to go throughout the territory of Jerusalem subject to Roman rule risking their lives with the message of the good news of the *Kingdom*.[4] Many were flogged, killed, and horribly persecuted for associating with Jesus and his message of reform. The Jewish leaders of course despised Jesus and his message of renovation. But that was then.

This is because the "son of man coming" was a prophetic reference to the destruction of Jerusalem—their motherland. It was scheduled for the most destructive assault in 70 AD according to Jewish history. And according to historical sources it happened just as Jesus predicted.

Unfortunately, most if not *all* of the biblical narratives associated with the destruction of the Temple and the Jewish order have been adopted for future use and an alleged coming modern apocalypse we have not yet witnessed.

This is necessary in order to keep the religion going and the Eros prison intact. Without the coming apocalypse it would be that much more problematic to solicit followers who fear the coming wrath let alone keep the one's we already have. This has been the model for the church for over two thousand years. Unfortunately,

4) The Kingdom of God, the Kingdom of heaven, and the family of God are all interchangeable references to the "authority of the kingdom" spoken of by Jesus. There are different beliefs surrounding this idea encompassing an invisible kingdom of enlightenment that resides within a person and as well as a literal walled city that will come out of the sky and land in modern day Jerusalem in the future.

the son of man never comes as this passage has been misinterpreted for as long as people have been waiting for its development.

Proclaiming what God wants and the punishments that will follow if rejected works really well for most, as no person actually knows for sure what is beyond the veil of death. If it were possible to prove there was no hell it wouldn't be likely that most people would care less what anyone did in relationship to their own life; they would be forced to come up with another punishment in order to draw the much-needed distinctions between *us* and *them*.

But as it stands, hell *is* believed to be an actual place by millions and its existence necessitates a need to impose upon others the rules of conduct most likely associated with its avoidance. All who truly believe an idea surrounding any belief or conduct will by necessity have to enforce this rule upon others and not just themselves.

Within the Eros system, it's impossible to believe I must never use course language while at the same time allow you to use it if you want to. According to the rules of traditional thinking, you are not allowed to live in the same world as I and do the things I believe are fundamentally wrong within that world system. The sheer discrepancy warrants action on my part. This is true with any person and any faith or belief.

This is why both the atheists and the religious claim offense when each party acts contrary to the other's beliefs in their world system—atheists own the schools and the Christians own the churches. But atheists want the churches to play by their rules and so does the church the atheists. It's madness. "Could you please not take the Lord's name in vain? Thank you." Or "You shouldn't be allowed to pray in school or set up a manger scene on school property. Thank you."

When atheists and Christians try to enforce their ideologies on others through whatever means, they are living in the Eros prison of performance and simply cannot *be* themselves among themselves. *Being* must be associated with whatever the believer or nonbeliever is doing; it cannot stand alone or apart from others. It's just not possible.

If my being *me* in any way (physiologically or emotionally) ends up costing *you* the freedom to be *you*, then I am in the Eros prison of performance. But if my being me is simply happening along side of you without the need to control or manage *your* behavior (as long as it isn't harmful to me or others), belief, or mindset, then I am free.

But if I am living within the walls of the Eros prison of performance and you say, "it is *not* wrong for me to take the Lord's name in vain," for all intents and purposes, I cannot believe it if it is wrong for me. This is a behavioral phenomenon.

But if I believe it is *actually* factually true that taking the Lord's name in vain is an actual *sin* and you still believe you are correct in believing that it's fine to use the offending language whenever you like, then why am I wasting my time controlling my tongue if you don't have to control yours?

This is where things begin to break down within the prison. The traditional mindset dictates that if I have to curb my tongue, you must by *necessity* have to curb yours or reap the punishment for acting contrary to my cosmic rule, lest I look like a fool for upholding the rule myself. When you believe what I believe, it ensures my beliefs all the more.

Unfortunately, at some point, might *must* make right within this scenario. Within the context of ISIS, they are already using their might to make things right within their world system. Given enough time, all will follow this course of action, as all human behavior subject to the Eros prison demands it.

The church believes this to be the *ultimate* end within their worldview as well, "Every knee shall bow and every tongue shall confess that Jesus Christ is Lord..." even if they don't want to. I have heard people say, "You might as well confess *him* now, as you will certainly have to confess *him* later."

Are We Really the World?

The problem with Eros-driven people is that it is impossible for them to allow other people who are outside of their in-group to live a life they choose, even if it has no affect on anyone else. This is why there is war. And this is why we have a current culture war. One woman believes she can make choices *for* her child while in the womb and another believes she cannot.

Each is constantly interfering with the other. Albeit, one believes one is representing the rights of the unborn child. The point is the *interference* in other people's lives while minding their own business not the rights of anyone.

The power of belief can be so strong that people are willing to make laws that promote their own ideas and support their own beliefs even if the law is at the expense of those who may not believe it. Whether abortion is good or bad becomes irrelevant—you cannot make another person stop doing what you don't want them to do, seeing you believe *you* can't do it yourself.

Lest you think I believe in aborting babies in the womb or harming people in any way, let me be clear—I do not. Freedom means we are free. You may influence others, but you should not be allowed to *control* them or their outcomes if their behaviors are only harmful to themselves alone. It's really none of your business what others do within their own right of possession.

Yes, we must create a society where harmony can exist or be initiated, and that includes laws and guides for cultivating harmonious societies and groups, such as stop signs, medicines that work, etc.

These laws are designed to keep us safe from others whose behaviors may cross over societal or personal lines and affect our own, but it's inappropriate to design laws to keep people "holy" in accordance to a belief you may aspire to if others don't believe it. Belief only presides within the mind of the believer—it doesn't belong anywhere else.

This is where the train leaves the tracks. If we see our beliefs as the *only* beliefs available for self-love within our authentic-selves, then it becomes impossible to love others who think and believe differently. Loving others becomes a task-oriented display of "playing by the rules" so we don't end up punished, more than an actual inward drive to *serve* others regardless of their beliefs.

Face it; it's easier to love those who believe like you, but difficult to love those who don't. Only duty and obligation can create an atmosphere for loving others in opposition to our beliefs. We easily love those who are aligned with our ideology, but must force ourselves to love those who mock it. This is a very hard pill to swallow, but it is true nonetheless.

Some believe you have to be religious to be good. You don't

have to "believe" anything to love appropriately and care deeply for another. Can homosexuals love children? Some don't think so. The standard for being a complete person should rest with the idea itself and not with a set of rules an in-group or individual comes up with.

Rules can be (and should be) placed into a forum for discussion and allowed to be proposed as a possible benchmark for creating a better outcome between peoples in a society, but to enforce our own ideas on others because one *believes* them is not entirely productive. Love allows others to live to the level of their own goodness or demise, provided they do not enslave or harm others in any way.

Thought Invader: Never judge what a person believes, but rather give your attention to what a person does regardless of what the person believes.

Some say there are plenty of people who are better by nature than others are through faith. Is anyone really better than another? Or are we all simply humans making decisions through different processes of doing and being that produce different consequences (decisions—con (*with*) sequence)?

This is another astounding phenomenon. Right and wrong are subject to individual beliefs. What one sees as right, another sees as wrong even within in-groups. Societies as a whole will make determinations based on community rules in order to establish peace and foster solidarity usually for protection, but in most cases isolated beliefs are not subject to whole societies unless the society deems it worthy. Laws are for lawbreakers.

All Performance Isn't Wrong

Understand, not all performances are need based. A circus performer performs because that is his or her job. We perform at work because we are being paid to perform. So why are we singled out for living in a performance prison when performance is necessary in so many areas?

The performance prison is not related to doing a job well or working at the circus. The performance prison is Eros in nature, meaning self-preserving. Unfortunately, religion by its very nature commands that actions diminish in the shadow of beliefs. In other words, within the Eros prison, beliefs speak louder than actions and actions speak louder than words as shown in the figure illustrated below.

This is why one may perform well by all human and cosmic standards yet still be punished for all eternity because one did *not believe* in the right message. This too is pointless. And this is the weakest link within the framework of religion and why it promotes the Eros prison. People should be judged (if judged at all) based on their intentions *behind* personal performance and not on the beliefs that allegedly drive their performance or their intentions.

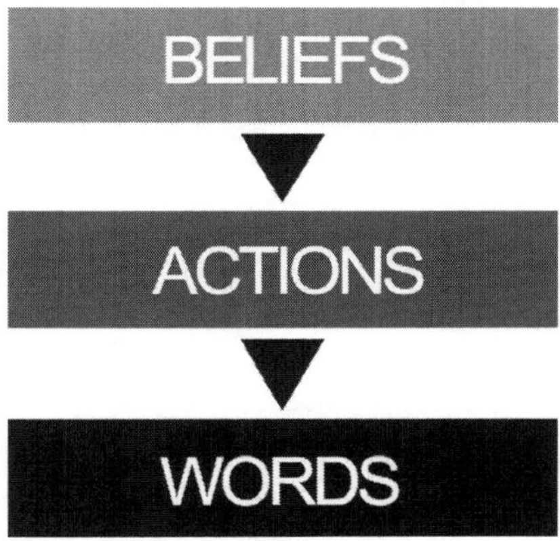

Fig. 1. The thought hierarchy within the Eros prison.

This is because a person can still help other persons even if they don't subscribe to the same beliefs about why they are doing it. We shouldn't have to *go* along in order to *get* along. My help for another should not depend on the beliefs we share or lack.

When living out of the authentic-self, people's beliefs cease to be a prerequisite for general engagement, friendship, or partnership. Although having similar worldviews can promote longevity between people, the relationship is not dependent upon it, motivated by it, or subject to it.

I heard a person on the radio say they never heard of an atheist humanitarian organization. It made me think a little deeper about the comment as this was on a Christian radio broadcast—the perfect audience for such a statement. The intent was to establish an association between Christianity and benevolence.

By saying it this way, that person left the listener assuming that atheists are incapable of caring about people at worst and an anomaly if they did at best. The statement underpinned the idea that if an unbelieving person did provide assistance to a less fortunate person it ultimately had no real merit because the beliefs behind the benevolent action did not necessarily support it.

This was a performance-driven statement made from within the Eros prison. In other words, if I believe in God and I'm working alongside an atheist (someone who does not *believe* in any god) who also cares for the poor or gives to the needy as I do, then what separates me from that atheist?

For fear of associating benevolence with an unbeliever, I must discredit the atheists by drawing a distinction between them and me through a negative comment targeting their belief or lack of it, seeing that I am unable to target their actions because they are in effect *equal* to mine.

I must do this because I am *insecure* and overly concerned with *not* being a separate individual that is associated with or acknowledged by a creator and its need for me to perform. In other words, my Eros attitude fears sameness or *equality* with anyone who differs in belief.

Because of this Eros insecurity, I must prove the differences between us lest we be the same in the eyes of others. This insecurity thus creates a gap or a *difference* between my humanitarian performance and the atheist's humanitarian performance albeit in the end the results are the same.

Likewise, if the atheist is happy to work with me regardless of my beliefs and he or she believes we both accomplished a good deed that deserves equal commendation, then the atheist is by all intents and purposes free and I am not.

If I am living out of my authentic-self, I can work side by side with an atheist, a homosexual, or a convicted felon; I can work with anyone and enjoy our work together for the poor or disenfranchised without having to draw attention to why I am doing it or make distinctions between our beliefs in an attempt to determine who is better, better off, or in need of the other's ideas. This is what real Eros freedom looks like!

As an Eros prisoner, it would be next to impossible to allow myself as a person of faith to work side by side with an atheist or agnostic and also allow them the same exact amount of kudos from God that I am receiving for the same accomplishment.

Although I may personally give approval for the deed itself, I mustn't credit an overall *celestial* approval from the gods, lest I muddy up the differences between us. So in all reality, who is this really all about? Them? No. Me? Yes.

Therefore, I *must* feel the need to either plant the seeds of my faith through conversation or collaborate with "the Spirit" in an effort to thwart their thinking, as I am likely under the assumption that I am safe and he or she is *not*.

Not only is this humanitarianly prejudice, but also it is sad—sad because I will ultimately miss out on the joy of knowing them as unique persons of intrinsic value and will be hard pressed to learn from them seeing that I believe they are *lost* and thus *lower* on the verticality ethics scale.[5]

Living this way ensures that the *beliefs* or statements of faith one uses as a ruler for measuring the quality of rightness for living become more important than the relationships the beliefs are designed to forge. Relationships thus become instrumental in their action rather than primary in their root.

On the other hand, if one happens to be an *unbeliever* in the sense that one has not adopted or been convinced of what others believe or consider truthfulness, one's involvement with that person will be limited at best. Unfortunately, most strong *believers* of any sect only associate with those outside their worldview in an attempt to get them in it.

One of the largest obstacles in the involvement with religious in-groups is the need to believe in the same things before being fully accepted into that community. And yes, if a community of people decides that certain beliefs are necessary to be a part of that particular in-group or tribe, then those who adhere to a different set of beliefs should not pursue involvement with that community

5) The verticality Ethics Scale measures the ethical value of an individual in light of any given religious framework such as sinner's and saint's.

as this would be highly disruptive to the group.

To add to this enigma, these communities are driven to expand their size, lest they suffer negative emotional feedback from the deities who demand that they build and expand to include the whole of mankind. Unfortunately, this creates the conundrum of "damned if I do" and "damned if I don't."

In other words, there is no such thing as the late Michael Jackson's powerful vision of "we are the world" while maintaining differences in belief. We will never be "the world" in this sense—it's just not possible.

Humans have been vying for the top position in regards to the best or most popular group since the beginning of time, dating back to the Tower of Babel. The Babel story is the picture of tribal in-grouping and its necessity for the survival of the species. The intervening deity is a picture of the requirement for subgrouping by culture, community, or language in order to bring personal and group definition and autonomy. This is the greatest thing religion does for us.

Therefore, religious communities by their sheer design must solicit those who have no desire to join in an effort to increase its numbers and influence in order to gain world or community supremacy, which in turn brings credibility to the group. The goal of every major religion is to dominate the world—either by love or by hate. Either way, the root need is personal definition and social separation in an effort to please the gods and feel worthy.

It is therefore the process of *misunderstanding* the authentic-self that becomes the driver behind religious solicitations and in-group building. People in religious communities feel pressed to disassociate with other groups because of eons of tribal in-grouping and definition building. The need to encroach on others, who may be busy minding their own business and living out their own authentic life, thus becomes irresistible.

Thought Invader: Leaving other people alone is not an option when it comes to social orders, structures, and frameworks where religious ideologies proliferate.

The compulsory *need* to convert the self of others is consequently a significant sign that one may be locked inside the Eros prison of performance and competition masked by evangelism allegedly spawned by *love*. But this is not what it actually *is*.

People's accompanying actions associated with any belief they hold are the greater part in regards to that belief, and it is these actions themselves that create the conditions for harmony and security if they are built upon a foundation of altruism *alone*.

Unfortunately, many actions done *to* others in the name of any religious deity or belief system are designed to *influence* another's *belief* as opposed to simply enjoy the relational differences while loving the person *as is*. It therefore becomes impossible to get along with anyone who believes differently.

For example, organized religious groups may give away sandwiches in the park to the homeless, but not without delivering a message of "*hope*" that for some at its root says, "You are not worth feeding for the sake of humanitarianism *alone*. We are feeding you only in an effort to *condition* you to accept our message."

The food is the baited-hook. I have actually heard this taught. This is known as *conditioning* (Figure 1.) and many groups practice it in one form or another for the specific purpose of lessening the chances of refusal.

"Greeters" are taught to make people *feel* welcome and many religious organizations have developed classes in order to modify their behavior. Of course, some of this reflects introversion on the part of a greeter; others simply don't want to do it. This brings us back to the Eros prison of performance.

We must *perform* in an effort to *persuade*. No longer is it simply about *being* because this ability to live free does not reflect the externals of religious association, competition, or campaigning.

Granted, not all individuals within these groups think this way, but the problem with this behavioral modification technique is that everybody knows what is going on except the persuaders themselves, and fortunately those living outside these tribal walls aren't buying it anymore.

But do these people groups really believe in their own message? Are the persuaders really that heart broken when outsiders refuse their call to repentance? Do people leave weeping and sobbing for their souls or do they go home and watch television?

The question remains, what affect does this behavioral framework have on the authentic-self? What about the shadow-self? The answers to these questions are worth finding.

Thought Invader: It's difficult to wake up each and every day and determine who is or is not in need of enlightenment.

When categorizing ourselves (regardless of the virtuous reasons we come up with) we end up categorizing everyone else by default. This inadvertently creates the "us against them" paradigm prevalent within and in some cases without religious communities.

Is it possible to simply love people and help those who may be in need simply because it's the human thing to do and not have a greater cosmic agenda? I argue that the answer unfortunately must be a *no* if you are a part of a religious in-group. Caring is glued to converting within most religious in-groups.

If people outside any given religious persuasion love people and help the people in need simply because it seems the right thing to do, but do not believe in any religious memorandum (most Abrahamic faiths) supported by those faiths, then the acts of righteousness, *without* the correct corresponding *beliefs* that support them, are believed by the religious to be *rubbish* in themselves and short of any material good in a cosmic sense.

Their efforts therefore must go unnoticed by the gods and unrewarded in the end. This is why the Eros prison pervades within religious systems, because it must. We find this scenario within the tenth chapter of the New Testament book of The Acts of the Apostles, when Cornelius, a leader of an Italian regiment, is confronted by an angel (messenger) with the message of The Way.[6]

> "At Caesarea there was a man named Cornelius, a centurion in what was known as the Italian Regiment. He and all his family were devout and God-fearing; *he gave generously to those in need and prayed to God regularly*. One day at about three in the afternoon he had a vision. He distinctly saw an angel of God, who came to him and said, "Cornelius!"
>
> "Cornelius stared at him in fear. "What is it, Lord?" he

6) This story unfolds in Acts chapter 10.

> asked. The angel answered, "Your prayers and gifts to the poor have come up as a memorial offering before God. Now send men to Joppa to bring back a man named Simon who is called Peter. He is staying with Simon the tanner, whose house is by the sea."

Later in verses 44 and 45 we read:

> "While Peter was still speaking these words, the Holy Spirit came on all who heard the message. The circumcised believers who had come with Peter were astonished that the gift of the Holy Spirit had been poured out even on Gentiles."

This story has been used for decades to infer that although helping the poor or doing any other humanitarian act may gain God's attention, it fails to qualify a person *before* God as one who is *acceptable* and an *integral* part of the Kingdom *of* God.

This is the heart of the performance prison: we believe we *must* perform a particular ritualistic act of obedience before a deity before being *accepted* by that deity. This is better known as *initiation*.

Unless Cornelius was "initiated" through the ritual of baptism, public confession, and in this particular case, speaking in tongues (Glossolalia[7]), he would remain *outside* the in-group (and heaven), regardless of any good deeds he may have done.

He would be destined for eternal torture for everlasting time simply because he didn't *believe* what they believed about the unbelievable, in spite of what he did for the needy—his deeds were ultimately irrelevant.

Someone recently told me that before they "found Christ," life was not working out for them, but since their *initiation* it has blossomed. Although this may be true, does it mean everyone who has not yet discovered Christ's teachings or has not yet been initiated into the "family" will have a terrible life that will not work out for them? To believe this would be preposterous.

Not everyone needs religious guardrails in order to function

7) Glossolalia, often understood among Protestant Christians as speaking in tongues, is the fluid vocalizing of speech-like syllables that lack any readily comprehended meaning, in some cases as part of religious practice. Some consider it as a part of a sacred language. It is a common practice amongst Pentecostal and Charismatic Christianity.

well, prosper, and treat other people with dignity and respect, but it's also obvious that some do. Because some find life *better* when they are *forced* to do well, does it mean those who don't need this religious mandate are suspect?

This person was obviously a self-centered jerk before being introduced to the teachings of Jesus. I'm glad he listened to them. But not everyone who doesn't believe Jesus is *God* is a self-centered jerk, although some are unmistakably viscerally problematic.

I have discovered that many *need* behavior-modifying laws in order to keep them from self-centered behaviors that will ultimately harm themselves or others, but this cannot be mistaken for something it is not.

Religion isn't the only means of solving this problem among people. Unfortunately, many believe it to be the *only* viable antidote, thus denying any other spiritually based process for learning to love the self and others. The fear of *punishment* and the fear of *displeasing* a deity is what drive most people to do well.

> "By faith Noah, being warned of God of things not seen as yet, *moved with fear*, prepared an ark to the saving of his house; by the which he condemned the world, and became heir of the righteousness which is by faith." –Hebrews 11:7

Unfortunately, because of the human dynamics we observe within societies at large, religion seems to be one of the most necessary evils to keep many people focused on something other than themselves. I therefore suggest when picking our in-groups and loyalties, we pick one that includes everyone.

We cannot afford another belief system that presently destroys everyone who does not believe in it or waits for his or her deity to do it for them through some apocalyptic event much later on. This idea only creates divisive and conquering mindsets that perpetuate the Eros initiatives we all long to avoid.

6

Our Need for Self-Validation

"I have no master plan for the religious reconstruction of the world, only a boundless confidence that the man who abandons his religious myth and is free from his idols will discover god in the growing *honesty* and *freedom* of his own life." —James Kavanaugh.

Many times our worth is discovered in what we *do* because it's impossible to improve upon our *being* who we *are*. Who we are remains precious regardless of our accomplishments or associations, but few see themselves as precious. For many, it's not enough to simply *be*—to simply enjoy who we *are* as our authentic-self and embrace it for what it's worth. For this reason many struggle to be noticed by others—to be validated.

They're forever refining and redefining their appearance and their credentials, or whatever else they can manipulate into a position of higher importance. Therefore, the objective for many is to cover up and, perhaps unintentionally, deface the beauty within by focusing too much energy on external accomplishments, deities, relationships, or whatever else that provides worth and significance.

Religion thus becomes the perfect host for validation and personal, social, and emotional rewards; everyone wants to hear the gods say, "Well done thy good and faithful servant. Enter ye into the joy of the Lord."

Decision Making and the Self

You may not recognize this now, but your authentic-self cannot be improved upon—it's touchless. It's that part of you that remains *eternal*—unable to be destroyed, marred, enhanced, or even distinguished by willing it to happen or by attaching external accomplishments or applying religious rules to it. Think of your internally eternal being as something akin to your intelligence quotient (IQ).

Our intelligence quotient is the same at the age of seventy-seven as it was at the age of seven—it doesn't grow because we read a book about Super String theory or because we finished high school or attended a high-class university. Our IQ always remains static not fluid because it represents an *established* amount of brain capacity.

People don't really become smarter as you might believe; they're simply more informed, equipped, or experienced through practice, engagement, and exposure to newfound realities. How one interprets or utilizes the new information determines the level of intellectual competence one actually has. We all know the so-called smart people (those with a huge information bank) who make very poor decisions with the information they possess.

Research has shown that your IQ is either high, moderate, or low regardless of how much information you may have acquired over the years—applying it can be difficult for some with a lower IQ.

Not only IQ but also wisdom is essential for good decision making. This innate ability to make good choices based upon the knowledge one possesses is many times referred to as *wisdom*—this is why many people outrival others more educated in life though only possessing a high-school diploma.

This also involves another element known as *emotional intelligence* (EI or sometimes called EQ—*emotional quotient*). Although the emotional quotient can vary between different people, unlike the IQ, it can almost always be improved upon.

Therefore, our level of knowledge does not affect our true authentic-self, our *spirit* being. Gaining knowledge does not enhance our authentic-self in any way. In all honesty, it has nothing to do with our authentic-self whatsoever.

Our spirit-self remains untouched by information, ritual, or rules. Our minds may benefit, but our true authentic-self does not change based upon an increase in knowledge or an upsurge of good deeds.

has the greatest impact on how we make decisions.

Thanks to the work of Dr. Hartman, we have a better grasp on value theory and the decision-making process. Our decisions and actions will always involve two elements: a *factual* aspect, which can be seen and empirically measured, and an intangible aspect, which can be *felt* and *believed*, but may not be immediately clarified in reasons, facts, and causes. For example, my request, "Please get my 'good' shirt" may mean for me my "blue cotton shirt which is thin and well worn."

The descriptive properties blue, thin, and well worn are easily identifiable, but the descriptive phrase "good" represents a different specific set of properties that I associate with shirts that I consider "good."

If the person to whom I make my request does not know what this combination of properties is, he or she may not only have difficulty finding my "good shirt," but more importantly, may disagree with me about what comprises a "good shirt" altogether.

Good has no universal definition, as everyone's value scale is obviously different. Of course, within the religious world, there will be a number of folks who believe it can only mean God. This is taken from the words of Jesus in the gospels when he says: "*Why callest thou me good? There is no one that is good except God alone.*"

The Hebrews believed no *good* people existed in and among themselves. They believed that God could not find one good person on the earth if he tried.

> "God has looked down from heaven upon the sons of men to see if there is anyone who understands, who seeks after God. They have all fallen away; together they have become corrupt; there is none who does good, not even one." –Psalm 53:3

It's this message of "non-goodness" that has proliferated Judeo-Christian concepts for thousands of years and has been the biggest culprit in the creation of the Eros prison—we are never "good enough" or we are only good because Jesus told his father we were good and begged him not to torture us forever in hell. So God tortured Jesus instead, but we for sure deserved it. But we will all get what we deserve in the end if we don't accept what Jesus did for us.

This is where the "*Santa Clause Concept*" comes from. Founded upon and within a religious framework, the story of St. Nicholas as it has trickled down through time brings with it the same religious trappings all other associations with religion do:

> You better watch out, you better not cry, you better not pout, I'm telling you why; Santa Clause is coming to town. He's making a list and checking it twice; he's gonna find out who's naughty and nice, Santa Clause is coming to town.
>
> He sees you when you're sleeping. He knows when you're awake. He knows if you've been bad or good so be good for goodness sake. Oh, you better watch out. You better not cry. You better not pout, I'm telling you why, Santa Clause is coming to town.[1]

This is the exact same premise we witness within the first-century apocalypse narrative spoken by Jesus to the Jews.

> "But about that day or hour no one knows, not even the angels in heaven, nor the Son, but only the Father. Be on guard! Be alert ! You do not know when that time will come. It's like a man going away: He leaves his house and puts his servants in charge, each with their assigned task, and tells the one at the door to keep watch.
>
> "Therefore keep watch because you do not know when the owner of the house will come back—whether in the evening, or at midnight, or when the rooster crows, or at dawn. If he comes suddenly, do not let him find you sleep-

1 Santa Clause is Coming to Town is a Christmas song. It was written by John Frederick Coots and Haven Gillespie and was first sung on Eddie Cantor's radio show in November 1934. It became an instant hit with orders for 100,000 copies of sheet music and more than 30,000 records sold within 24 hours.

ing. What I say to you, I say to everyone: 'Watch!' "–Mark 13:32-37

The Eros prison of performance exists because at root level we believe we are not good. Perpetuated by concepts such as Santa Clause and the return of Jesus, these feelings of low self-worth pervade within all societies.

Thought Invader: "We are not our mind" –Eckhart Tolle.

Songs such as "Jesus loves the little children" mask the distortion and leave one with feelings of better self-worth when *associated* with Jesus, but only until one understands these deeper concepts later to be revealed. Sadly, others feel no self-worth seeing that there isn't any human worth in itself apart from the religions sanction. The Eros concept, birthed through the Hebrew traditional stories, has had a profound *negative* impact on the world at large.

Faith, Religion, and Spirit Being

I want to help you understand the power of performance through the venue of faith, relationship, religion, or spirituality and further expound on the ideas we just talked about. One of the most misunderstood areas of "being" falls within matters of faith, spirituality, and religion.

I understand many Christians speak of *relationship* as if it's able to replace religion, but religion is still an organized collection of *beliefs*, cultural *systems*, and *world views* that relate humanity to an order of existence believed to be both here on earth and beyond the stars.

Whether based on biblical ideas and concepts or elusive idealistic notions rooted in the universe or subjective realities, beliefs that affect actions through organized systems are always religious at its root.

Having spent thousands of hours reading and studying Christian philosophies, Judaism, and other sects, it's appropriate that I speak through that particular lens although *any* religious affiliation will work, as the language of behavior is cross cultural in regards to beliefs and will fit any social or religious paradigm. It's important that we understand how religion and ideology impact the Eros prison.

The Christian message is about a rebirth (this is known by the term *born again*) of the authentic-self. It's one of the most widely held beliefs on earth and one of the most *attractive* lifestyles in the Western world although there has been a recent shift in this.

The concept of a spiritual rebirth is frequently understood strictly within the framework of Judeo-Christian concepts and is highlighted around the *spirit*-self on the *inside* and not an external (flesh-body) person including the mind, feelings, and emotions.

According to this line of thought, it is believed the *whole* person physical, mental, and spiritual can be divided into three parts, known as the trinity of man. They include the spirit, the soul, and the body respectively.

Thus according to many spiritual frameworks (not just Christianity), we are a *spirit* (the invisible ethereal *us*), we have a *soul* (mind, emotions, desires, thoughts, uniqueness), and we live in a *body* (skin, organs, brain matter, fingernails, etc.).

Jesus referred to this imagery when he spoke of "white washed sepulchers filled with dead men's bones," when addressing religious leaders who publicly appeared (what you would see through observation *externally*—the human body with its actions represented as a tomb) one way, while secretly (hidden *motives* of the soul—that which one cannot see represented as dead men's bones) *being* another in private.

This on all counts is a *contradiction* within the self and it's known as a "me-me" conflict. It's akin to a kingdom divided against itself. Pious religious leaders knew Jesus for pointing out the obvious and publicly condemning these divisive and conflictive actions.

It is these actions that speak of a deeper confinement with walls that cannot be as easily overcome—deep within the Eros prison. Therefore, when Jesus spoke of freeing people, he was freeing them from the Eros prison of religion—deliverance.

> Jesus said to him, "Today *salvation* has come to this house, because this man, too, is a son of Abraham.'" — Luke 19:9

This is a story about a Jewish tax collector. A tax collector in the first century was an extortionist—a thief. The Romans controlled them and thus many Jews believed they had sold out to the Roman machine. Tax collectors were akin to the mafia today. Enter Jesus:

> "Jesus entered Jericho and was passing through. A man was there by the name of Zacchaeus; he was a chief tax collector and was wealthy. He wanted to see who Jesus was, but because he was short he could not see over the crowd. So he ran ahead and climbed a sycamore-fig tree to see him, since Jesus was coming that way.
>
> When Jesus reached the spot, he looked up and said to him, "Zacchaeus, come down immediately. I must stay at your house today." So he came down at once and welcomed him gladly. All the people saw this and began to mutter, "He has gone to be the guest of a sinner."
>
> But Zacchaeus stood up and said to the Lord, "Look, Lord! Here and now I give half of my possessions to the poor, and if I have cheated anybody out of anything, I will pay back four times the amount." –Luke 19:1-8

This is another astounding account of Jesus influencing another through pure unconditional love. Zacchaeus' response to Jesus inviting himself over for a meal is simply mind blowing. Jesus says, "Today salvation (deliverance) has come to this house, because this man, too, is a son of Abraham."

Thought Invader: Religion creates walls between the one in need and the givers of life before them.

The Jews did not want to identify with the tax collector. But Jesus reinforces the idea by spelling it out to the crowd that "This man, too, is a son of Abraham." Jesus was saying, "Like it or not, he is one of you." Both Jesus' lack of correction and his unbridled love toward Zacchaeus tear the walls of his Eros prison away only to leave a generous and repentant authentic-self behind.

There is no prayer, no fanfare, and no hoopla. Just a simple transaction between him and Zacchaeus through pure agape (selfless) love and generosity. Why no one else could accomplish this is anybody's guess. I suspect it is because they could only see a *distorted* figure of him through the bars of their Eros prison.

Our Insatiable Need to Convert the Self

The insatiable need to convert the authentic safe-self never seems to go away. People never seem to feel good enough. Some will tell you this is the sign that they are not, but I would respectfully differ. It's because it's all we've ever heard.

According to early Christian text sources, the writers claim Jesus believed the human spirit or *being* could be changed from darkness to light—or possibly better known by Easterners as the process of *enlightenment*, but is this what Jesus really believed?

It says in John 1:9 that "There was the true *Light* which, coming into the world, *enlightens* every man." According to the writer of John's gospel, Jesus was able to *enlighten* all those who believed it possible. Drenched in darkness by religion and selfish living, the authentic-self was hidden from almost everyone.

It was Jesus who was able to strip away the layers that kept Zacchaeus' authentic-self hidden for years. He exposed *it* without exposing *him*—by preserving *him* without socially ridiculing *him*.

According to the writers of the biblical texts (mainly St. Paul according to theologians), the spirit-self (of humankind) could be affected—altered in some mysterious way although by all scientific accounts, this process remains quite undetected and wholly and *completely* immeasurable.

This concept is birthed in the idea that our first entrance into existence begins in a *darkened state of being* rather than an *enlightened* one based upon ancient Hebrew garden theology.

In other words, our authentic-self, rather than *being* the divine nature it is, can only *partake* (sample) of the "supreme" divine nature (of God) not having any of its own. This concept unfortunately misses the mark and thus perpetuates the performance mentality in all people. We are all *working* towards the *light*, but sadly, only a handful will ever reach it—so they say.

Therefore *only* eight souls were saved as by water. –1 Peter 3:20 (The Noah story.)

In order to better clarify the possible existence of the authentic spirit-self, we must contemplate this statement: "*I've got to quit doing this to myself.*" This is believed to be the authentic sign that we are a spirit, we have a soul, and we live in a body—a three part being. Although the reality of such a notion escapes the human eye, many believe in this hypothesis.

The "I" reflects the mechanical body and/or soul-mind whereas the "myself" component represents the authentic spirit-self that is the divine nature deep within the *middle* of us all (Greek for middle; *kardia,* meaning the *heart*).

Let's look at another example, say I have a drinking problem. I might say something such as "*I've got to get a handle on myself*" or "*I cannot live with myself any longer.*" Eckhart Tolle mumbled this later statement many years ago. He claims it catapulted him and sparked a revolutionary process *within* him that led to his rethinking of what life was all about.[2]

According to these double self-styled statements (and we all make similar statements), it appears there are two selfs, the *self* that has the drinking problem (the natural-self likely effected by the shadow-self) and the *self* that cannot live with it anymore (the divine nature or authentic-self).

If this is indeed true, and perhaps it is as I'm inclined to believe so, then it would make sense that the drinking *self* would need the more attention and not the other *self* that remains tired of it. But according to many religious belief systems, *both* selfs are in need of improvement through a conversion. Thus the *authentic-self* is utterly and *wholly* corrupt according to mainline Christian doctrine and others.

It is said that the *authentic*-self is changed in an instant (from darkness to light) through belief in Jesus as God (conversion), but the *natural* soul-self is changed over time (known by theologians as the process of *sanctification*) although never *fully* changed until full redemption of the flesh-body, which is supposed to take place

2) The Power of Now by Eckhart Tolle, copyright© 1999 New World Library, 14 Pamaron Way, Novato, CA 94949.

in natural death or through the great vanishing (Greek, parousia) when Christ returns in the sky on a white horse to fully redeem the earth and its inhabitants after destroying all his enemies by fire from heaven. This is the conundrum. According to these philosophies there is no *safe*-self within these concepts apart from *converting* the most inner authentic-self through a religious framework or formulaic processes.

If the innermost self is not converted through this particular redemptive process (many times heavily scrutinized by leaders in the know), according to present day Christian concepts, the inner-self remains *corrupt*, wholly separated from God, and awaits what is known as the *second death*, which consists of eternal fire and torture of the body, the authentic-self, and the soul-self in hell forever, the eternal naughty step.

This concept by its very nature brings the Eros prison to a level of possibility beyond comprehension. Interestingly enough, many theologians argue that the theory of evolution with its ideas of chance and accidental happenstance have had horrible affects upon our society while not realizing that the idea of a darkened corrupt self has the same implications.

School shootings and the like have also been attributed to the teachings of evolutionary concepts as they render students *causeless* through belief that they are accidental occurrences brought on by time and chance happening upon matter. I fully understand the reasoning. Unfortunately this has trouble holding a candle to the idea that the authentic-self is utterly *corrupt* and doomed to hellfire and torture if one fails to adopt religious particulars and beliefs in unprovable ideologies set forth within ancient texts.

The idea that the authentic-self is *not* a divine nature leaves us little hope of believing it could be, seeing we must all *begin* within the Eros prison of hopelessness if disassociated with Christian concepts.

No Safe-Self

I've seen countless mini-posters on Facebook depicting a lighthouse and storm surge or pictures of Jesus holding a lamb or an angel hovering over a sick child in the hospital. These images are meant to portray the safety that comes only from converting the self. They are meant to force our imagination to wonder what will happen if we fail to let it happen. They are an ingenious approach to emotional manipulation.

You may have heard that "*You must be born again.*" These are the words attributed to Jesus when speaking to a Jew named Nicodemus in the first century in the third chapter of John. This passage is related to the very well-known John 3:16 discourse.

> "How can a man be born again when he is old? Can he enter a second time into his mother's womb and be born?" This was Nicodemus' reply to such an astonishing claim by the rabbinical teacher.

> Jesus replied, "That which is born of the spirit is spirit and that which is born of the flesh is flesh. Marvel not that I said unto you, you must be born again." –John 3:16

This idea that our very authentic-*self* must be *fixed* or reborn has its origins as far back as the garden story within the Hebrew Genesis narrative. Disobedience of God's instructions by the first authentic humans after listening to a deceptive talking snake ruins the authentic-self for all time. According to Christian thought, since the time of this alleged *fall* of humankind many thousands of years ago we have been endeavoring to repair and renovate our broken *authentic*-self, but to no avail.

Subsequent formulas, religious rituals, and man-made rules have all been but unsuccessful attempts at rescuing the broken-self from the eternal state of sad insufficiency and the promised destruction that awaits behind the veil of death. Unfortunately, this irreversible "condition" is likely responsible for the groundbreaking and the initial foundation upon which the Eros prison of performance has been built.

The Book of Beginnings tells a story of a young couple and depicts the prison of performance when the couple decides to *mask* their *nakedness* and bolster their appearance by creating aprons with leaves from a fig tree. This symbolic action is suggestive of the two pillars of performance: shame and guilt.

These two pillars become the towers that not only generate a deep fear *of* the gods, but also initiate a hiding *from* the gods whose righteous anger must be appeased through the barbaric ritual of animal blood-sacrifice.

Amazingly, but not surprisingly the garden myth has been believed to be an *actual* occurrence by millions of people for many hundreds of years. Moreover, the fig-leaf aprons are the first Eros attempt at *performing* for the gods within the Hebrew Bible.

Although the garden myth is a simple moral tale that speaks of poor decision-making and the unfavorable consequences that follow, the Eros prison has since pervaded among millions. This same Eros prison of performance is later seen in the legend of Cain and Abel. Cain apparently kills his brother Abel in a desperate attempt to quell the misgivings within his wounded-self after he finds out the deity is unsatisfied with his offering, but not his brother Abel's.

Cain becomes exceedingly offended and further wounded within his soul-self because God refuses his sacrifice and accepts his brother Abel's gift instead. Rather than making attempts to right his wrong and endeavor to bring the correct animal for sacrifice, he throws his ball down and goes home in a heated rage of jealousy.

It isn't long before he kills his brother after allowing his feelings of inferiority to simmer. Fueled by his shadow-self who decides getting even is the only option, Cain is the first among many millions who will not be able to bear the shame of not living up to the expectations of others. Does this sound familiar?

Interestingly enough, there is no mention of a deceptive serpent in this story or an exterior influence to raise questions of allegiance. This begs the question: what does this story ultimately reveal about us as people? I'll suggest this story is about the competitive self. It's about performance anxiety, jealousy, and the wounded-self that remains in competition with others. Within the Eros prison of performance, nobody wins.

Cain became jealous because the gods looked favorably upon Abel and his accomplishments while looking upon Cain's with disappointment and disapproval; both are necessary elements for low self-worth—something Cain was already experiencing in the shadow of his brother's more notable performances. We see this over and over again within later biblical narratives including David and Saul and others.

These ancient types and shadows reveal not only the emotions of the ancients, but also our own sense of inferiority, our own sense of brokenness and our apparent inability to measure up to others or the high gods and their celestial standards. As unfortunate as it appears, these behavioral gymnastics between people and the gods have been in play for a very long time.

The inescapable Eros prison was already underway within the minds of those dwelling in the Fertile Crescent many millennia ago. Whether it is the Epic of Gilgamesh or some other ancient writ, competitive actions and performance-driven behaviors among people and people-groups have been a fundamental framework within all societies.

Thought Invader: The concept of appeasing an angry and difficult God may be the oldest and most grim ideological barrier to overcome in the entire universe.

If we are indeed broken at the deepest level of the self, then according to ancient storytelling, our *authentic-self* is not safe without religious influence, instruction, or a divine roadmap that can lead us to the only place that can right this wrong—the converted self by a deity through performance initiatives.

The problem is that there are thousands of religious frameworks laying claim to the *only* way to accomplish this most coveted act of redemption.

This again begs the question: are people actually born *damaged* goods? Are we truly doomed from our humble beginning? I was taught for years that we were, but after much thinking, I have reached a better conclusion that I believe makes better sense and has better outcomes.

Self-Distortion

The authentic-self *cannot* be corrupt or broken in my opinion—ever. I have thought very long and very hard about this concept. Think of high school; everyone starts out with an A as opposed to an F as a freshman. Imagine we are all born into the cosmos with an A+ self; imagine we are completely devoid of wrongdoing, wrong being, or in urgent need of any religious restorative processes—simply and utterly *authentic.*

Imagine the exterior influences, people, negative experiences, traumas, and the like, all crashing against our inner selves like a storm out of control. Imagine our self-organizing minds (souls) beginning to corrupt the truth about who we *really* are as religion permeates our societies. We look at our self through the soul—a distorted place of being influenced by feelings and emotions under the stress of inadequacy.

To add to this enigma, during our formative years (if born into a religious framework) all those we look to for direction, correction, and guidance are always telling us that they are the only ones holding the key to our much-needed *spiritual* restoration.

The beliefs we receive from *trusted* guardians while young tend to be the beliefs we ultimately believe with little exception until forced to think on our own. Statistically, if one is not converted to any religious belief system before age fourteen, the odds that they will not convert at all dramatically increase.

This is why the children's church is one of the top three tiers within modern church development. Leaders are taught that if they "get to the children first," the parents will follow. It's interesting to note that in regards to Abraham, the father of the three major religions, it is said:

> "For I have chosen him, so that he will direct [*train*] his children and his household after him to keep the way of the LORD by doing [*performing*] what is right and just, so that the LORD will bring about for Abraham what he has promised him [*reward*]." –Genesis 18:19 (brackets mine).

This was the beginning of the Eros prison of performance in regards to pleasing the gods and passing on the traditions believed to be of utmost importance. Those who develop within religious households will be strongly persuaded towards the need to convert the self. This is stamped in all our minds if raised traditionally.

The years of excessive repetition and emotional influence will strongly influence the behavior to wholeheartedly believe by the age of puberty or not at all. Although many faiths are harmless, the unfortunate belief that the *self* is completely broken and incongruous has profound implications later on when children leave the nest.

Remember our former statement that describes the double-self theory: "*I have got to stop doing this to myself!*" The "I" must stop speaking evil *against* or attributing evil *to* the authentic-*self*. This is primarily the reason for behaviors that seem to run amuck among many young people and why many go haywire when they leave the home and attend a college or university. The authentic-self is desperately trying to get out of prison.

This distorted view of self doesn't take place in people until there's an influencer or a people group to *imprint* it. Only when there are two or more people committed to this idea does this competitive influence have opportunity to raise its head within children.

This Eros prison process is what the brain executes in order to "protect" the authentic-self, as one understands it. In other words, it becomes as much a *survival* mechanism as it does an *approval* mechanism.

Thought Invader: Competition is a survival instinct.

The physiology of the mind has been under study for centuries, and it's very complicated. We shall see as we move forward in the coming chapters that the authentic-self is truly safe and by all accounts neither in need of performance initiatives nor an Eros prison to carry them out in.

The key to experiencing the beauty of being "free" to be yourself can only come when others are not seen as a threat, but rather they are seen and *understood* to be a part of the whole of creation. We are all connected, but most of us spend an inordinate amount of time drawing hard and clear distinctions between others and the self in an effort to feel important and further socially acceptable.

This process of drawing hard lines and distinctions rather than looking for similarities and complements distorts our view of self and establishes opportunity for the Eros prison to materialize and take hold.

This is why we have thousands of subgroups within our social and religious in-groups. Once we appear to be similar to those within our in-group, we must create another group with new social distinctions in order to bring new definition to the soul-self. As we do this, those left behind after the new distinctions are drawn are viewed as having *less* meaning while those who disconnect themselves from the larger group move on to an alleged *better* place of being.

According to the Genesis narrative, Adam moved on from Eve after she allegedly *ate him out of house and home* and Cain moved on from Abel after killing him. Baptists move on from Catholics, Protestants move on from Catholics, Pentecostals move on from Protestants, Conservatives move on from Liberals, and so on ad infinitum.

Because of this framework, those who become most secure within their authentic-self will ultimately be seen by those who are on a quest to convert their wounded-self as arrogant and lost. Unfortunately it must be this way. With 95% of the world in search of salvation from the corrupted wounded-self, is it any wonder religion abounds and the prison population expands? Is it any wonder religious groups are trying to dominate the world?

Super Groups and Power Plays

The concepts used to support ideas such as light and darkness, saved and lost, and us and them, like in-groups and out-groups they draw distinctions and perpetuate the prison rules. "You are the *light* of the world," is what Jesus said to his followers *after* they believed and incorporated his message into their lives. In the same way Christian doctrine states that if one is "*born of the Spirit*" they are renewed or *washed* on the *inside*—enlightened—by God, the supreme deity.

This concept is actually rooted in the Hebrew philosophy of the purification and the *cleansing* of the corrupted self. In this line of thought, *light* is *good* while darkness is *bad*. This goes for many other contrasts such as *up* and *down*, *heaven* and *hell* concepts, and *in* and *out* ideas.

Because of this reasoning, heaven must by all accounts be *above* and the idea of hell must by necessity be *beneath*. It's interesting to note that once one leaves the earth and moves to the outer regions of space, the concepts of above and beneath cease to exist and altogether lose their meaning.

To be clear, there are perhaps four major religions in the world vying for the authentic first position and the title of *The Way* to healing or *saving* the wounded-self. Until we understand how these groups formed and where these ideas actually came from, we are doomed to the prison of performance fueled by our ignorance and artfully masked by religion.

Thought Invader: "Did you hear the Jones' were moving on up? They finally got a piece of the pie."

Religious traditions fall into what are known as "super-groups" in comparative religion, arranged by historical origin and mutual influence. The largest super-groups in the world are Christianity, Islam, Hinduism, and Buddhism (And in that order). The first two are Abrahamic (as is Judaism, a medium sized group) and the second two are Indian.

The medium sized religions (I will list the largest to the smallest) are represented by Shinto, Sikhism, Judaism, The Baha'i Faith, Korean shamanism, and Caodaism. Jainism, Cheondoism, Hoahaoism, and Tenriism follow these. There are other groups, but they are obviously too small to make a noticeable impact on society as a whole so I won't bother listing them here. It's from people and their social in-groups that any idea of religion in the world has its deep roots.

People do the inventing, interpreting, wondering, writing, persuading, killing, and believing—people do these things, not supernatural deities although many maintain they are influenced by them.

Many allege magical encounters, divine instructions for killing opposing foes, fire from the sky, wrestling matches with the supreme God, secret revelations, meetings face-to-face with the divine, voices booming from the sky, etc., but none of these stories are any more tangible than another—all are equally subjective, bizarre, improvable and nuanced throughout time.

Interestingly enough, all stem from a fascination with solar mystery, celestial bodies, and *light*. Although there are many religious persuasions in the world (and likely some we have never heard of), there is a set of common denominators distinct among them all—people. With their ideas, emotions, needs, and complex personalities, people perpetuate religion. Since the beginning, all religions seem to have in common a fascination with the sun and the celestial canopy.

No matter where we find people and no matter how long ago we find them, they are wondering the same things—who are we and where do we come from? What are we? Where are we going? The next question inevitably seems to be, *what is that giant ball of light in the sky?* All these celestial occurrences were virtually unknown *mysteries* to the ancients with a tremendous causal effect on humanity and its survival.

As in all people groups (people always create groups in order to define, redefine, and defend themselves) whether it's nationalism (i.e. The Third Reich) or the Elks Club (local chapter president Dale Smith finally has a position), there are always a select few who rise to the top by way of election, perceived perfection, magician, motivation, or usurpation.

We will address the concepts of light and the self in a minute. This "rise to power" dynamic within all people groups creates position power, which feeds the wounded-self in need of performance and ultimately, celestial acceptance.

The Prison of Position Power

People within the Eros prison in need of excessive identification will inevitably maneuver themselves for position power while the passive and less driven fall to the bottom. We must understand that it's the people in power that make all the rules.

They write all the books, create and pass on all the myths, and define the parameters for indoctrination. If they can get away with attributing their ideas to a deity and convince the ignorant, they will likely be in charge—wardens within the prison.

In the example of Christianity and its early narratives, it appears that Peter, James, and John rose through the ranks and were established at the top although some would argue based upon other first-century gospels that the Magdalene was also a part of this upper leadership sect—either way, we see the pattern of position power emerge as in any in-group.

This need for power became so strong that at one point in the gospel narratives we read, "*An argument started among the disciples as to which of them would be the greatest.*"[3] This was right after Jesus tells them he is going to be "delivered into the hands of men" to be crucified. Jesus wasn't even dead yet, and they were jockeying for position so they could capitalize on his absence.

In Judaism we see Caiaphas and others in top positions. Ultimately, it is the top leadership tier that determines the course of the entire in-group while the passives follow along in order to belong and be safe. Another clever insight worth mentioning is it only takes about 3% of a "power populace" to determine its entire course and cultural persuasion.

This is why a small portion of society, such as a few popular media outlets and Hollywood, can determine the entire American culture although they're only a minute percentage of it. Whether they are true or false is irrelevant.

All ancient stories depict our human dilemmas, personality conflicts, natural competitive needs, the need for a safe-self, and our longing for answers to the unknown mysteries around and above us. People look to leadership for these answers as a general rule as opposed to within himself or herself—from someone else they believe is more qualified.

Seeing we have been taught by *qualified* individuals and authority figures to *believe* we are corrupt, incapable of good decision making, and in need of supernatural redemption, these thoughts pervade. This explains why we have all forms of organized religion in every place you find people.

The majority of humans both want and *need* to be led by those at the top and they want to be part of a purpose or cause much larger than himself or herself in order to foster feelings of worth, goals, and have something to do. This is also why countries will continue to follow governments even if their government is corrupt and blatantly bent on its own convoluted interests.

Unfortunately, each person's soul-self is not easily believed in, trusted, or seemingly capable of decision-making without authority figures to decide if we are making the correct choices. It's just the way people are. History repeats itself simply because people repeat the patterns that come naturally. It's not as much history

3) Luke 9:46

repeating as it is people repeating natural instincts, thus making history.

As long as there are people groups, it will likely never end. Few notice this and when they do, their numbers are never significant enough to oppose the larger super-group bent on following behavioral patterns through misshapen instincts brought on by traditional frameworks bent on a *bad* self in the subsequent need of behavioral Eros imprisonment.

Thought Invader: Ignorance of science and ignorance of history are the two great bulwarks of religious error.

But we must understand that both science and faith have the same size black eye, and we should not pit them against one another. They both can overlap, and at times, they can be in opposition to one another. The problem isn't science and the problem isn't faith; the problem is the people who hold these ideas in their minds. It's how they act and *react* to those who disagree with them.

The problem is always people as they are the more complex, irrational entity within all these equations. Facts can be fabricated, distorted, and disguised, while faith can be subjective, elusive, and mysterious. Unfortunately both get away with murder in their own right.

The Mystery of the Sun, Night and Tumult

As far back as ten thousand years, humans have been obsessed with the sun and the stars, both perpetuating a fear of the unknown and the unsafe-self living within it. Part of feeling safe within the self means we must understand the unreachable parts of the universe that have a tremendous impact on our lives on earth.

Numerous carvings, drawings, and scripts have been discovered that prove this need to know what is happening beyond our own planet and ourselves. Nevertheless, its profound impact on all people groups has had lasting implications.

These celestial mysteries have driven both math and science to unprecedented levels, while leaving the unknowable anonymities in a place all by themselves. The human need for safety within the self has never ceased to have impact on people groups throughout all history. The mystery of death and birth has both plagued the human soul-mind for many thousands of years and still do for some in the most remote areas of the globe.

Abundant artifacts also attest to these points, such as from the sun-worshiping cultures of the Egyptians, Indians, Babylonians, Greeks, and many others, including the peoples of the Levant and ancient Israel (biblical claims of making the sun stand still in the sky in order to win a battle).

We can understand why when we understand that every morning the sun will rise, bringing warmth, safety, crop yields, and comfort, along with the dispelling of fears of darkness and the mystery and obscurity of night. All peoples, as far back as we can find them, understood that without the sun our crops would fail and life itself would cease to exist.

This need to be safe was the beginning of sun worship and according to some it may also be the reason for Christian *Son* worship as well. Jesus makes us safe before the scary God by shielding us from his wrath through personal sacrifice.

These mysterious realities associated with both the *Son* and the sun have made these two suns the most adored objects in all of history as their presence has brought peace, hope, and safety to the self. Like Jesus the "son," the celestial sun has been venerated as an object of worship for generations.

I was recently spending Christmas with my daughter in Montezuma Canyon in Utah where she lives. The evening sky was so brilliant you could actually see the Milky Way galaxy. One evening I was walking from the main ranch to the guest house where my wife and I were staying.

It was pitch black and I couldn't see my hand in front of my face. I was instantaneously filled with fear of what *could be*. This was when I speculated what the ancients felt like with such limited knowledge of the many then mysteries such as fire, wind, and rain … and the darkness of night.

Stars were mapped and catalogued into constellations upwards of ten thousand years ago (as in ancient Sumer) as they measured seasons, eclipses, and numerous other important happenings, which had a great impact on the peoples below including how safe or unsafe they felt as a people.

The ancients were also responsible for the knowledge of stars, systems, planets, moons, and various celestial objects such as Pluto, not discovered by modern man until the twentieth century. Needing to know *why* has never left the sphere of human endeavor, and the need to have a safe-self in light of any misunderstandings associated with the daunting celestial mysteries has continued to this day.

It is the best reason why this obsession with *light* has been around since the beginning of time. Sages, teachers, and prophets such as Jesus and the Buddha have incorporated the terms within their philosophies and teachings with striking differentiations between itself and darkness in a spiritual sense.

The idea of being bathed in *light* or full of light brings comfort and safety to the self. When traveling teachers included light concepts into their way of life, they got people's attention—nobody wanted to be *full of darkness*.

How did we as a people become so engrossed with darkness? The answer? The wounded-self can only focus on what it fears the most. When one embraces the authentic-self and *loves* and *trusts* the authentic-self as Zacchaeus did, their need for religious rituals and superstitious beliefs to dispel the unpleasant darkness as a means to *redeeming* the unsafe-self all but ceases to exist.

When one fears darkness, rituals are invented to keep the darkness away from the unsafe-self. We are by nature against what we do not understand. Therefore, the ideas surrounding death and the *afterlife* bring fear and an unsettling to the soul-mind thus ill-affecting the authentic-self within.

Therefore, religion becomes a means to define these mysteries, name them, and give them a residence. This makes the self safe and free from the fear and anxiety manufactured by focusing on the unknown.

Safety and the Unsafe-Self

Regeneration is a sure way to make the authentic-self safe and secure. This *regeneration* or *washing* of the human spirit-self (enlightenment out of a place of darkness), which is the *real* self according to writers of the New Testament, is allegedly accomplished by the Spirit of God.

This regenerative occurrence *cannot* be reversed easily once it has taken place within the believer. Although there are different interpretations on this matter, they all generally agree to its necessity for salvation.

For thousands of Evangelicals as well as other religious sects outside of Christendom across the world, focusing on a *new* self is imperative. Focusing on this new self creates a sense of *being* unlike anything one may have ever experienced before a conversion from darkness to light.

Unfortunately, this idea is impossible to reject for fear of being stuck with a wounded-self forever—or worse. Religion, therefore, is the most popular antidote to bring the unsafe-self to a place or position of true safety.

As a matter of fact, the better one can communicate this idea of an unsafe-self becoming safe to an outsider (one outside the in-group promoting it), the better the chances the listener will sign up for it. This idea once believed has had a pretty good track record for many people—especially if it brings about a *positive* effect on the self.

Statistically, negative behaviors such as drug addiction, poor decision-making, harmful habits, loneliness, self-hatred, and the like are more apt to *change* seeing they now intensely *believe* these issues are no longer a part of who they *are* in light of this new birth of the self they experience within their mind, and the redemptive transformation they *believe* takes place within their wounded spirit-self.

In other words, once an individual can separate their *actions* (flesh-body behaviors) from their spirit-self through *belief*, a new behavioral dynamic usually ensues. Unfortunately, this is a poor method of curbing behaviors that ill effect the authentic-self and others—religion simply cannot stop it; it can only create short-term delays or redefine the purpose and consequence of behaviors.

For example, prejudices may continue within a religious framework, being justified by a perceived greater principle such as when the Jews were allowed to hate Samaritans because they were a product of violated Deuteronomic breeding Laws.

How Faith Affects our Behavior

This is how the concept of regeneration functions: according to mainline Christian thought and doctrine a person's center of being or *heart* (the true-self) is regenerated (enlightened) or *purified* (in Jewish thought). In effect, redeemed by the Spirit of God. Redeemed actually means "to rescue and deliver from the bondage of sin and the *penalties* of God's violated laws." The penalty is the scary part.

This may be better known as "*putting on the new man*" (or woman as this was a male-dominant term for people in general in this patriarchal society) according to the apostolic teaching of St. Paul, who is said to have written two-thirds of the information in the New Testament.

Putting on the new man meant consciously and intentionally *adjusting* one's behavior to line up with the idealist embodiment of the *new* condition of the *self* at the point of *regeneration*, which is believed to be the acknowledgment and the *acceptance* of the message of Jesus as God through faith and then copying it.

Although there have been many twists and turns since the days when these philosophies were penned, the simplicity of the ideas surrounding the safe-self can be harvested if one approaches these ancient texts in light of their cultural contexts within the ancient world that they were written in.

According to this philosophy, an individual has been spiritually *translated* (through a mysterious invisible conversion) out of an invisible "kingdom of *darkness*" and virtually placed into a new invisible "kingdom of God" or "*Light*," sometimes called the "kingdom of *his* (God's) dear son (Jesus)."

According to this philosophy, there is a new *awareness* of their actions and how these actions reflect or correspond to how Jesus lived and the *new* self on the inside reflecting *his* actions and ideals—their authentic *being*.

Wholeheartedness and the Self

This *new* knowledge will translate into new *behaviors* for those who fully and *wholeheartedly* believe something has actually taken place within their true authentic-self—they will have *better* corresponding actions that mirror the new *beliefs* about who they are *now* in light of this perceived process of regeneration—the unsafe-self is now safe or *saved with actions to prove it.*

Although our actions characterize our *beliefs* (if I believe it is cold, I will *put on* warmer clothes), many claim the new set of behaviors to be in direct correlation to the Spirit of God within them and not an automatic conformity with the mind's new thinking pattern known as the *consistency rule*.

Although simple enlightenment on these issues would suffice, many need large buttresses of religious enormity in order to *feel* safe within the system that allows for real changes in behavior lest they lose to the soulish-self who acts and reacts based upon the current mood of its surroundings or its brat child the undisciplined self.

This behavioral modification occurs within every faith and culture although through differing means. Islam, Judaism, Christianity, Mormonism, Taoism, Wiccan, Buddhism, you name it. Every serious convert to any belief *system* will easily create the corresponding actions that reflect the new *system* or *self* whether good or bad if one believes it *wholeheartedly*. When we tell children they are smart, they will excel at school. When we tell them they are stupid, they will drop out.

As another example, a well-socialized pharmacist may modify his or her behavior to the point of becoming a *terrorist* if he or she believes *wholeheartedly* (with his or her whole unsafe-self and soul-mind) the message of extreme Islam and will have a *safer-self* through negative corresponding actions to prove it.

These actions always correspond to the *belief* embraced although the actions in themselves do not prove that anything actually took place. These corresponding actions only prove that one *believes* something took place within the self.

Many individuals do not have the corresponding actions to prove their conversion. In the book of James found in the later part of the New Testament, the writer claims that "Faith without corresponding actions is dead, being alone." The writer also says, "Now someone may argue, 'Some people have faith; others have good deeds.' But I say, 'How can you show me your faith if you don't have good deeds? I will show you my faith by my good deeds.'"[4]

This is a fundamental framework that works in any religious structure. And it's exactly why society appears to *need* religion in order to cultivate true solidarity, better behaviors, hope, and thus the survival of our species. Religion can be virtuous when it sees others as important and worthy of unconditional love and when it's rooted in altruistic values.

But it can be extremely destructive if the religious see themselves and those outside a particular in-group as *less* or in need of spiritual or behavioral modification because they contain a perceived unsafe-self or they become a threat to an in-group's mission of taking over the world.

But religion all but falls apart when people take it upon themselves to moderate those around them in an attempt to put right others' perceived unsafe or wounded-selfs. This is why religion cycles through the ages with times of peace and also times of horror. The tipping point occurs when the leading dominant influencer's make everyone else outside the group (everyone who thinks or believes contrary) their business and then begin to amass emotional and physical *control* through manipulation, societal laws, shaming, judgment, or war.

Unfortunately, even this philosophical scenario over time runs out of natural gas, and the same feelings of low self-worth and performance, originally thought to be obliterated through the creation of a new self, can reemerge within this new social system and community of shared beliefs once one *relaxes* into the status quo within the new social order and assumes a repositioning.

Thought Invader: People are like water; they inevitably seek their own level.

Once the charm wears off, our behaviors fall back to their *original* position within any new system, regardless of what it is. We revert to an unsafe-self *within* the new community of supposed safe-selfs in light of *others'* ability and social prowess.

Correspondingly, the new social order itself ultimately falls back into the same original pattern of dysfunction, and it's the black hole need machine all over again while the Eros prison

4) James 2:18.

eventually follows, this time under new management—the clergy.

In other words, people with alcoholic type behaviors (this does not necessarily include a continued action of drinking alcohol) will transfer these behaviors to the new system if they fail to embrace their safe-self wholeheartedly in spite of religious claims that it isn't possible without spiritual guidance—these are those who *hope* it is true, which according to St. Paul is everyone, i.e., "*we are saved by hope*."[5]

Dominant influencing styles rise to positions of authority within these new religious social systems. People's personalities and misaligned feelings take on new dimensions within these redefined social systems, but will remain the same behaviorally.

Nothing really changes other than the stage upon which people perform. Although they may believe they now have a safe-self, it will actually start working against them when others claim to be safer or closer based upon the verticality ethics scale (we will discuss this later).

The bottom line is this: nothing changes. This is clear when we think of the bumper sticker that says, "I'm not perfect, just forgiven." In other words, "I'm still a jerk; I'm just under new management." Sure, some behaviors are modified, but we are still human with needs, wants, and independent ideas not completely changed through our alleged purification of the soul. The prison may have been painted, but it is still a prison.

Safe Does Not Mean Secure

Many believers within all religious frameworks fall prey to the same need-oriented problems they escaped earlier having only changed the environments known to foster them—venues for them to play out in.

Without loving and embracing the authentic-self wholeheartedly apart from traditional regulations set up by leadership hierarchy, simply *believing* our true authentic-self has been regenerated will not eliminate the deeper emotional needs associated with ourselves and others, as well as our imperfections highlighted through people comparisons.

---

5) "For in this hope we were saved. But hope that is seen is no hope at all. Who hopes for what they already have?" Romans 8:24 NIV.

Thought Invader: You cannot make an authentic-self safe. It already is.

The result? We create behavioral and verbal acrobatics in order to escape the confusion and illogical outcomes produced by *believing* the unbelievable. For instance, some may *believe* they are not perfect, just forgiven as stated above.

They accept the fact that they are *broken* even though they *believe* they are no longer a wounded-self because they followed the formula for converting the authentic-self already authenticated at birth.[6]

We come up with clever statements such as "God's not through with me yet" or "I live within the space-time period of *now* and not *yet*" or some other contrived sleight-of-word statement to ensure some semblance of reason for not changing completely.

The whole process begins again within the religious system only there's no way out this time. People are now worse off than they were before they were told they needed to heal and regenerate the wounded-self not withstanding it is already safe—it is only hidden from view. This is the same problem earlier Hebrew followers of The Way had as we see it addressed within a New Testament Hebrew letter.

> "Dear friends, if we deliberately continue sinning after we have received knowledge of the truth, there is no longer any sacrifice that will cover these sins." –Hebrews 10:26

When the only recipe for success fails, there is no other cake to be baked. Creating strict guidelines for behavior and spiritual reformation compounds this problem. Rather than working through behaviors that work against us, they are *forbidden* altogether creating an immovable, frustrating dilemma that lowers not only personal expectation, but also the necessary drive for better behaviors.

They say there's nothing worse than being hurt or betrayed by a *believer* of any kind. This is true because merely believing does not heal the soul-self or the wounded-self affected by the shad-

6) We are born perfect: flawless, innocent, and pure. Later on we develop habitual behaviors that are contrary to the authentic-self and need readjusting. Many times religion provides a forum for this, but lacks authenticity itself thus perpetuating the Eros prison.

ow-self; it only changes a person's community group where their emotional maladies can play out upon other unsuspecting victims, naïve of the shadow-self's ability to mask reality.

By creating opponents to the self such as the devil, we inadvertently place our ladder against the wrong house and wonder why we don't get paid for doing a great job of painting it. The wounded-self may have an excuse for missing the mark, but the healthy self does not nor ever will because it isn't designed to shoot a target.

This is why the redeemed-self theory does not work. People remain the same. All they are doing is identifying with another social system in hopes of feeling better about their unsafe-self. The problem is they have misdiagnosed the true authentic-self in the first place by calling it bad or *desperately wicked* as the Prophet Isaiah claimed. Saved people act no different than unsaved people.

The desire to please an all-powerful deity can be overwhelming during these faithful exercises. Knowing we aren't perfect simply adds to this unfortunate enigma. We continue to pursue religiously driven performance rituals within the new social framework while conveniently convincing ourselves we're still in good standing with the deity.

Ministry, voluntarism, leadership roles, etc. will not be enough to complete the so-called deficit that remains within our soul-self thwarted by our shadow-self. This creates a cyclic sense of performance that never brings total freedom of being, thus perpetuating the existence of the performance prison we painted white.

External disturbances remain the same, but our definitions of them must change. We may be going through the same storms in life, but we now believe *Jesus is with us*. We may lose our partner in a nasty divorce, but *God has someone else for me* now. We may at times act contrary to what we actually believe, but *we're still under construction*.

This behavioral twisting perpetuates the insanity religion creates. No longer is our soul-mind affected by the shadow-self and its complex differences as the problem within this new social order is now the work of the devil, which means it will never be fixed seeing we are no longer to blame.

Competition and Completeness of Being

No matter what the social or religious framework is, it will still solicit competition among insiders as long as there are people and a central place to perform—the only survivors will be those truly connected with their authentic *safe*-self, not the belief system people have cleverly designed to support or improve it.

Those who are happy with themselves and see themselves as *children of God* in a simpler and purer sense without the religious trappings and performance rituals necessary for full acceptance will find more completeness of *being*.

Knowing that your authentic-self is *safe*, without having to buy into a new social order designed to promote the new self at the expense of others who allegedly still contain the wounded unsafe-self, is truly life changing.

Believing Jesus protects us from God and his holiness only keeps us in a position of forever trying to improve, but never getting it done. It's very difficult to square the conundrums we've created around these ideas. God loves us but can kill us or God is just and thus will throw people in hell, etc.

We default to "*His ways are higher than our ways*"[7] or "*The secret things belong unto the Lord our God, but the revealed belong to us ...*" from the Torah.[8] When these scenarios refuse to make any sense at all, we simply ignore them or build walls of ignorance in order to protect them.

For this reason, Jesus must never cease to be God for who else can calm his father or stand in the gap between us and him for our much-needed safety? Believing all peoples have utterly failed the test of humanity leaves little room for belief in the authentic-self having any chance of emerging apart from Jesus or any other figurehead to supernaturally heal and protect it.

Within this petri dish of a new social order where Jesus protects our unsafe-self from his father God, feelings such as, they

---

7) "For just as the heavens are higher than the earth, so my ways are higher than your ways and my thoughts higher than your thoughts." Isaiah 59:9 NLT.

8) "The secret things belong to the LORD our God, but the things revealed belong to us and to our children forever, that we may follow all the words of this law." Deuteronomy 29:29 NIV.

don't allow me to sing, or they don't allow me to lead the ladies group, or they have not recognized my benevolence or my acts of courage among the heathen will begin to emerge if one misdiagnoses their truly safe-self in this way. It's unstoppable.

It's human. Even Christianity cannot completely solve these complicated issues of *being* and performing. No matter who you are or what religious affiliation you belong to, we as people are primarily unsatisfied with who we *are* when competing in social groups of any kind because we fail to realize the truths about our true authentic-self.

And when transferring between social and religious in-groups, unfortunately the only thing that changes is the scenery. Our sick and twisted souls always come with us.

We and our need to compare ourselves among ourselves remains the same. Although there may be a social change in what one allows themselves to participate in, the self may still be looking through the bars of the Eros prison in hopes of experiencing personal acceptance from the soul-self after overcoming the shadow-self who previously lied about our beautiful authentic-self.

People will ultimately obsess over perceived imperfections in themselves in order to become more acceptable within any community order if they remain disconnected with who they *really* are and continue to focus on what they do and how well they do it in light of those around them and the deity they must now serve and please or be destroyed.

7

The Power of Thought Reform and the Self

The part of maintaining ideas about the authentic-self that are not in step with reality can only be accomplished through thought reform. I read an article that not only intrigued me, but also it may have been the one article that solidified my suspicions about the way we trick our soul-minds into believing the unbelievable.

The article summarized some work done by Dr. Robert J. Lifton[1] called *Criteria for Thought Reform* in which key indicators are identified that suggest whether an organization or in-group might be seen as a cult.

Cult is a pretty strong word, so I'll use Dr. Lifton's term *Thought Reform* as I move through this chapter. The sacred authentic-self belongs to you and you alone. But for whatever reason, many who have been tired of "*living with themselves*," using our former *Double-Layer Theory* as an example, have inadvertently surrendered their authentic-self to the church or some other religious community for safe keeping.

I understand why, but do *you* understand why? Coming to terms with our soul-self can be great and terrible at times. It's great when we see things more clearly and make the proper adjustments, but it's terrible when we assign someone else to do the job for us or approve of the job we have endeavored to do.

This is how cults thrive—they thrive on those who have believed the lie spoken by or sanctioned by the shadow-self that says, "*Last time you were in control of your own life, you ruined it.*"

1) Robert Jay Lifton (born May 16, 1926) is an American psychiatrist and author, chiefly known for his studies of the psychological causes and effects of war and political violence and for his theory of thought reform.

We allow an institution or a leader of a small cult-institution to cater to our emotional and spiritual needs, and oftentimes without question. Let's take a look and see how this happens, and maybe we can spot it in the lives of those around us who are captivated by a new sense of self-worth brought on by people who may not really have their best interest at heart after all.

These same criteria can shockingly be prevalent within mainline denominational institutions and go unnoticed, as there is a fundamental acceptance by thousands. Note to self: we must always endeavor to successfully drive our own cars instead of handing the wheel over to someone else for fear of driving off the road again.

I've condensed the key components according to Dr. Lifton's work and I will present them below.

Control of the Environment

Controlling the environment is essentially controlling what people read and think, and with whom they relate thus creating an "us against them" scenario that keeps people focused on where they are, where they should be, and where others' are *not* in an effort to create solidarity and leave bad habits behind.

This environmental control is so subtle that it is nearly impossible to detect. That being said, I do not believe this is a purposeful occurrence in most cases. In other words, I do not believe people are purposefully trying to control people's environment in an effort to manipulate them for selfish gain—at least not everyone.

However, I do believe people make a strong effort to *influence* other people in ways that have the exact same effect as manipulation although they may not believe that's what it is. Although their intent may be virtuous, the outcomes never are.

I have experienced this many times. Being influenced or told what to read or what not to read by well-meaning people who believe they have a better understanding of the "truth" than I have. I've been told how to think about a matter and what to believe about ideas and texts associated with the supernatural, the unexplainable, and the spectacularly weird.

Dr. Lifton is correct in that Environmental Control works as I have seen it in action for almost a half century. Although I did put up with it by giving people the benefit of the doubt, I do so no longer.

"God told me" or "I woke up this morning and the Lord said" and other statements endemic within the church are statements that leave the listener ill-equipped to comment or even make a standing rational judgment.

This appeal to the "highest" authority works really well when influencing others, especially the weak or feeble minded, which are unfortunately more than you might like to believe. But it's only within the confines of religious frameworks that this behavioral stonewalling finds any merit.

The Roman church practiced this for centuries on the poor, the benevolent, and the illiterate, resulting in enriched coffers with extravagant monetary assets and loyalties. It is prevalent today in Evangelical circles, and especially, the charismatic branch of Christianity.

Environmental Control, although extremely subtle and mysteriously attractive, is highly effective in not only identifying adherents, but also essentially creating the in-groups that support them. Giving away the keys to your authentic-self will always result in having your house robbed blind—not by everyone, but certainly by someone.

Mystical Manipulation

Otherwise known as planned spontaneity, this is the process of assigning supernatural significance to things and situations that take place even if they can be explained in ordinary ways. This practice is extremely common. I remember several years ago the church I attended went through a series of events that had the entire in-group looking for dimes, yes dimes.

After a sermon and several key people sharing their "experience" from the platform, an overexcited audience began finding dimes in ordinary places as well as some peculiar places. These dimes were said to represent both the "battle" and the "blessing." In other words, they were supposed to represent the tension between success and failure in all of our lives; a common bond we all share equally.

Because this is a true occurrence for all of us, on the surface it immediately speaks to our soul-self and gains our attention. If some members of the congregation lost their job for instance, they would soon after find a dime on the sidewalk or in a pants pocket or perhaps on the floor of their car.

Although former dime-finding would go unnoticed, this time it stands out as the idea had been harmlessly planted in the minds of the faithful in need of a sign by a trusted leader and friend with a direct connection with the divine. Although there was seemingly no ulterior motive or malice within this particular situation, people latched onto this idea as if it were the only hope of getting out of their unfortunate circumstance.

Finding ordinary dimes meant God recognized your plight and was promising a blessing by allowing you to spot the dime, or as some outliers claimed, by *creating* it out of thin air. Yes, some went as far to say that God was actually *placing* dimes in people's way by some supernatural power. This is the power of human need unchecked within apparently otherwise smart people.

This Mystical Manipulation was so powerful, even I found myself hoping for a dime when I was faced with a certain difficult situation. It is this kind of manipulative influence that will rally the troops, increase one's belief in certain theological theories, and strengthen one's resolve in particular beliefs no matter how absurd they are.

Be careful what you expose your mind and heart to. Don't believe anything until you can *know* it for sure and it makes sense. Although some may successfully argue we cannot know everything, I think you know what I mean. Always remember, once one is within the forest, only some trees are visible—only some.

The Demand for Purity

This is one of the most powerful tools for getting a response to what "safe" looks like or what is deemed as "acceptable" behavior. This form of control comes not only from most shame-based cultures, but also from strict Judaism itself of which Christianity is a sect.

There is no more powerful tool than making people feel dirty within the wounded-self. Without going too deep into this form of control (I discuss this in the section coming up on disgust and contamination psychology), using shame as a tool for soulish socio-alignment is exceedingly effective.

I heard a person a few months ago give advice to the distraught father of a ten-year-old thumb sucker, "Take a picture of them sucking their thumb and then show it to them. That will fix it!"

This is an attempt to shame the child into more suitable behavior. Not only is this a terrible choice, but also it is manipulative and self-serving. Shame is one of the strongest tools for controlling behavior and the worst for obtaining healthy consequences, and much of the church has mastered it regardless of the reason. Shame comes in many forms.

Like a Christmas present, it can be wrapped up with a pretty ribbon and go unnoticed for years. The only sign can be the fact that you have not really changed—if one can admit it. You still feel hopeless, helpless, and dirty on the inside. Your efforts in religion are merely keeping your feelings at bay, but they don't eliminate them altogether. If this is what you are experiencing, you are still in a prison—the Eros prison.

Confession

Confession creates control by devaluing the person who confesses and strengthening the person who listens to the confession. Revealing mistakes and sins to others makes an individual vulnerable to shame, fear, and ultimately manipulation.

Make no mistake: I understand the power of confession as it does cleanse the soul and free a person from unwarranted guilt and shame, but confession can also be used for more merciless means. Confession is good, but it can also backfire if used inappropriately.

The Roman church figured this out centuries ago. Admitting wrongdoing creates a knee-jerk reaction in the victim to perform for the one who now holds your cards in their hands. I believe in confession and I practice it with close friends whom I trust, but it *must* be voluntary.

When leaders demand it, it is nothing more than behavioral manipulation designed to produce shame and performance-based living in order to solicit something for themselves.

Relationships within these people groups should be peer-to-peer not master to disciple. Master-disciple relationships are out of balance and leave some at the expense of another. This type of group classifying such as clergy and laity or teacher and disciple are not only unhealthy, they can pave the way to manipulation.

Sacred Science

Sacred science happens when ideology is given special sacred status and cannot be critiqued by normal thinking people. This is a big one. The church has become expert in creating dogma, weird beliefs, and bizarre interpretations of sacred texts in order to control in-groups and in many cases extract money.

I remember working with a friend in 1982 who would wear long-sleeved shirts in one hundred and twenty degree weather for fear of hell because he was showing the skin on his arms. This would be the sacred science of clothing. I visited his church out of courtesy and wanted to gag after being there for only about twenty minutes.

It was brimming with sacred oddities such as specified length of hair, percentages of money that needed to be given, wearing pants or not wearing pants, jewelry, etc. Unfortunately, it was more insane than peculiar.

The church youth had to contact the lead "shepherd" and ask if they could go bowling; "Yes, as long as you wear a dress." This was a tax-exempt functioning community church in a rural neighborhood of wonderful people looking to be loved and accepted for who they were, but *could not be* in this religious order proclaiming their freedom.

One individual controlled the entire in-group, and the parishioners dressed according to his demands—at least when in church. This is no isolated event. This happens in all church in-groups in varying ways and most of it goes undetected by adherents. Questioning these beliefs is not only frowned upon, but also it is extremely disruptive to your social circle.

This also according to Dr. Lifton is what keeps groups of people in groups which they would otherwise abandon if given enough time to really think about it. One of the key ingredients for keeping people in groups they would otherwise abandon is the power of *Social Acceptance*.

When all your relationships revolve around your in-group loyalties, it's nearly impossible to leave the group and maintain the lifelong friendships you spent your lifetime building as they were *only* built upon *similar* beliefs and not the authentic-self. This by far is the most disappointing attribute to in-grouping. It's really not about the authentic you *as* you; it's about conforming to the image of someone else.

Loading the Language

There are literally hundreds of thousands of clichés within modern Christendom that will solicit certain behaviors. Loading the language takes place when the language of the totalistic environment is characterized by the thought-terminating cliché. In other words, one-word or one-sentence phrases that have this innate ability to turn others' and our brains off.

This again is rife within church in-groups. From calling people "brother" and "sister" to calling simple servants "pastor" or "bishop" sets people up as higher and in some instances better in most minds.

"Thus sayeth the Lord" may be the biggest controlling device within the charismatic movement. Many people add this to their decisions and commands and encouragements to others in order to foolproof themselves against push-back or when outcomes end up sideways—some may blame it on God or the devil. People resort to King James' English for effect and authenticity.

I heard a leader publicly call a man fat and tell him that God was going kill him if he didn't go on a diet, in front of thousands of people. This kind of bold brash behavior only takes place when the power to do it is given to them by the spectators who crave it.

Loading the language is one of the most effective manipulation tools when performed with expert precision. Behavioral science proves this. Never give another person this kind of power over your own personal decisions. Your personal decisions should come from within your safe authentic-self who has the interest of you alone and not the need for the acceptance of others.

Doctrine Instead of the Person

This form of control takes place when we place ideology and religious doctrine and dogma over the person it is allegedly designed to help. When ideology is more important than the people who believe it, behavioral control ensues. "The Bible says" may be one of the most powerful phrases for shutting down a weak person who you disagree with and annoying outsiders.

Citing so-called doctrine will keep people apart quicker than hate or prejudice. When people passively believe doctrine without doing personal research, they subject themselves to control, leading thousands of people with loaded words. Adolf Hitler mastered this.

If you have ever seen the footage of his birthday bash in the late 1930s, it is clear that millions upon millions of Germans had been manipulated to the point of total insanity. Ultimately, lazy makes hazy when we fail to check in with our authentic-self, which by and large is good at baloney detection.

I heard a woman call into a Christian radio station the other day with what she called a "praise report." A praise report is when a Christian reports something they believe God did for them or on their behalf. It almost always represents the supernatural work of God in a person's life through an interruption into the physical world with his power, and it's sometimes referred to as a "God thing."

This woman said she had been a believer for 38 years. And all the while she was a believer though her husband had 30 heart attacks, multiple surgeries, and devastating circumstances physically. She also went on to say she had recently developed a disease that affects her tongue and throat. After her delivering all this awful news, I was wondering where she was going with her story.

And then she dropped the bomb I expected, "*But the Lord has been with us through it all.*" This is a clear case of doctrine over person. The scriptures say, "I will never leave you or forsake you."[2] Although her life was a series of devastating physical hardships, Jesus was *there* the whole time. Not that he did anything to help. This is a level of irrationality millions are walking in.

2) Keep your lives free from the love of money and be content with what you have, because God has said, "Never will I leave you; never will I forsake you" Hebrews 13:5 NIV.

What was really going on was the consistency rule of personal persuasion. She had to live consistent with her confession that Jesus Christ is Lord of all. The lives of the religious are no different from the lives of the nonreligious.

The rain *and* the hail fall on the just and the unjust alike. The *only* difference is what one believes and what another does not believe concerning the joy and devastations that will ultimately occur. That is all.

Dispensing of Existence

When personal value is attributed as an individual's relationship to the in-group, followers are only valuable to the aims and objectives of the group leaders or the group expectations. Dr. Lifton's theory was developed in response to his studies of North Korean brainwashing techniques in the 1950s. At first they may not seem completely transferable to an evangelical context, but after close examination, I find they are worthy of supplementary study.

When you contemplate your own local evangelical church, you might think it a far cry from the manipulative techniques of North Korea, but take a look at the following thoughts that bring together Dr. Lifton's ideas and a few of my own.

The insistent need for evangelical churches to forcefully define the *core beliefs* is a worry for numerous reasons. When beliefs are used to prescribe *inclusion*, then the brain and common senses are no longer required—believing anything apart from our own ability to reason and work out our conclusions is not only dangerous—it's highly destructive. Honesty has to be an essential component of any healthy culture.

But sadly, honesty is rejected or frowned upon in many churches. One is discouraged to think beyond the bounds of any given ideology as if God is waiting with a giant bat behind the theological door. Belief should never be the grounds for inclusion, but unfortunately this is how these dynamics are set up. Actions should determine trustworthiness, *not* belief—ever.

Belief *never* makes a person a better person, behavior does. When groups allow actions that are inconsistent with beliefs, but will not allow the denial of illogical beliefs even when the correct actions towards others are present, there will be enormous tension points. As soon as thoughts are limited to those deemed as acceptable by and large, we enter the area of mind control suggested by Dr. Lifton.

In more moderate evangelical churches, this may not seem so explicit, but ask yourself this question: "what will happen to me if I disagree with the idea of any major doctrine or talking point?" In truth, most people are ostracized at best for thinking beyond established theological boxes and at worst removed from the group altogether.

Or what of the stories of genocide, infanticide, and tribalism that seem to be offered as holy or acceptable criterion for the adherence to the Hebrew God? I understand there are exegetical or religious explanations for the methods for dealing with such notions, but for most people much of this is highly problematic at best and irrational at worst.

This is compounded by the fact that people are not encouraged to think, engage, and admit openly any sensible reasoning to the contrary.

Thought Invader: The discouragement of human reasoning is a sign there's a controlling agent at work.

It's thought provoking how many people believe that healthy conversation and dissection of the bizarre ideas within the Bible and the church are somehow related to non-commitment or disbelief in God.

Ridiculous and irrational ideas defended so powerfully are often left to find their own way out of the religious maze of absurdity. How often have we heard loaded words and language such as "you cannot out-give God" or "God always answers prayer" or "bless this food to our bodies"?

Although traditionally cherished, these phrases leave many people grasping for straws of reason. Out of respect, many give up trying to make sense out of these phrases assuming they may be too critical or offensive if they decide to question the status quo. "God always answers prayer, but sometimes he says no" is tantamount to "whatever, I'm too afraid to talk about it or enquire of its absurdity."

These might seem like innocuous sayings, but think about

how they both control human behavior and suggest a view of God that is distinctly unsustainable. I suggest we reconsider some of our beliefs and reassess how we treat others who think differently, scientifically, and perhaps more sensibly.

I suggest we might want to check our manipulation detectors and upgrade them if they're not working properly or if they are only designed to protect their own outcomes no matter how bizarre.

8

Everyone Loved Jesus

This chapter will deal with the self and the Eros prison of special groups and differences. Having engaged in many conversations with many people over the last thirty years, I have come to a startling conclusion.

Ordinary people struggle to like Christians at all today. Albeit Christians will tell you this is because people hated Jesus, and it's only normal to be hated by the *world*, but this is not entirely true. The scriptures tell another story that becomes very clear if one looks critically.

Thought Invader: In the first century, the "common people heard him gladly." –Mark 12:37

It was the Jewish zealots that hated Jesus, not the common people. The common people were elevated and loved by Jesus whereas the religious of that day looked down on the people and saw them as outcasts, outsiders, illiterate, and unlovable—pagan. The common people were a standing threat to the religious who lived for position power because of their numbers.

Jesus said:

> "But this is to fulfill what is written in *their* Law: 'They hated me without reason.'" –John 15:25

Whose law? That's right, the Jewish Law (it is written in *their* Law). Jesus always disassociated himself with tribalism and geographies as he does in relationship to the Jews, the law, and the geography of Israel.[1] It was the zealous Jews (the *they* in verse 25) who hated Jesus—not all Jews, just a certain group of Jews—the

1) John 4:21: "Woman," Jesus replied, "believe me, a time is coming when you will worship the Father neither on this mountain nor in Jerusalem.

religious and pious Jews. Jesus was actually an *advocate* for all the Jews, being a Jew himself, but only accepted by a small minority.

Jesus came unto his *own* (the Jews beginning at Jerusalem) and his own received him not according to the gospel of John. But the common people loved Jesus because he didn't show favoritism and he believed in the true safe authentic-self.

We never see Jesus "saving" people; only forgiving them for wrongs done to the self and others. He held nothing against an individual that was willing to *be* without pretense and adopt his ideas about the Jewish state of affairs or the lack of integrity within their own soulish-self. Jesus was all about *authenticity.*

Thought Invader: Nowhere in the scriptures do regular everyday people hate Jesus.

As a matter of fact, scoundrels, tax collectors, prostitutes, the disease ridden, the poor, the nut jobs, and even a religious leader named Nicodemus, a ruler of the Jews, all loved Jesus. In Matthew 24, Jesus tells his disciples they will be hated all over the "world" because they followed him within a Jewish context of self-absorption and high-minded in-grouping.

What many fail to realize is that this is the same "*world*" in Luke 2:1—"And it came to pass in those days, that there went out a decree from Caesar Augustus, that *all the world* should be taxed." Did Caesar tax the whole earth? Of course not. Caesar only taxed the Roman world—all the territory Rome occupied including Judea.

Being hated all over the *world* meant they would be hated throughout the Jewish world mainly Jerusalem and its outlying cities.[2] There was no reason Christians would be hated in Japan or North America because there were no Christians there.

The Jewish Authorities who competed with Jesus for power would only hate the first-century followers of Jesus. With no means of transportation and no reason for it, believers in Jesus were local at best and in some outlying areas at worst.

This idea that necessitates Christians be abhorred by the whole *world* is not only completely unwarranted, it's unreasonable

2) The term "world" within the scriptures typically denotes the "known" world and not the entire planet.

and ridiculous. The Eskimos in the "new world," which had yet to be discovered, did they hate Jesus? It's more likely a clever way to appear distinctive and important. These characteristics help formulate the "us against them" mentality, leading to the Eros prison.

It allows many Christians to not only appear unique, but also can be further concocted to allow certain people within the in-group to act in ways that are unbecoming of a Jesus follower.

An individual in the Eros prison stands on a street corner with a bullhorn and condemns everyone to hell, and when he or she gets arrested for it, he or she can claim the world hates him or her just as it hated Jesus.[3] This elitist in-group behavior has gone on for hundreds of years, but no longer. The generation after this millennial generation (19-29) will very likely be the least religious in American history.

Thought Invader: Jesus was not in the in-group, therefore not in the Eros prison.

Some believe selective Psalms prophetically point to Jesus of Nazareth contending with religious Authorities within the first century (although written hundreds of years earlier), including Psalm 35:19 which states: "Do not let those gloat over me who are my *enemies* without cause; do not let those who hate me *without reason* maliciously wink the eye."

This again is not a reference to common everyday people around the world at large, but rather it represents the present condition during the days of Jesus and those bent on his social demise *locally*.

It's referencing Jewish people in the first-century Roman province, those few who refused to *hear him gladly*. It was the Pharisees and their religious rulers—the religious who were malicious towards him because he was stealing their show.

People don't realize the whole of the scriptures are related to the Hebrews *only* and not the world at large. It is *their* story and understanding of the gods, not ours. It is *their* heritage, *their* history of deliverance and setbacks, and *their* desire for a messiah figure to rule the natural world and make them special again like the rest of us want.

3) Granted, many times this kind of person is suffering a mental illness.

Christianity came much later and was at that time a small *Jewish* sect which followed the teachings of Jesus about 10 to 30 years *after* his death. Those who followed him while he was alive were known as those of *The Way*, a *Jewish* group of vagabond disciples (probably Essenes) who believed Jesus would overthrow Roman rule and establish a literal physical kingdom on earth—of course it never happened.

Non-Jews didn't start becoming a large part of the initial following until *after* St. Paul redefined Jesus' mission and created the idea of *spiritual Jews* (Romans 2), thus perpetuating the more modern version we are familiar with today. Unfortunately, the tables have now turned rather considerably.

America the beautiful now looks like the first century, but backwards. The common people have problems with Jesus, and the religious people (like the first-century Jews) are the only ones who love him—nobody else does. Is this as disturbing to you as it is to me?

The first-century pagans, people holding *many* superstitious beliefs other than those of the main world religions (especially Judaism) loved Jesus in the first century; but today for some odd reason, they don't like him *at all*. Could this be simply because he has been grossly misrepresented to our modern world?

Many outsider Jews with less national significance also loved him in the first century and would even climb trees just to get a glimpse of him coming down the road. Jesus was thronged in his day like President Barack Obama on an African tour in our day.

Women also loved Jesus and followed him everywhere. Remember, pagans were villagers who had many beliefs in many gods whereas the Jews were monotheistic (they believed in one supreme God) as were the Muslims. But after Jesus' death, pagans became better known as the *heathen* or nonbelievers.

This behavioral phenomenon can only be expected seeing people need to have personal definitions that set them apart as *special*. Today people are placed in two essential groups, believers and nonbelievers according to Christian beliefs. Initially, this kind of thinking came from the Jewish community during Jesus' time.

The Jews believed they were *chosen* by God above *all* other people groups and assigned the position of *special* through their beloved patriarch Abraham—a sign they were deep in the Eros prison of performance. They were the *special* ones whereas everyone else was either tolerated or outright ignored by the deity as in this holy passage, "*In the past he (God) allowed all nations to go their own ways . . .*" Acts 14:16.

Thought Invader: The soul-self desires total uniqueness and acceptance when locked within the Eros prison and guarded by the shadow-self.

This is why pagan villagers were so easily dismissed and destroyed including their women, children, and animals. This psychological phenomenon is catching. When people groups are considered "unclean" or "heathen," behaviors reflecting their disdain will sweep an entire landscape, as it did in the majority of groups in Nazi Germany in the 1930s and 1940s.[4]

Everyday people dismissed the Jews as subhuman filth. Remarkably, this is the very same behavior the Jews displayed in ancient times towards others. Karma is a real problem.

The surest way to justify selective hatred today is when we attribute it to the actions and ideas of a deity. Modern day evangelicals are close but not quite there as they claim God *hates* the sin, but loves the sinner. This is a very slippery slope as it disallows one to truly love without strings.

People in general won't hire, marry, work with, or hang around people who do the things they hate. What makes us believe we're going to actually *love* them when we hate what they do? This idea is ridiculous at its root.

The destruction of Jericho in ancient times by the Hebrews under the direction of their God and Moses' lead protégé Joshua was tantamount to ISIS taking over the Middle East today—brutal beyond words. As it was in Germany in the 1940s, German Christians stood by and did nothing during the Holocaust because they were more proud to be part of the German in-group than a Jesus follower, or maybe they believed they were one and the same.

The Eros prison of Nationalism held them fast through fear

4) Please excuse the use of Nazi Germany again, but unfortunately this makes the point really well.

of the furor. Unfortunately, this Eros thinking and sect building during the Nazi reformation, which entrenched millions, is still alive and working today in many parts of the world. For millennia, people groups have believed they were the most important while everyone else wasn't.

The Pharaohs, the Caesars, the Nazis, the Russians, all of them. People have been clamoring for the title "most *special* race" since Nimrod and the Tower of Babel. This type of human behavior has been around since man walked the earth, and it will continue unless we are freed from the Eros prison of performance and embrace our authentic-self and release its power to others.

Spirituality *embraces* everyone, but religion attempts to *change* everyone. Christians today are taught to believe they are a *royal priesthood*, a *peculiar people*, and a *chosen generation* not of this physical world because we have been *reborn* from above according to Pauline and Petran thought.

> "But you are a *chosen* people, a *royal* priesthood, a *holy* nation, God's *special* possession, that you may declare the praises of him who called you out of *darkness* into his wonderful *light*." –1 Peter 2:9

This begs the question: where does this leave everyone else? This of course sets believers *higher* on the verticality ethic's scale and places everyone else on the lower end by default—a prison of perceived specialness. This kingdom of *darkness* we are allegedly called out of could easily mean the darkness in our unbelieving neighbor's home.

It's this *need* to be more special, closer, or more forgiven than others in the eyes of God that creates divisions and hardships among people groups. If everyone is equally forgiven, then why can't we just leave everyone alone?

I want you to imagine that the whole world becomes Christian tomorrow. What would things look like in one or five years? Fifty years? I suggest it would look just like it does now. It would be filled with factions, fights, in-groups, and competitive leaders jockeying for the top positions while claiming large groups of "others" are not "in" for one reason or another.

The only way to stop this unnecessary fighting is to realize *no* differences actually exist between people in spirit—we are all one.

The Verticality Ethic and Spiritual Categorization

People groups have also developed another psychology that some psychologists call the *verticality ethic*. This ethic turns the created order of living beings into a vertical scale of importance beginning with God and ending with a devil in the Judeo-Christian model, which is just one of many models. This scale is used widely and encompasses many subgroups within the in-groups and perpetuates the Eros prison of performance.

Beginning with the higher element and working towards the lower elements on the scale it looks something like Figure 1. This scale is not a conscious scale, but it's always applicable when defining in-groups or how one believes God sees the world within an evangelical religious framework.

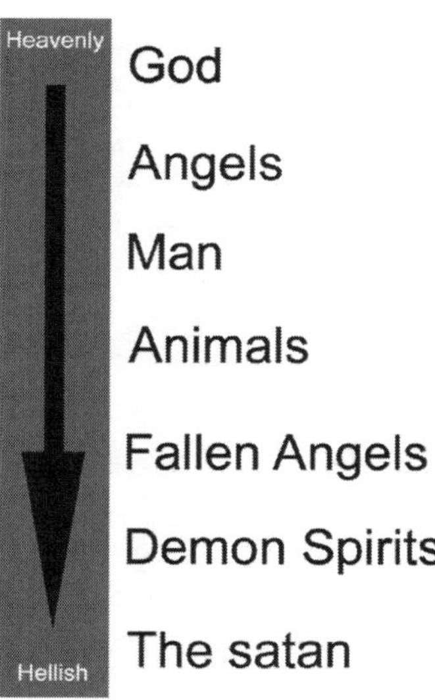

Figure 1. The beings scale.

Within the context of "beings" in the figure above we have the subgroup called "man" or mankind (man on the verticality ethic scale above). Within this subgroup of man, I want to introduce another scale (a scale within the above scale scale). This new scale resembles the first with a scale of zero to one hundred with a 50% line across the middle as in figure 2. on the next page.

According to this subscale, mankind is supposed to have been created to be "*a little lower than the angels*" according to Psalm 8:5, but higher than animals in importance or possibly authority—this is seemingly a sliding scale, as we shall see.

According to Christian thought and doctrine, when a believer *backslides* within the church, they slide lower (towards the animal kingdom) and when they are considered to be "*walking in the Spirit*," they rise above 50% and therefore are closer to God (behaviorally) and the angels, regardless of what they may be thinking or doing behind closed doors.

This method of evaluating others is a powerful tool for building communities of people with more militant aspirations. I've known people who've made it their mission in life to live *above* the half way point on this scale.

Unfortunately, they inadvertently make everyone else around them feel insignificant or *less* spiritual by comparison. Their constant conversation typically revolves around all the worldly things they avoid, such as movies or television and even sugar and soft drinks, and the scriptures they refer to constantly.

Conversations are therefore unmistakably forced into a tit-for-tat competitive awareness, and before you know it, you find yourself taking personal inventory and coming up short in comparison. This is another unfortunate result of living within the Eros prison of performance. Although quite harmless, the results speak for themselves.

This up and down psychology is not only rampant in most religious groups caught within the Eros prison; it also perpetuates moral classifications (Christians vs. homosexuals, sinners vs. saints, Pentecostals vs. Baptists, and Liberals vs. Conservatives). Because of this vertical psychology, Christians see the world and people associated with it as being "of the flesh" or "of the devil" and a part of the devil's kingdom of darkness.

If one is *born from above*, that person is part of an *otherworldly kingdom of light* distinctly different from the rest of society.

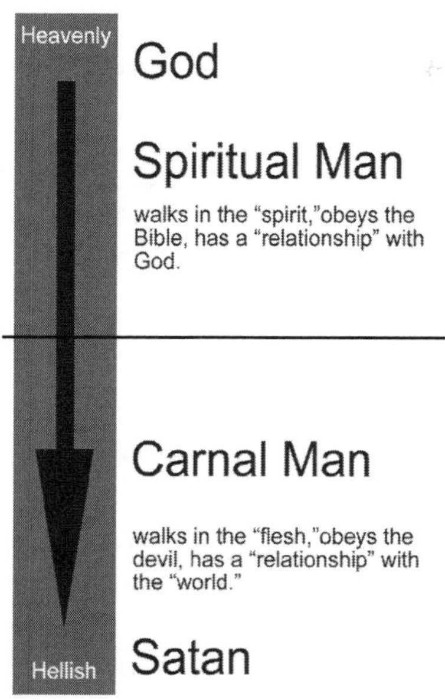

Figure 2. The man scale.

This plays into the idea of why *hell* must by all accounts be *below* and the idea of a *heaven* must necessarily be *above*. The Pharisees of Jesus' day practiced the verticality lifestyle as they thanked God they were not like the "sinners" or "a woman" as they saw them as *lower* in relationship to the human verticality ethic just like believers are taught today (fortunately most don't lessen women anymore although most believe they are inherently a *weaker* vessel according to Pauline thought).

Religious groups endeavor to *love* the world's inhabitants, but sadly many people's efforts are less than ambitious. When these same people sit and eat next to so-called "sinners" on their way to a hypothetical fiery hell forever, it becomes difficult for many to emotionally shoulder the weight of responsibility associated with it.

I understand this enigma as I lived at this address for many years. When we view our "self" and the "self" of others as initially corrupt, bearing the co-responsibility for its safety becomes a performance we fear we'll fail. Although many are up for it and find their spiritual worth in their ability to become conversion machines, many ignore this mandate altogether.

Within the Christian concept, Jesus takes on this role of responsibility *for* us, but not without our free will to allow it to happen. This is where the problems arise albeit very subtly.

If we think deeper about this methodology, it becomes clear that God is utterly unable to *save* the human race without the obedience required by his servants to show them how to get it done. This is primarily what keeps people within the prison of performance while we justify our being there.

Thought Invader: Spiritual classifications create animosity and inner differentiation between people groups throughout society.

People's ceremoniously driven weekly attendance at their local church gathering and the giving of their money is typically the authentic sign that we are *in*. Although behaviors may not change fully, the ideas *and mental assent given to this process on many occasions is the only* significant difference between people within the kingdom of light and those within the kingdom of darkness.

Unfortunately the idea and satisfaction that comes from believing we have the *only* working key to life is enough to replace the behaviors these ideas should reflect. Yet the efforts in *saving* the lost from the wrath of Jesus' father and the devil are less than passionate for many and for good reason—we can't emotionally shoulder the responsibility.

Most adherents to any faith system have to attend weekly meetings simply to remain connected to what they believe. Within Christianity, without strict support from others in believing what Jesus allegedly believed, the soul-self quickly seeks its own level. In all actuality, it is no longer God who sustains us, but the in-group we create in his name.

This is what makes these ideas so suspect. Since the beginning, people have had to be taught to care within religious communities. People compete. And it's this competitive edge that allows the religious in-groups to continue. It's no longer an inward drive to live out of our own authenticity, but a life of trying to live up to the standard the in-group propagates.

For this reason people's attention thus turns *inward* to the personal soul-self or their personal positions, doctrines, in-groups and loyalties, and newfound knowledge created by the order. This creates what I call "spiritual *masturbation* sessions" where everyone feels better about themselves and thus leaves with goose bumps and emotional self-sufficiency, but nothing actually happens to the world outside of where they live.

> "The harvest is past, the summer is ended, and we are not saved." –Jeremiah 8:20

In the passage above, Jeremiah weeps for the Jewish people because although they writhed in pain like a mother with child, and as the prophet Isaiah said, they only gave birth to wind—no significant or lasting change takes place. This is still the outcome today.

> "We were with child, we writhed in labor, but we gave birth to wind. We have not brought salvation to the earth, and the people of the world have not come to life." –Isaiah 26:18

We are excellent with going through the motions, but many lack the proper e-motions necessary for true authentic spirituality because it has been institutionalized, not personalized. True spirituality, much like a duck, doesn't come in an organized row. Not surprisingly, the classic behavior of attendees after a religious meeting can be stunningly predictable.

Adherents will flock to a local eatery and continue to encourage each other in the in-group *way* while exchanging war stories designed to promote purpose, solidarity, and acceptance among one another, yet without significant change to their continued behavior dynamics as a whole. All that takes place is a reevaluation of their own personal significance within the group.

Granted, some have a lot of change within their lifestyle, but after being absorbed by the larger community, the cycle of behavior begins all over again at a newer level than before—a higher one in comparison, but the same competitive behaviors play out within the new system.

Instead of competing with Bob, the drug dealer they now compete in Bible-Quiz. Solomon says, "A wise man keeps his knowledge to himself," but this is difficult to find within religious groups behaving in accordance to the verticality rule. Only within *authentic* spirituality will you see behavior morph without competitive frameworks. Think about it; think about not having to submit your behavior to others within a group for observation and approval.

Imagine living to God alone without outside interference or authorization. Imagine communion with God being whatever, whenever, and however you wish. This is the authentic life lived from within without the consent of others becoming interference to our being.

Performance only takes place when the approval of others is within the spiritual equation. Unfortunately, many within evangelical in-groups believe having certain extras means operating at a different level of faith. Ideas such as having an "infilling of the Spirit" makes one *higher* on the verticality scale.

Some subgroups also believe possessing certain "gifts" makes one *closer* on the verticality scale or makes their inner wounded-self *fuller* or more equipped, hence the term *filled with the Spirit*. This creates another performance group within the subgroup. These community-driven frameworks sadly have a way of creating people who categorize and characterize others in accordance to the texts they pattern their behaviors after.

In Christian sects, people will view their peers as *inner court* Christians, *outer court* Christians, or those within the *Most Holy Place* after the Jewish temple model.[5]

There are also *thirty-fold* Christians, *sixty-fold* Christians, and *hundredfold* Christians based upon Jesus' parable of the sower[6] and the amount of fruit certain trees were able to produce based upon the condition of the soil that was representative of the heart *self*.

There can also be the *children*, *young men*, and the *fathers* model taken from the epistle of John. These are all classifications born out of the Eros prison of performance. This is prevalent among other sects such as *Pentecostals* or *Word of Faith* groups.

They believe one has more of God when they show behavioral

5) "Put the atonement cover on the ark of the covenant law in the Most Holy Place." Exodus 26:34.

6) "Now listen to the explanation of the parable about the farmer planting seeds." Matthew 13:18.

signs of the *Spirit* by operating within the examples listed in foundational Pauline Theology including special wisdom, healing powers, speaking in foreign languages formerly not known or one's own personal foreign language assigned to the self by God, etc.

St. Paul writes about the competitive spirit (attitude) these demonstrations created among leaders and "laymen" within the first century. Nothing has changed because these are inherent behaviors not accustomed to change for fear of loss of social recognition by the soul-self. There can be no such thing as loving God apart from a group who decides whether or not you are doing it properly—it's downright impossible.

Moreover, many people within these closed religious systems believe ministers are in a *higher* position of honor and thus call them father, pastor or bishop in order to distinguish the difference—another verticality scale.

But again, Jesus does not do this. The example of Jesus washing the feet of everyday people is a significant picture of his humble attitude. He places himself on the same level as everyone else, if not *lower*, as a sign that he is *not* within a performance prison.

> "But you are not to be called 'Rabbi,' for you have one Teacher, and you are all brothers. And do not call anyone on earth 'father,' for you have one Father, and he is in heaven. Nor are you to be called instructors, for you have one Instructor, the Christ [anointed one].

> "The greatest among you will be your servant. For those who exalt themselves will be humbled, and those who humble themselves will be exalted." –Matthew 23:8-11

Consider Jesus a liberal thinker if you are able to disassociate with the word itself. He spoke of loving, caring, and fairness and reciprocity, but when speaking to the religious conservatives of his day he generally spoke of their failure to care and their phony pious actions (Matthew 25:33).

He spoke of their need to be seen as important and their lack of ability to see themselves as anything but better than or *higher* than anyone else on the verticality ethics scale, both within and without.

Think about the bumper sticker that reads: *my child is an honor student*. Where does this leave everyone else's child? It may be true that someone's child made the honor role, but that's not really the point with most people who sport the sticker. Rather than simply being glad that our child did well, we have to contrast them with those students who didn't make the honor role—another sign of personal imprisonment.

So what do the parents of the lesser children do? It's a simple adjustment. They come up with their own sticker that reads: *my child beat up your honor role student*. This is what people do when confronted with religious ideas that create categories, levels, and the corresponding attitudes they reflect—they want to beat them up.

Jesus Preserved People's Dignity

This is all religion is. It's a giant bumper sticker war. Religious people are like those who claim the honor role and everyone else wants to beat them up because of the way they make everyone else feel who didn't make the cut. But how did Jesus make people feel?

Well, from the looks of the literature available, pretty good. Surprisingly, when not encompassed about by the prison walls of performance, we are free to promote others rather than compete with them.

People gave up their businesses and followed him around just to hear what he had to say. Sadly, today we have to go to school to learn persuasion techniques and become professional evangelists in order to hopefully snag a few unsuspecting sinners suffering fatalities of the self.

People have to create institutions designed to train people in how to influence others in their faith. The prison walls are too thick for authentic, meaningful, and spiritual interactions void of any need to convert others to their cherished in-group.

It appears Jesus transformed more lives by accident than many ministers do today on purpose because he loved without a personal agenda driven by the performance prison. Unfortunately, religion disallows this at every turn.

Who Did Jesus Consider Lost?

> "These twelve Jesus sent out after instructing them: Do not go in the way of the Gentiles, and do not enter any city of the Samaritans; but rather go to the *lost* sheep of the house of *Israel*." –Matthew 10:5-6.

This again is a statement taken right out of the first century. The only *lost* people in Jesus' day were those associated with the *house of Israel*. These were those within this *house* (a cultural community) that had lost their way. They lost perspective and lived through performance and competition. They forgot how important people outside their own community of beliefs were.

They practiced isolationism and separatism. They became self-important, spiritually introverted, and spiritually and communally convoluted—they were captive in the Eros prison of religious performance—spiritual masturbators.

> "My people have been lost sheep; their shepherds have led them astray and caused them to roam on the mountains. They wandered over mountain and hill and forgot their own resting place." –Jer. 50:6

This is why Jesus called himself the *way, the truth, and the life*. He demonstrated *the way* they were supposed to be—the *way* they were supposed to live in light of others. He represented a *true* servant.

The Hebrew people were led into metaphorical mountainous regions of duty and obligation by its leaders who were only thinking of themselves and using the common people for selfish gain while holding them captive to frivolous laws of performance.

They were not helpers, but rather they were hinderer's—performers acting on behalf of the overlord—the shadow-self. His or her whole life's work was to be better than everyone else—chosen.

> "You have not strengthened the weak or healed the sick or bound up the injured. You have not brought back the strays or searched for the lost. You have ruled them harshly and brutally." –Ezekiel 34:4

This ancient Hebrew text written long *before* the first century proves this had been going on for centuries. The *lost* does not refer to people around the world going to hell nor did it ever (Jews didn't believe in a hell).

Jesus' lost terminology was referring to those who had been neglected, used, abused, and broken by selfish, brutal, and harsh spiritual performance-based leaders locked in the Eros prison of performance over millennia. It was referring to those who were *lost* within the system of Judaism with its laws and ordinances—lost within the prison system.

Every reference to a lost sheep in any biblical narrative will always represent Jews in its context. The Jews who were a part of the Eros prison of performance including both the leadership and those subordinate to the leadership such as Zacchaeus whom Jesus referred to as "*that* which was lost," meaning the intimacy and relational aspects of the divine nature.

This was the only definition of *lost* in the mind of Jesus. If there are any *lost* people today, then this same idea must apply—they are again lost in religious performance.

In the account of Zacchaeus (as mentioned in chapter 4), Jesus invites himself to his home for dinner, which was a sign of Jewish *intimacy*. It was this invitation to an intimate meal on the part of Jesus that freed the soul-mind of Zacchaeus to believe the truth about his being a son of Abraham, an idea that had been *lost*.

It wasn't that his lineage didn't exist, it had slipped his mind and become lost, which is why his behavior disagreed with his original purpose—to love and serve others. This was the *way* he should have lived but didn't.

All who fail to recognize the divine nature within the authentic-self—the understanding that we are created in the *image* and *likeness* of God who represents love and respect, are lost whether religious, atheist, agnostic, or otherwise.

To be *found* is to recognize the divine element within all of us. This is what being enlightened or a child of the *light* is all about. It's true spirituality—a private journey we must all embark upon without a need for recognition *from* or competition *with* others.

Thought Invader: What always begins as a revelation will eventually be subject to crystallization.

The only people who can contextually and legitimately apply for the category of "lost" within biblical narratives would be those *bound* by the rules of the Eros system of religious performance *not* those outside the system.

Those outside the Eros performance system are not subject to prison rules any more than I am subject to the rules of a foreign country. This does not mean those outside any given in-group are not *lost* within another Eros performance system.

The only *free* people in the world today are those free from performance initiatives subscribed by the shadow-self and imposed upon the soul-mind. These people live without any excessive *need* for approval, recognition, or religion.

Can We Love Apart From Religion?

Can we really change our ideas about what it means to be *lost*? Is there only one view? Can we only understand the term *lost* as it was handed down by leaders one after the other—those around us on every side who don't go to church or subject themselves to institutional mandates or rules derived from a verticality ethic from *above*?

Do we only see *lost* souls as people who don't believe as we do? Do we only understand the term *lost* as it relates to hell and damnation?

What about *purpose* and *direction*? What about freedom of thought and the divine-self as it relates to the universe and the mastermind behind it? Can *lost* be associated with the inability to find our true authentic-self within the universe?

Thought Invader: Religion has focused far too much on belief rather than behaviors, on a person rather than people.

Religion has neglected people's independence and liberty to be themselves without interference from others who feel the need to do God's bidding as if he cannot do it himself. It has failed to teach people how to love their own authentic-selfs by teaching them they are unfortunate lowly worms sold into sin and in need of rectification or that their own deeds are nothing more than filthy menstrual rags (according to Isaiah the prophet).

> "For all of us have become like one who is unclean, and all our righteous deeds are like a filthy garment; And all of us wither like a leaf, And our iniquities, like the wind, take us away." –Isaiah 64:6

What are we doing and why are we doing it this way? What do we believe and how do these beliefs add to or take away from the quality of our lives and the freedoms of our associations as bishop Carton Pearson asks?

Do we really *believe* in people or do we only see people as fish that need to be caught and placed on our emotional mantle for our fishing buddies to envy or applaud? Does religion only promote loving people *into the exclusive kingdom* rather than simply loving people where they are?

Have *outsiders* only become a means to a religious end, a means of fulfillment to certain required duties and obligations to appease an angry God that must be satisfied? Or are those outside our religious systems merely representative of a reason to feel accomplished or worthy of love? What is our problem?

Can we love and care for people apart from any religious duty or compulsively driven responsibility? Can we do anything in regards to *others* simply for the sake of it, for the humanitarianism of it—simply because we care? Is there no real value apart from a religious system that ensures only God is love, and everything else is a cheap copy? Can we be spiritual without the dogma? Can we love out of the divine nature already within us?

God is love, but does that translate into something completely separate from our own actions and ability to love others sincerely out of our divine nature? Can we only love with the *love of the Lord* or else its love is meaningless? Is there any meaningful life outside of mindless belief in ancient myths and stories written by men? Is there no safe-self apart from these systems of religion and those men who define them?

I suggest there most certainly is—and with no strings attached. We can and should care because it's human—spiritual, not because we fear an unseen abyss or a God who may put us there. We should help others navigate their way because it's right, not because of religious duty or because God or his followers will be upset with our lack of performance or religious etiquette.

We should be motivated to rescue disoriented people void of purpose and direction because that's what we would want if we were confused and in the woods. If we can't do this because it's a human right to be loved, important, appreciated and free, then by all means, let your religion help you, but don't allow your religion to oust everyone who struggles with believing in the same ambiguities you believe in.

Allow your authentic divine-self to embrace those around you with meekness and care without the need to create hoops for others to jump through. Allow others to enjoy their own authenticity without out your insatiable need to critique it.

Thought Invader: Christians are not the only people who can love fervently.

Compulsory acts towards others is not love; it's obedience to a perceived standard or rule. Somebody once told me in 1990, "I love you with the *love of the Lord*," which translated means, "because I'm a Christian I am forced to love you." This bizarre strategy is why the church is shrinking. People aren't bamboozled this easily anymore. Everyone knows when someone driven by the performance prison is selling him or her.

As human beings I suggest we become more available to mentor others who don't quite know where to begin without the need to announce our performances. We must allow our authentic-self to overcome the shadows within that claim we are not worthy to love apart from a system regulated by men or religious machinery.

I suggest we renew our soul-self with wisdom and unconventional clarity while reading wisdom literature including the words of Jesus and others like the Dali Lama, Deepak Chopra, Wayne Dyer, Rob Bell, and Eckhart Tolle, to name a few.

I posted an Eckhart Tolle quote I found amazing on Facebook a few months ago. A Christian friend commented, "Isn't that one of Oprah's New Age deceivers?" I was stump dumb. There were no longer any words . . . I just shut the computer off and stared at the wall in silence. My soul aches for those within this prison of performance.

Allow yourself the expansion of your own ideas that may have atrophied through non-use or wasted away covered in dust within your religious attic deep within your soul-self. Be encouraged rather than afraid of a spiritual life outside your favorite box and breathe freely the fresh air you thought too dangerous to previously inhale.

9

Lateral Thinking

When Greek thinking entered Europe during the time of the Renaissance, all schools, universities, and thinking as an exercise was completely in the hands of the church—the Eros prison. The church had no use for creative thinking, perceptive thinking, or thinking in terms of design or spiritual *freedom of expression,* as these did not necessarily accomplish the church's main goal, which was to convert others.

Moreover, the church's main method of thinking was in terms of *absolute* truth, logic, and argumentation based on the Eros prison rules. This mode of thinking came in handy when proving heretics wrong and making arguments in defense of the dogmatic positions the church held. This was primarily the church's mission during the time of the Renaissance.

Traditional arguments or "argumentative thinking" meant the church would take a side, which was an opposing position in relation to the *adversary's* (everyone else) and then seek to attack it in an effort to prove the opposing party wrong.

Within this form of debating, each opposing side seeks to prove the other side erroneous. This is similar to postmodern debates by Hitchens and others on subjects such as evolutionary theory and religious dogma.

According to Edward de Bono[1], this type of judgment making was first established by the Greek Gang of Three (Socrates, Plato, and Aristotle) about 2400 years ago and was how the traditional church (around the time of the Renaissance) approached nearly

1) Edward de Bono (born May 19, 1933) is a Maltese physician, author, inventor and consultant. He originated the term lateral thinking, wrote the book Six Thinking Hats and is a proponent of the teaching of thinking as a subject in schools.

every subject. This was a bold move and was sadly designed to regulate, influence, and *convert* large people groups, whether they wanted to convert or not.

We find this form of thinking serves well when endeavoring to find the *truth* about something when there are known measurable components involved. Forums such as court, mathematics, the sciences, and even religious dogmas are areas where this type of reasoning thrives, but it falls short when deliberating in terms of life, the future, spirituality, creative innovation, and rethinking subjective ideas.

In the religious sector, it was deadly to disagree in those days when conveying specific truths to those within the church structure. Modern day creative thinkers such as Dr. Edward de Bono understand that the old order of logic-based argumentation works well when endeavoring to discover certain facts within a closed system, but it has no real merit when trying to create value in an open system such as the authentic-self or the soul-mind.

Freethinking people possess their own set of separate considerations, sympathies, experiences, feelings, emotional frameworks, and backgrounds. Hard-lined or dogmatic thinking does not accommodate free thinking simply because the internal derivatives of the self are fluid.

The more static an idea, the more one loses control of its outcomes. Here is how things traditionally worked under the old religious prison system. When the traditional church would state an argument, it always began from a *fixed* or a *static* position of dogma and according to a written text or edict rather than an indirect creative approach that would encompass progressive ideas and possibilities. Lateral thinking[2] is typically avoided out of fear of disrupting traditional systems and establishments much like the religious leaders of Jesus' day.

This fixed position based upon a lack of lateral thinking was usually in stone and based upon a presupposition of truth based in a tradition or on a specific biblically based idea from within the

---

2) Lateral thinking is a way of solving problems through an indirect and creative approach, using reasoning that is not immediately obvious and involving ideas that may not be obtainable by using only traditional step-by-step logic. The term was coined in 1967 by Edward de Bono.

Eros prison of dogma.

Thought Invader: The letter kills, but the spirit gives life.

In other words, people who didn't hold to the same subjective ideas were defeated from the get-go. People today are still considered either a part of the kingdom of God or a part of the Kingdom of darkness. Within other faiths, you are either chosen or an infidel. There are no other choices within these Eros prisons of religious confinement.

Unfortunately, human beings (both within and without the organized religious prison) do not begin from a "fixed" position of dogma regardless of what they believe or don't believe, but rather they begin from a position of *perception* based upon what their brain understands.

Brain Terrain

Perceptual Psychology and the brain sciences have come to understand and emphasize the way that people experience reality. According to an article in Scientific American, cognitive neuroscientist Geraint Rees, a professor at the *Wellcome Trust Center for Neuroimaging* at University College London—undoubtedly the world's leading fMRI center—published a trio of studies that relate to "differences in the way people experience things with differences in gross aspects of their cerebral neocortex, the highly convoluted part of the forebrain that crowns the brains of all mammals."

To help you understand what scientists have learned about the brain, current research has brought amazing results. According to an article by Christof Koch, thirty subjects looked at the *Ponzo illusion* (figure 3. Next page) while their brains were scanned.

Whereas everybody who looks at the *Ponzo* illusion perceives the upper bar as larger than the lower one, the magnitude of this effect differs substantially across individuals. The size of the illusion is recognized by asking subjects how much larger the lower bar has to be in order to make it look the same size as the upper one.

Surprisingly, these differences are reflected in the surface area of the primary visual cortex at the back of each individual's head. For unknown reasons, the area of primary visual cortex can differ by a factor of three among people. Dr. Rees and his collaborators discovered that the smaller a person's primary visual cortex, the more powerfully he or she experiences the illusion.

Those individuals with a large primary visual cortex judged the size of the bars to be more similar than those with a smaller one. Interestingly enough, the size of the two immediately adjacent visual areas did not influence the amplitude of the illusion. This was a stunning discovery.

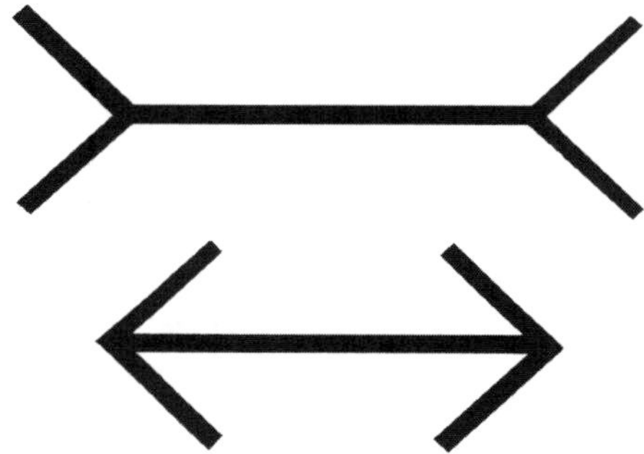

Figure 3. The *Ponzo Illusion*.

In the same way that the Ponzo illusion differs between individuals with differing brain structures, so also our perceptions surrounding various concepts and judgments completely unknown to us can differ widely. The *God* concept is widely viewed in different ways as people are inherently wired differently, both physiologically and emotionally. These differences cause people to feel, think, do, or help in different ways as a general rule.

Forcing everyone's personal judgments to fit into the same Eros box is impossible. People are not static, but rather, we are organic; people are *fluid* in nature. In other words, people are *fluid*-based like a basin of water as opposed to *solid*-based like a table or a chair.

The self is emotionally and *creatively* self-organized and virtually impossible to understand. Therefore, for all intents and purposes, the authentic-self, as fluid as it is, cannot be separated from the mind, but only distinguished within it.

Our brains are self-organizing—like a sandbox and less like

a table. If an individual's perception is off the mark by just a little bit, their logic by default will be completely faulty. Information received pertaining to subjective material arrives like water being poured into a sandbox—it becomes self-organizing.

This self-organization is why the Ponzo illusion differs between people; our brains are *different*. One size does not fit all when it comes to perception. Everybody has a different sandbox containing different amounts of sand.

Thought Invader: According to logicians, 90% of errors made in thinking are errors in perception and not in logic.

Therefore, depending upon the authentic-self and the soul-mind a person possesses, the information is *perceived* differently based on the brain terrain they have. Everyone does not have the same brain terrain. Right and wrong in regards to *perceiving* subjective ideas are just that—subjective. What is right for me is wrong for you. But within the Eros prison, what is wrong for me *must* be wrong for you as well.

Within the world of static thought, ideas are lodged within our minds and become unmovable. Like the Ponzo Illusion, what we believe is not necessarily what is yet we will typically not relent or release our lodged thought stream. Everything becomes either/or and nothing is both/and. Creativity ceases to exist and we are left with unparalleled thinking processes much like a politician endeavoring to explore the art of creative thinking.

Parallel Thinking

Dr. Edward de Bono, known to some as the father of creative thought, introduced the term "parallel thinking"[3] in his astonishing book, *Parallel Thinking*, published by Viking, London and Penguin Books, London. Parallel thinking is probably best understood in contrast to traditional argument. According to de Bono,

3) Parallel thinking is a term coined and implemented by Edward de Bono. Parallel thinking is described as a constructive alternative to "adversarial thinking", debate and in general the approach the GG3 (Greek gang of three) has been known to advocate. In general, parallel thinking is a further development of the well-known lateral thinking processes, focusing even more on explorations—looking for what can be rather than for what is.

"argumentative thinking completely lacks a constructive, creative or 'design' element and therefore lacks the ability to create value."

Traditional argument was intended only to discover the truth about what one believes *is*, but it was never meant to shape or create anything by utilizing what *can be*. Where religion has lost ground, not to mention credibility, is its refusal to think imaginatively, creatively, spiritually, or laterally.

Out of fear, religion, because of its static root, disallows any room for what *might* or *could* be. For instance, logic can be better understood in the rear view mirror. If I ask you to take a shortcut you are unfamiliar with, I may get an argument from you about it. But if I'm driving and force you to come with me and I inevitably shave off a mile from your original route, you will likely understand its logic, but only in *hindsight*.

In your limited foresight you didn't see it and in your dogma you refused to believe it. Not until you *experienced* it did you fully receive the power of the new information. Creativity requires seeing things before they are in the rear view mirror; it's more like peripheral vision—you feel something first, and then you can see it.

Logic is confined to see only what *is* in the line of sight. Creativity on the other hand, is free to perceive in every direction, revealing contextual insights that otherwise would be missed. Religion will align experiences to coincide with beliefs regardless of whether or not they support one another. This is what Jesus hated about it and why he spoke out against traditionalism.

Religion forces people to drive one way to work without the benefit of thinking crosswise and discovering creative shortcuts. Forcing ourselves to cut across our cognitive highways can aid us in discovering creative shortcuts when we may have formally (in ignorance) denied their existence. This progressive continuance is typically frowned upon within the Eros prison less we establish an alternative road to the *same* destination.

This is why many believe there are alternate routes leading to paradise while others are forced through limited foresight to deny its reality. The Eros prison thus disallows creative experience and real *spirituality* based upon our own divine perceptions.

Black and White Thinking

When all is said and done, many religionists believe a person will either enter heaven for an eternity of bliss or enter hell for an eternity of immense torture. And it all hinges on whether or not one believes in or disagrees with a specific static position of dogma.

When decision-making skills are rooted in either/or -based thinking, you can only experience right or wrong—there is no creative flexibility or creative spirituality. There is really no longer any freedom at all. Religion thus becomes a strait jacket we wear while swimming in the pool.

There is no movement. There isn't any room for discussion, exploration, creativity, or crosswise thinking within the Eros prison. This is why people become stagnant within the prison. Beliefs become etched in stone forever while we boast about our ability to maintain allegiances to old improvable ideas birthed in superstition.

True spirituality does not come from an either/or place, but rather it comes from a both/and soul-set. For example, Jesus was a both/and thinker while the Pharisees were steeped in either/or traditionalism. This is why Jesus claimed their religious traditions made void the *logos* (logic) of God, thus leaving their acts of religion of no effect in the real world.

True spirituality can see everyone's point of view without killing those of others who may need to tweak their process for better outcomes. When Jesus was faced with the infamous woman caught in adultery, he dealt with her from a both/and mindset.

From Jesus' perspective she *both* broke the Jewish Law *but also* deserved the mercy available to all people. Because Pharisees were merciless, they denied any outcome that would not lead to her death. The only way out within the Eros prison is by way of the green mile.[4]

If you were wrong during the dark ages, then you had to suffer the consequences at the hands of the organization—the green mile would be calling your name. Many are evolving out of this black-and-white sphere today, but the fear of being ousted from

4) The green mile represents the short "mile" from cell to chamber that a prisoner walks before he is executed on prison grounds by the force of the law.

important in-groups keeps many from totally abandoning their green-mile theology of death, punishment, and destruction.

Unfortunately, religion's either/or mindset is currently responsible for holding the gates of the Eros prison tightly closed for millions. For this reason, many struggle to find rescue, as they are unable to open the gates from the inside because there are no keys within the prison. Our experiences are limited to the prison courtyard where the wardens of the state can oversee our activity.

Prisoners Can't Create Value

However, it is interesting to note that during the life of Jesus, he rarely answered questions or acted in an atrocious or barbaric way towards others like his predecessors:

> "All who came before me were thieves and robbers . . . but I came to give life . . ."—A portion of John 10.

He either answered with another question or with a simple story conveying an idea. His goal was to help people move into a position of both receiving and creating value through parallel thinking strategies. Jesus was not in the habit of giving people ammunition in order to shore up their next static-truth assault.

Jesus was not dogmatic. His "I am the way" statement was not an either/or edict, but rather he was communicating to people that the *way* he pursued God was in fact a way everyone should emulate. He believed God should be one with the authentic-self—*I am my father are one.* God was *realized* humbly and simply without fanfare and religious duty or obligation.

Because the Jews would not budge from their traditional venue of spirit connection and the way with which they communicated to God, Jesus was offering an alternative. His alternative method would *both* release the bonds of the unsafe-self *and* provide opportunity for spiritual exploration within as opposed to the bondage surrounding external rituals and routines.

This is why Jesus created value with and in the people he encountered. He allowed people to *think* and *believe* by helping them percolate an idea through a series of questions and stories meant to grow their authentic-self.

People came to their *own* conclusions about his message and he allowed them to do so in their own course without Eros coercions or standard religious manipulations. Only those deep within the Eros prison were *unable* to perceive and receive his gesture.

When Jesus asked a rich young ruler to sell his possessions, give the proceeds to the poor, and follow him, the young man went away sad as he was unable to free himself from the prison of possessions that owned him. He misplaced his values for virtue.

When the rich man approached Jesus about eternal life, Jesus humbly pointed it out that its only road was paved with selflessness. Unfortunately there is neither true value nor virtue within the Eros prison.

Thought Invader: Jesus never commanded worship or that an institution be built around him.

However, Jesus was more punitively minded when dealing with religious mindsets and traditionally prejudiced people who refused to think outside their own convoluted Eros prison. He dealt strictly with those who claimed freedom while they themselves were slaves to performance. He stood between them and the wounded souls of others. This was mainly because they were more about protecting their position and performance than they were about loving other people.

> Jesus said, "For judgment I have come into this world, so that the blind will see and those who see will become blind." Some Pharisees who were with him heard him say this and asked, "What? Are we blind too?" Jesus said, "If you were blind, you would not be guilty of sin; but now that you claim you can see, your guilt remains." –John 9:31-42

Like between Jesus and the religious leaders, most interactions between religious and nonreligious people end up in argumentation with the religious trying to prove the nonreligious faulty in their thinking. This is changing a little bit as Americans are moving away from traditional ideas.

This perhaps is happening because the black-and-white model creates a defensive posture when interacting with those they consider *outsiders* making it difficult to sell their story to the thinking masses.

With the Internet age upon us, it has become much easier to gather facts and draw our own conclusions on matters we were formerly taught to trust others with. This is a welcome relief. In the past, we were taught to point out the error of someone's way and then feel pity for him or her when they didn't comply.

Of course not all are advocates of this tactic, but many fall into it without realizing it. It becomes a mission of mercy, which is why it's so easy to uncover. I suggest if we want to provide opportunity for the exchanging of ideas with those of another persuasion, we must be perceived as messengers of good will, we must create value, and we must be free from the Eros prison of performance and the *I know everything* club.

Second, we must be of good intention while remaining open to ideas different from our own. This means we must have another's best interest at heart, not our own interests. The problem is too many religious people have set themselves up as the only ones in the know when it comes to the unknowable.

All exchanges become nothing more than a means to an already decided end—an attempt to change the mind of others rather than living in harmony *with* others regardless of what their minds perceive.

Thought Invader: Relationships become instrumental rather than primary within the Eros prison.

Exchanges with others who contain closed regulated mindsets are nothing less than dealing with an impassible fracture—we have no options. It seems more pleasurable to eat glass than to try to make exchanges with closed minds. And third, we must have creative ways of making differing ideas worth listening to.

If not, religious institutions will continue to close their doors throughout the country, and many thousands will not have the opportunity for enlightening discussions surrounding life and eternal values. According to current figures, 1500-1700 people leave the organized church every day as of 2014.

The Relationship Model and the Self

Another religious model for bringing meaning and acceptance

to the authentic-self is the *relationship* model. This by far is the most defended. When certain people within certain religious sects are accused of being "religious," they rebut by saying they are not religious at all.

In order to avoid the religious in-group stigma, many will claim a *relationship* with the creator, which they believe is something altogether different from religion, but is it really?

This of course eliminates any self-sabotage for appearing religiously devout while providing a private although a subjective and irrefutable interpretation for what they believe. I know how this works because I lived at this address for forty years. I'm amazed at what I attributed to God over the last fifty years—shocked actually. But self-preservation has a way of convincing ourselves of unimaginable beliefs.

As humans, we are exceedingly vulnerable. We are vulnerable to attack and shame—emotionally, intuitively, and physically. Our inner-self (the wounded-self) many times lives in a *defensive* posture. Many of us live in a shame-based state, but unfortunately we don't know it. It is because of this that most of our allegiances involve those within the in-group who think the same way.

It's rare that we would have meaningful relationships with those of any other religious persuasion, if at all. Adjusting one's beliefs therefore becomes more and more unlikely as it will ultimately mean a total loss of intimacy and friendship on the deepest level.

Therefore, having a *relationship* with the creator is a way of defining and *defending* our celestial popularity while onlookers only imagine the extent of this relationship with the all powerful. In other words, being *in* with God is by far the better position within the universe. Although we have never seen God nor have we met God, we somehow feel we completely *relate* to God on a very *personal* level.

This posture again points to our *need* to be safe within the self. Whether it's Jesus, Mary, or St. Jude, we all need a connecting point to the deity. This makes the self feel good and somewhat safe.

The Need to Partner with Perfection

It's good to know why people can become extremely *certain* in their attempt to subconsciously obstruct their own vulnerability and turn it into reliable conversations with God. Many are convinced they know and understand God, [his] mind, motives, and perfect plans for their lives.

Believers can become more and more certain and dogmatic through this subjective relationship within the mind along with many pervasive ideas they receive from the Bible or mentors they trust. The power of the imagination in need is breathtaking.

Fear of the unknown creates exaggerated certainty. People have a habit of becoming over certain when they don't know the end game. The more we wonder, the more we say we know. Psychology defines this as an inability to become vulnerable within the self.

Thought Invader: Vulnerability easily says, "I don't know" whereas fear must say, "you don't know."

Although the Bible teaches there is no fear in love, people are still very fearful they could be wrong about their beliefs, which is why dogmatism is allowed to creep in unannounced.

I believe many relationships are possible here on the earth with real people, but a relationship with God is more a relationship with an impression or an ideal—an inner *awareness* that defies definition, rather than a real physiological person who holds real conversations about concrete facts.

This *idea* of God can be highly subjective and impossible to dislodge once one believes wholeheartedly they are connected through *conversations* and *feelings* to a personal divine being outside themselves.

Our emotions and attitudes will support these ideas to the death as well as the outcomes that are believed to be created by them, no matter how conflictive. This is harmless. Unfortunately, Eros prisoners receive their worth from the idea of connecting with the gods. We all have inner voices that we both listen to and ignore.

Counting on these voices for direction is one thing, claiming we are chosen because of them is quite another thing. Everyone has this divine ability to discern between good and evil if they listen long enough.

There's really no way of knowing what is *really* going on here other than possibly our brains making small talk around its information gathering, but many make a reasonable stab at deciphering it.

The problems come when we claim we know things that are only speculative at best. The unsafe-self fears looking imprudent or getting it wrong, as it believes it must be responsible for the information although sometimes pretending it's not.

Thought Invader: God is not a person. Jesus was a person.

Many will point to those martyred for their beliefs as an example of the facts of their faith, but this is in reality no fact at all. It simply proves people will die for what they believe in wholeheartedly as long as it makes the self feel safe.

Jim Jones convinced many people to commit mass suicide once they believed his message wholeheartedly. The Eros prison of specialness and fear swallowed them all.

There are countless examples of people dying for things they *believe* in, even crazy things. Believing wholeheartedly should never be the sign we're correct. It merely proves strong belief in something. All faiths believe with equally wholehearted strength. Who's right? This is the sixty-four-thousand-dollar question.

Our wounded-self has a realization that it's vulnerable and in need of a partnership with something perfect or flawless—something that will bring safety and affirmation to an unsafe or confused self. But this *relationship* is not defined in very precise ways. Rather it is defined subjectively by each personality ascribing differing details to the *divine* relationship as it understands it.

Countless believing people may describe in minute specifics what *God* might have said to them. I have heard it all during the last fifty years, and although there are thousands of interpretations of interpretations, there are a few main ingredients everyone seems to subscribe to. From purple bears, dimes, and butterflies to halos, monsters, and mist, everyone has a unique experience with their own imagination and the gods they attribute it to.

I have been in the unique position of knowing people on the opposite ends of this ideological spectrum, and I keep seeing similar patterns on both sides. Generally, both sides are clearly misinformed about what the other side actually believes, and when I have tried to communicate between sides, I usually find an identical knee-jerk response. I get arguments so baseless that it's obvious the clear intent is to frustrate the understanding of the other party.

It's not that one side *cannot* understand the other—they typically make an effort *not* to understand the other. This is the power of identification, and it's a *must* if one is going to remain *different* from the other in-groups and loyalties. It's our differences that many times bring our definitions.

While our imaginations differ, there are a few "musts" that all in-groups have to identify with in order to remain separate from everyone else. Within evangelical circles, this would be Jesus is God, hell and eternal retribution, water baptism, sin, and the second coming. This is because we can't simply have *anyone* in relationship with the same God we are in relationship with, lest we end up diluted into a malaise of soulish mish-mash with conflicting value streams.

This is paramount to behavioral group identification. In-grouping endeavors to create strict rules that must authenticate the incoming and keep out the riffraff—those with opposing views. The Eros prison feeds off these behaviors and thus continues to confine its inhabitants.

Stereotyping

Both religious and nonreligious people fall prey to stereotyping one another. When intellectuals see religious believers emitting incorrect stereotypes, can you possibly blame them for not taking religious believers seriously? Here are a few of the most glaring as understood by Professor Steven Dutch of the University of Wisconsin.

"Believers see intellectuals as those who lead haunted, unsatisfied lives left by the gaping void created by non-belief in the supernatural." But according to many of those who don't hold religious beliefs, they are pretty satisfied with their lives as they are. They don't seem haunted by some aching need to relate to a distant deity or the need to believe in subjective ideas that remain lost to the faculties of reason.

Or another idea according to Professor Steven Dutch is that

"intellectuals are jealous of the high moral ideals of the religious, and hate what they cannot attain." But many of the people who scorn religion do so because of the many moral failures of religious believers, *as measured by the standards of believers themselves.*

They often see the moral standards of the religious as *lower* than those of most nonbelievers. Who, apart from a few diehard Vatican theologians, takes the Catholic Church seriously any more as an educator of sexual morality after the child sex-abuse scandals involving thousands of priests?

Fundamentalists have also lost moral ground with the many scandals of high-powered evangelical leaders, but at least *their* sexual misconduct was with consenting adults. The point being *regardless* of what one believes, our conduct reflects what we *really* are within our soul-self.

People all over the world struggle with the same behaviors and temptations. We all wrestle with misfortune, malevolent behavior, and at times, conduct most unbecoming of a civilized human being.

But beliefs are a separate issue all together. They are used as signposts to justify our existence or as comfort in a world where our future is uncertain. Beliefs *reinforce* our intentions although not always lining up with our actions—they make us feel safe when we fail to do the right things but make restitution with the deity.

Those who live truly authentic lives, whether within or without religious systems, are far happier and *freer* to love those of differing persuasions. Realizing they are a part of the divine nature allows a life of trial and error without fear of hell or retribution. I find this creates a better outcome for behaviors more in line with a better destiny. It allows an infidel or us to see others as on the same playing field rather than lost.

One Way

When I was a child (in the 1970s), there was a Christian slogan that went around in the form of stickers for cars and other things that said "One Way" with a picture of a cross and a hand pointing upwards to the sky where God is supposed to be living. It meant there is only one way to get there, and *I am one of the lucky ones that found it.*

"*I found it*" was another slogan that had its day in the 1980s. I didn't like it then, and I don't like it now. It divides unnecessarily and devalues everyone else's solemn search for *meaning*. It hurts when people call other people's search for meaning "*illegitimate*" when it falls *outside* their spectrum of subjective experiences.

In the Christian faith, there are several popular formulas for getting our authentic-self *saved* from hell and eternal retribution. The development of the "sinner's prayer" has become the most popular door into this in-group within evangelical communities. Based upon St. Paul's words within his Roman letter, we have developed an initiation process or an *admission* (every religious sect has one) gate into the in-group that defines us as partners in this relationship.

This is changing a bit as general spirituality is on the rise again, but the fundamental ingredients are still the same. Verbal confession in public followed by the ritual of public baptism has become the most popular model with hundreds of variations depending on the subgroup.

It's through this process that people bring others into their relationship circle and ultimately a relationship with God, thus creating the illusion of a safe-self based upon these rites of passage. It is similar to children creating rites of passage to personal clubs and in-groups within their relationship circles beginning at a very young age.

In other words, people allow others to participate *with them* if they follow certain patterns that prove solidarity. Similarly, the pattern laid out by St. Paul and in accordance to known traditional formulas establishes the rite of passage into Christianity.

In fact, this process is the flash point as to whether or not one will be in *true* relationship at all with the rest of the in-group. This process determines whether or not one will eat with people or be in business with another person or even marry in many cases.

This is one of the tightest of the four main religious super in-group initiations, and it will determine one's spiritual *worth* as a human being or if they can participate in religious doings or whether or not one is in God's kingdom or the devil's kingdom.

I typed into Google "Is Jesus the only way to God?" and the

first thing that came up was this:

> "Absolutely! I love The Father and The Holy Spirit just as much, but if you don't believe that Jesus IS God, you will never see the gates of Heaven!" –Yahoo Answers

To be truthful, this cannot change and there remains the in-group loyalty we will discuss in the section on ethical platforms. I'm not discussing other ways among the four main world religious sects here.

I'm simply affirming that according to human nature and the behavioral dynamics of social in-grouping there can only be one way per group with regulatory thinkers and all other groups will be wrong according to whichever group you are a part.

I saw a Facebook post today reflecting a recent Muslim controversy within our government. The United States House of Representatives allowed a Muslim imam to give the opening prayer last Thursday morning, in which he praised Allah, the god of Islam, who is according to Christians the enemy of Christ and America.

People are demonizing the imam calling him demonic among other things. Post's such as "a Muslim should not be allowed to pray in *our* house" and others are rampant. Apart from agreeing or disagreeing, I find it interesting how one in-group claims freedom of religion while denying the other the same—venomously.

Sadly, this is always the outcome of religion, exclusivity, and in-groups driven by a fear of the devil, each other, and the Eros prison warden. In order to establish our self-worth, we must by necessity belong to an *exclusive* group—the right group. Airlines play upon this mindset along with everyone else who has a potential public display of human worth for manipulative reasons.

Have you ever walked onto an airplane and passed all the *special* people in first class? Better yet, have you ever sat in first class and enjoyed watching those assigned to coach walk by? This is the same medicine religion hands us—it makes us feel better—more important on the *inside*—inside the Eros prison.

Special Relationships and True Worth

As adherents to any faith system, like it or not, people believe they are in a celestial first class while everyone else flies coach. It has to be this way in order to remain a viable in-group necessitating loyalty. Moreover, we believe everyone is invited into first class, but they have to pay the ticket price just as we did.

There is no way we will allow another person in coach to sneak behind the curtain and get a free seat with no strings attached—no way in hell—and this notion we will fight for to the death.

There is only one way in—the *way* as defined by St. Paul, Mohamed, or Joseph Smith. Throughout history, powerful influencer's have defined all passages to eternal life. When Jesus was speaking to the Jews who were trying to reach God through religious and empty ceremonial means, he also claimed his *way*—a way rooted in humility, love, mercy, and forgiveness as its access point. Later, St. Peter and St. Paul defined theirs as well, as did many other influential people.

Jesus spoke harshly when it came to tribal groupies and formulas for attaining God's favor when dealing with pious Jews who believed they held the only keys to God's house.

> "You study the scriptures diligently because you think that in them you have eternal life. But these are the very scriptures that testify about me, yet you refuse to come to me in order to have life," Jesus said.

The Torah was the way, the truth, and the life for all pious Jews who placed a tremendous amount of effort in ceremoniously "serving" God. Jesus' "I Am the Way" statement demolished their arguments. It was an ingenious way of saying *I am* the Torah—watch and learn.

Jesus taught that humility and servanthood not *exclusivism* were the only true entry points to the heart of God. He didn't teach one formula or one sect or people group, he spoke of belief like a child in a message of love, forgiveness, and acceptance. It was later that people created strict guidelines in order to keep out the abysmal and bring definition and specialization to the growing group.

Thought Invader: We should spend our time looking into what Jesus said about God rather than what the church says about Jesus.

I suggest we think about the effects of in-grouping and deity selection and realize we are all divine beings—divine within the safe authentic-self. Even Jesus when questioned about his alleged claims to be God answered, "*Is it not written in your Law, 'I have said you are gods?'*" What?

This divine nature within us is far better than the exterior deities people create and their strict rules for acceptance. This nature is smarter, more accepting, and less judgmental than people who fight for personal worth and belonging among each other by creating standards and worth scales. Only the wounded soul treats people like this.

> "By the sweat of your brow you will eat your food until you return to the ground, since from it you were taken; for dust you are and to dust you will return." –Genesis 3:19

In the end, everyone will be in the same in-group of the dead without classification. Unfortunately, most do not believe this, and that is why we struggle to create in-groups here on earth while we are still living. Many Americans believe there are two groups in the end: the good and the bad.

Loyal Christians believe in two groups: believers in Jesus as defined by St. Paul and unbelievers. Even after death, according to St. Paul, there are more levels of reward, including crowns, jewels, and thrones.

> "Each man's work will become evident; for the day (of judgment) will show it because it is to be revealed with fire, and the fire itself will test the quality of each man's work. If any man's work which he has built on remains, he will receive a reward. If any man's work is burned up, he will suffer loss; but he himself will be saved, yet so as through fire." –1 Corinthians 3:13-15

We just can't help it. Our insatiable need to be important seems to follow us all the way to death and then chases us down on the other side to beat us up some more. In-groups will allegedly be in heaven as well. Some will judge angels, some will sit next to the risen Christ, and some will have their long awaited prize burnt to a cinder in front of everyone—pitiful.

This system of rewards and punishments is one of the most

superlative systems for behavioral modification of people. This is highly reflective of our insatiable need to compete projected *upon*, and thus becoming, the desires *of* our deity in the afterlife.

As long as our world continues, there will be people groups with narrow doors for entrance into them. Although we are all the same species, we are not fully family as long as there is an ability to choose sides and show others what we can do. People will keep themselves in groups in order to bring personal definition, value, and purpose to the wounded-self.

> "Whatever your hand finds to do, do it with all your might, for in the realm of the dead, where you are going, there is neither working nor planning nor knowledge nor wisdom. All go to the same place; all come from dust, and to dust all return. Even if the other man lives a thousand years twice and does not enjoy good things—do not all go to one place?" –Solomon, Eccl. 9:10.

Judeo-Christian Performance Concepts

I recently saw a video posted on Facebook that showed a young man telling me how much God loved me no matter what I had done or how broken I was within my authentic-self and how God wanted to use me to touch the world today.

As I listened to this message, I could feel the emotions swirling around—emotions attracted to the idea that no matter what, God loved me.

And then it happened—the inevitable left shoe. This can all be yours if only you accept (believe certain unproven claims by faith) Jesus as your Lord and savior, believe what we believe about what only we can imagine, and enter our treaty and follow our rules for living.

Thought Invader: The idea that we need to put videos on Facebook of ourselves performing for God is a sign of low self-worth.

As someone who was raised in the Christian world, I fully understand this message and its implications. As he continued to speak in the video, I thought of how wonderful this message was and how many people could benefit from the idea that God loved them *no matter what.*

But I also knew this idea was only partially true. It can be mine only *if* I follow its principles correctly as outlined in the New testament; love others, forgive, be content, have money but don't let money have you, etc., *and* I believe a particular statement of faith.

The difficulty with this *underlying* message is this: none of this can be yours if you *do not* believe exactly what we are told to believe about God and what this deity might be thinking as interpreted by others allegedly in the know. I have struggled with this conundrum for forty years.

God is great and he loves us so much that he killed his son in our place, but it does *not* include you *really*, unless you follow these certain steps. I've heard it told that we must *receive* (believe the ideas about the deity and its plan) the gift handed to us (like being given a gift at Christmas).

For years I saw people walking forward in churches while the crowd clapped and emotional appeals rang from the platform. The leader then feels the sense of accomplishment while the crowed only imagines what it must be like to lead a sinner to God. I've been there, and the feeling of euphoria can rival any other means to a full-on dopamine explosion. I would imagine my master saying, "well done my good and faithful servant ... enter in to the joy of the Lord."

This scenario now looks a bit unsettling to me. Who do I think I am? The audacity to think that I'm chosen and "empowered" from above to assist in or in any way determine the eternal life of another person. My intentions were pure, but there's nothing like having a mandate from God and carrying it out for him in front of the masses. But when you're in an Eros prison, it merely looks like another room in the house you are accustomed too. This is the height of the performance prison—lights, camera, action.

Suzerains, Vassals, and the Self

Is there really such a thing as "no strings attached" when it comes to any faith framework? We might expect this to be prevalent within the general populace between people or people groups, but does this occur between people and a deity? The answer is unfortunately a resounding *no* for many people who find themselves within an Eros prison of performance.

The idea of "*if you do this, I'll do that*" began early with the ancient Hittites and Sumerian's and then found its way into the communities of Hebrews who used this same model. This is readily seen within the Genesis narrative in the Old Testament when the character Abraham makes "treaty" with God known to theologians as the *Abrahamic Covenant*[5] (Genesis 15).

Not only was Abraham a benefactor of this model, but also Moses who was said to have made a treaty with God (Deuteronomy 28) and David who made a covenant with Saul's son Jonathan (1 Samuel 20:16).

In ancient times, particularly in the Persian world, the sovereign or *suzerain* would enter into treaty with his subjects or *vassals* in which he would agree to protect them and be their king so long as they submitted to his laws and ordinances. But if they refused, they would be killed without any question or remorse.

The Hebrews modeled their own religious affairs after the Suzerain model and therefore made laws allowing their deity to exercise an alleged sovereign dominion over their dependent state. This dominion extended beyond physical property and ordinances, and encompassed their authentic-self, their internal *state* of being.

These Hittite and other treaties took one of two forms in the ancient East—parity or suzerainty. A parity treaty was between equals whereas a suzerainty treaty was between a sovereign (suzerain) and a vassal (subject). It was typically drawn up by the greater power and imposed on the inferior.

Both types of treaties contained clauses including a title identifying the chief partner, a historical prologue to show how past benefits from the chief partner (God in the Hebrew treaty) should inspire the vassal to a grateful response (Moses and the Israelites), and a list of stipulations (obligations, laws to be followed).

They also contained a provision for the preservation of the document (usually by deposit in the vassal's chief shrine, which

5) The Abrahamic Covenant is comprised of nine sacred steps: the exchanging of the coat, the exchanging the weapon, the cutting of the covenant (blood), the mixing of the blood, the exchanging of names, the making of the "scar," the covenant terms, the memorial meal, and the planting of a tree.

would be the temple or ark in the Hebrew case), the witnesses to the covenant (usually the gods of both parties), the blessings and curses that would result from keeping or breaking it, a prescribed regular public reading of it, an oath ratifying the covenant in a solemn ceremony, and death to the violator.

The Sinai Treaty

The Sinai Covenant is seen in the account of the plagues upon Egypt. Moses delivered God's message to Pharaoh: "Let my people go, so that they may worship [or serve] me." At Sinai, Israel was to commit itself to their God in the form of a covenant based upon the model Abraham followed.

Yahweh, the terrifying male God, established his call to covenant commitment based on his prodigious acts of deliverance (Exodus 19:4), while the Israelites seemed more than happy to oblige when tested. It would only be through *obedience* to this covenant (treaty) that Israel could fulfill its responsibility as "a kingdom of priests and a holy nation" (Exodus 19:5-6).

Having no bearing on the authentic-self, these acts of homage as well as the obedience-driven systems they created were to become the sole means for *acceptance* by the deity. It was here where the Eros prison of performance gained an exceptional amount of ground within the Jewish system of thought. If they obeyed, the deity would respond in kind, but if they didn't the deity would destroy them without remedy.

Unanimously of course, the Hebrew's concurred. Moses prepared to ascend Mount Sinai to solemnize the arrangement in Exodus19:7-15. As Moses was about to go up, Yahweh comes down to earth, visiting the mountain with a show of thunder, lightning, and smoke. This is when Moses warns the people to not only respect and heed the holy and dangerous deity, but to commit their life to it (Exodus 19:16-25) by *drawing a line in the sand.*

As suggested already, the Sinaitic or sometimes called *Mosaic* covenant was in the form of a "sovereign-vassal treaty text" well attested from the ancient Near East. The treaty established the relationship between a King, which in this case was the Hebrew deity and his servants who also in this case were the Hebrews.

This treaty in no way addressed the authentic-self, but rather it *ignored* it in place of external acts of obedience that were supposed to reflect the authentic-self's intentions.

After a brief narrative interlude (Exodus 20:18-22), the Book of the Covenant (Exodus 20:23-23:23) gives the specific stipulations of the treaty including the Ten Commandments among many others. In fact, the Old Testament contains around 2,713 total commands.

Contracting parties often sealed their agreement with oaths and a ceremony that included a fellowship meal. The Sinaitic covenant also had its familiar animal sacrifice, sealing of the oath by the animal's blood (Exodus 24:1-8), and a covenant meal of bread and wine (Exodus 24:9-11).

This is where the cake and wine at our modern weddings finds its origin. The covenant or treaty texts also had to be prepared in duplicate and preserved in a safe place for regular, periodic reading. Moses therefore brings down from the mountain the tablets of stone to be stored in the Ark of the Covenant (Exodus 24:12-18; 25:16 or see the movie).

By now you may be wondering where this is leading and what Israelite history has to do with the Eros prison or the authentic-self. Helping you understand the history and the level of commitment cultures have towards performance rituals should give you insight into why these methods of reasoning have become so pervasive.

Performance within the arena of religion may well be the deepest and most concrete reason why we struggle with personal freedom and decision-making. These ideas go back forever and have strong ties with the ability to see ourselves as worthy or lovable.

Parents within the baby-boomer group typically received their ideas of parenting from the religious institutions they were raised in, thus millennial children will have experienced it while not always agreeing with it. Baby-boomer parents are typically highly traditional and are laced with an either/or mindset. This is known as the O.T.P. or the *Old Testament*

Parent, signified by the "I brought you into this world and I can take you out" mindset.

Therefore, in Exodus 19:5-6, the deity is said to have formulated his requirements and stipulations for those whom he had chosen as his servants just as the O.T.P. does with their children. This type of covenant was very common in that era between any sovereign and his subjects.

As long as the people served the sovereign, the deity blessed and protected the people, but if not, the deity would kill the people with plagues, enemies, or through some other horrible means showing no mercy.

When I was in grade school my parents formulated a strategy for gaining the truth out of us kids that went like this: "Steven, did you take that piece of candy?"

Steven: "NO."

This was in an effort to protect himself from the inevitable consequences that will likely follow if he did.

Mom: "Lord's truth?"

This meant that if I was lying, I was lying *to* or *before* God and not my mother, and thus I would reap the whirlwind for doing so. This frightened the *hell* out of me as a kid; therefore, I would tell the truth when asked "Lord's truth." This formula succeeded in gaining the truth, but it also succeeded in creating a fear-based strategy for obeying God.

This is why Baby-Boomer's who experienced O.T.P. guardianship from their own parents became a little more lenient with their own children. It's these subtle strategies during the formative years that instill beliefs in the "if you do this then I'll do that" philosophy that have promoted the Eros prison of performance for thousands of generations.

Divine Pest Control

In the ancient Hebrew book of Malachi it says:

> "If you do not listen, and if you do not resolve to honor my name," says the LORD Almighty, "I will send a curse on you, and I will curse your blessings. Yes, I have already cursed them, because you have not resolved to honor Me."

–Mal. 2:2

I have never found this insatiable need for the deity to be loved and served by its creation comforting. It appears the deity itself is also stuck within the Eros prison and caught up within the emotional need machine. Apparently the character of the kingdom truly emanates from the character of the king. God seems to be the first being who ever signed up for the "look at me" club.

We also see the Hebrews were required to give a percentage of their belongings to the priests who resided within the deity's "house" and who controlled the homage, rituals, and rules the servants were required to give and obey. These tactical performance rituals sealed the idea of *performance* and *acceptance* and allowed them to set like concrete for generations.

> "You are under a curse—your whole nation—because you are robbing me. Bring the whole tithe into the storehouse, that there may be food in my house. Test me in this," says the LORD Almighty, "and see if I will not throw open the floodgates of heaven and pour out so much blessing that there will not be room enough to store it." –Malachi 3:8-10

This *testing* text from the book of Malachi allows us to peek into the window of performance and why the ancients believed the gods brought the rain that watered their crops based upon their *actions* in relationship to the covenant rules. They weren't loved for who they were, but rather for what they did or didn't do.

Without a deity to reward their good behaviors they believed they would die or starve. This still happens today with the modern day *tithing* concept. It was under these emotional building blocks that the performance prison was built.

I was consulting a twenty-two-year-old girl several years ago that feared she would go broke because she failed to give her ten percent at church the previous Sunday. She sped to the church office Monday morning to *get it in* before God punished her that week by perhaps allowing her car to fail or being fired at her job. I don't blame her for these behaviors and mindsets, but I blame the church for creating them in innocent people like this young girl.

In the Malachite excerpt above, the Israelites followed the rules so that God would bless them with rain and food. The most important ideas of the ancient world were food, shelter, sun, rain, and sex (i.e., *that there may be food in my house*). In this ancient text above, Malachi threatened the Hebrews with a curse of bugs and drought on their crops if they did not comply.

This was tantamount to *divine pest control* if they obeyed and devastation by the celestial mafia if they didn't. Nothing has changed today; we see these same ideas of performance surrounding not only Christianity, but also all faiths. If I give to the local church, I won't go broke; if I don't, I'm on my own.

Within these strict concepts, there is a servant-vassal relationship that must be obeyed (Allah and Jesus are examples) in order to receive both eternal life after death and physical blessings such as health and wealth here on earth. Ministers at times will speak of curses and financial ruin if one does not comply with the rules of the covenant when it comes to our money and great blessing if we do.

Although there is no evidence this is true, nonetheless people believe it for fear of the retribution that follows the breaking of the treaty. I don't think I know *one* person in fifty years who has had their "barns filled to overflowing" with riches because of giving faithfully as the scriptures promise.

This is why I am not moved by sexy appeals to be loved by God in this way. It's conditional like every other rules-based religion on earth, as it must be. This reflects the ideas of men in charge more than it reflects a God of love and acceptance.

Thought Invader: Systems of rewards and punishments and shame and guilt are used as motivators for behavioral modification within all religious systems.

People will always be making other people jump hoops in order to benefit from whatever they're offering, and then shamming them when they don't, with scary gods and consequences. I don't know about you, but in every area of my life I want to be loved simply because I'm worth it. People don't *need* treaties with God; they need to make a treaty with themselves.

We need to promise to love ourselves. We need to believe we

already measure up instead of measuring down to the superstitious standards of insecure people groups claiming an inroad with the gods. We need to understand and embrace our divine nature already within us and welcome its realities.

We must separate the soul-mind from the spirit-self and clarify the difference. Only when we escape the Eros prison of religious performance and allow the beauty of being to infiltrate our minds will we have a safe-self free of performance initiatives.

10

The Five Ethical Platforms and the Self

If we can understand religion and ethics as a means to *protect* the authentic-self and appease an aggressive God through blood sacrifice, duty, and obligatory acts or treaties, we will understand why the bars surrounding the Eros performance prison have become so thick.

According to Jonathan Haidt[1] there are five moral foundations upon which every society rests. I will list them for you here because they are significant building blocks for understanding the religious implications associated with *being* and what Jesus referred to as *enlightenment* or being "children of the *light*."

The first of the five moral foundations referred to by Haidt involves caring for others and protecting them from bodily harm. Haidt calls this the *Harm and Care* foundation because the idea of not protecting or giving the right amount of care under the right circumstances would be considered wrong within a community of people that has adopted this attitude.

Although any wrongdoing is separate from the authentic-self, it is believed that it can negatively *affect* or *influence* the self and the mind.

The Double- Self Theory

This is how St. Paul teaches what is known as the *double-self* theory:

> "We know that the law is spiritual; but I am unspiritual, sold as a slave to sin. I do not understand what I do.

1) Jonathan David Haidt is a social psychologist and Professor of Ethical Leadership at New York University's Stern School of Business.

> For what I want to do I do not do, but what I hate I do. And if I do what I do not want to do, I agree that the law is good.
>
> "As it is, it is no longer I myself who do it, but it is sin living in me. For I know that good itself does not dwell in me, that is, in my sinful nature. For I have the desire to do what is good, but I cannot carry it out.
>
> "For I do not do the good I want to do, but the evil I do not want to do—this I keep on doing. Now if I do what I do not want to do, it is no longer I who do it, but it is sin living in me that does it." —Romans 7:14-20

This is another example of the *double-self.* Here the writer explains the concept of the two selfs—*I* do not understand what *I* do. This again is the dreadfully antagonistic parallel between the real-self (the divine nature) and the other-self (the natural soul-self) and it shows the *me-me* conflict between them sustained by the shadow-self. Every human being suffers this same dichotomy.

St. Paul was a consistent "sinner"[2] yet he did not claim ownership of those sins as part of his authentic-self that inwardly desired a different and better strategy for life.

He was able to separate his *actions* from his *intentions* (all things are lawful for *me*) when it came to his *own* behaviors, but I'm not convinced he was as generous with everyone else. His decision to blame "*sin*" and make *sin* the culprit, frees *him* (his authentic-self) from the burden of responsibility of these unwanted and unappreciated actions in relationship to Judaism, thus perpetuating his *new* message of what he calls *Grace.*

This effort protects and makes *safe* the authentic-self while at the same time allowing one to be human. As we move through the remaining four foundational ethics platforms, we will see how religion sees the world outside itself. This is how we survive our own misplaced rules.

---

2) A sinner is one who consistently misses the mark set up by a deity or those who create performance initiatives on the deities behalf. It's equal to needing to hit the bulls eye, yet never hitting it consistently.

The next foundation is a justice model and includes treating others in proportion to their actions, sharing, and egalitarianism. This foundation is known as the *Justice and Reciprocity* foundation. This attitude says it's wrong not to share, reciprocate, or enact justice within certain frameworks.

This is akin to the "eye for an eye" model of rewards and punishments, but it doesn't always go as far as a death penalty in many cases. This attitude is emotionally moved by injustice and inequality. The third foundation involves loyalty to your in-group, family, nation, and religion. The *In-Group and Loyalty* foundation is largely associated with beliefs, patriotism, nationalism, and being loyal to certain causes and missions.

With this frame of mind, an individual or group considerer's it wrong not to participate through solidarity or loyalty to one's cause. This foundation fuels religious affiliation, denominations, offshoots, differences, prejudices, and subgroups within subgroups or branches of like-minded beliefs and philosophies.

The fourth foundation deals with respect for traditions and perceived legitimate authorities and includes things like respect, duty, and obedience. This is known as the *Authority and Respect* foundation, and it typically involves parental or patriarchal models within communities, social in-groups, families, companies, the military, and religious institutions. Not removing one's hat when entering a church building or allowing the flag to touch the ground would be considered disrespectful and wrong within this framework.

The last foundation is known as the *Purity and Sanctity* foundation, and it is related to avoiding disgusting things, awful foodstuffs, and actions and activities that profane the sacred. Sex before marriage, fondling, French kissing before marriage, not covering one's head, and eating certain foods such as pork can be considered wrong within this thought pattern.

We must bear in mind that the gauge of these violations is very broad within this in-group and will differ widely between subgroups. Out of all the foundations listed, it's primarily the *Purity and Sanctity* foundation that affects the authentic-self in the most negative way.

Believing that something or someone is constantly at watch

over the unsafe-self can not only be debilitating for many, but also it is emotionally unsustainable and paves the way to the performance prison. If acts of performance do not take affect within the believer, outright rebellion towards the foundation will likely result.

Many observations surrounding these foundations made by two important psychologists, Jonathan Haidt and Jesse Graham[3], are insightful, one being that all people do not deploy these specific warrants evenly.

For example, there are discrepancies within cultures and people groups depending on social standing and demographics such as the Bible belt in the Southern region of the United States. And there are variants within variants, within in-groups within in-groups, subgroups within subgroups, and so on.

Identity issues among people within certain in-groups can and usually does create subgroups, which is why Christianity now sports 41,000 denominations worldwide as of 2012, according to the Barna Research Institute and this number is still growing. Give it enough time and fundamental Christianity will be unrecognizable in the next twenty to thirty years.

Both Haidt and Graham discovered that similar to the contention between Jesus and the Pharisees in the first century, in-groups such as liberals and conservatives today, for example, differ in how they view and appeal to the five moral foundations listed above. These differing approaches to ethics means a different approach to the self and how one views they're standing in the universe.

For instance, when making normative judgments about decisions made within specific people groups, liberals tend towards *Harm and Care* and *Fairness and Reciprocity* while conservatives tend to employ all five most of the time while playing heavy towards the *In-Group Loyalty and Purity and Sanctity* rules.

This thinking relies heavily on dos and don'ts and alleged rights and wrongs determined by a narrow view of interpretative text sources and subjective ideologies.

3) Jesse Graham is an Assistant Professor of Psychology at the University of South Carolina. His work is reliable and profound.

According to Richard Beck,[4] Professor and Department Chair of Psychology at Abilene Christian University, in his thoughtful book *Unclean, Meditations on Purity, Hospitality, and Morality*, studies show that although liberals do employ the other three foundations from time to time, it is much less frequent than in conservative groups.

Clearly if we can understand that the formation of groups among people within a social order is standard for reasons of social identity and importance, it will bring clarity to the following ideas. For example, when employing the idea of a specific social difference such as homosexuality within the Christian church, liberals will focus on the question of *harm*, asking if their decision to uncover their sexual preference is harming or unfair to anyone else.

They will underscore the idea of being treated unfairly or maybe even question the *justice* of in-group and out-group decision-making as it relates to people of different persuasions including sexual persuasions.

While these differences abound within all people groups, the standard operating procedures for making them paramount is perpetuated by performance. In other words, the need to highlight the *harmless* differences between us is only fueled by competitive behaviors triggered by a *need* to be better, different, or morally superior. These *triggers* are born within the Eros prison of performance and drive deep wedges between people groups.

Typically driven by fear and insecurity, competitive attitudes driven by purity metaphors are what separate us from one another. Insecurity fuels the need to be different, while religion justifies its outcomes.[5] In the end we all lose. Jesus saw everyone as a winner. His stories and his relentless pursuit of social justice has become one of the most powerful representations of what being free from the Eros prison of performance looks like.

---

4) Richard Beck is a professor at Abilene Christian University whose blog Experimental Theology, which explores the intersections between psychology and theology, has revealed him to be one of the most intelligent and provocative voices in world of theology today.

5) Beck persuasively argues that the church's obsession with purity is a costly pursuit, one fraught with serious psychological and sociological consequences.

The Real Meaning behind Purity Rules

Most conservatives see sexual difference or deviation as a blatant violation of the *Purity and Sanctity* foundation which is, according to Beck, rooted in what is known as disgust and contamination psychology. For this reason those who see this as a violation will by necessity determine these actions as choice rather than birth differences rooted in chromosomes and DNA subtleties.

The thin-minded and regulatory-driven think tank will never believe this to be an internal physiological mechanism, but rather a poor choice rooted in rebellion against purity and sanctity standards.

This thinking is designed to protect the god author of the flesh-body who would *never* allow a contradictory set of circumstances to muddy up long established interpretations surrounding humans and what is believed to be their acceptable co-mingling with one another.

According to Beck, purity metaphors trigger revulsion and are typically synchronized with the *sexual* characteristics of the human condition within religious conservative groups, dating back to the time of Moses. All other violations of any social or moral code are simply not treated in the same way.

Christian doctrine markets sexual violations as the *only* sins *against* the flesh-body itself—a representation of the larger *body of Christ* metaphor in biblical thought. All other sins are without or *outside* of the body envelope according to Pauline thought and are therefore not against the body according to 1 Corinthians 6:18:

"All other sins a person commits are outside the body, but whoever sins sexually, sins against their own body."

Terms like *missing the mark* or *sin* are associated with external conditions or *actions* like stealing, but according to the Hebrew tradition that St. Paul was highly trained in, *purity* violations run much deeper—touching the soul and spirit of a person thus affecting the entire *true-self.*

This is why many will simply say, "get up again," or "get back on the straight and narrow," or "dust yourself off and pick yourself up again" after sinning in a *venial* manner, or making a sincere mistake in judgment.

Conversely, divorce, fornication, and adultery as well as many other *perversions* (there are many levels of sexual violation within certain religious in-groups) are emotionally and psychologically *unredeemable* within these in-groups seeing that they run deeper in the Hebrew purity tradition and are against the person's own body. In the Old Testament, you were killed for violating purity rules.

This *mortal* infraction may be tantamount to sinning against God himself within this mindset, as the great apostle believed was the case with eating meat formerly sacrificed to idols in the first century.

> "And when you sin against other believers by encouraging them to do something they believe is wrong, you are sinning against *Christ*."—1 Corinthians 8:12

In many evangelical groups one might commit murder and then after coming to faith (conversion) become a minister within that social order, but if you are divorced or remarried a second time, you can be banned from ministerial duty in many sects—for life.

Seeing that the body metaphor is representative of Jesus' body (Body of Christ, etc.) in both a corporate and singular sense within this philosophy, it makes sense that these in-groups place such an overwhelmingly hard line on the implications associated with violating it.

It's equal to bodily harm within this *emotional* framework. Sexual union, sexual desire, sexual promiscuity, and everything associated with sexuality therefore become a greater taboo within purist social groups.

Moreover, sexuality inadvertently becomes a performance-based act within the Eros prison. Much of these rules are designed to keep oneself *pure* before the deity who cannot and will not tolerate impurity or contamination of the body or mind.

The outcome of such thinking creates a "*be ye holy even as I am holy*" (set apart *from* others) mindset that powers the Eros prison of performance within people groups who believe their God requires a standard of celestial excellence in order to be accepted within the cosmic community.

Purity rules therefore have the strength of an ox when used to manipulate or control people groups who have been taught from a young age that violations are unacceptable. This form of control thus perpetuates sexual temptation much like a wet paint sign tempts an individual to touch the wet paint to ensure the sign's claim.

It is because of this religious cycle of attempting to live up to false ideals that are by and large impossible to meet that we as people are living discouraged lives before the gods. Our feeble attempts the solicit their favor fall to the ground with a deep thudding sound.

Our creating more personal/tribal hoops to jump through in an attempt to curry a simple turn of the head by the gods in our direction becomes the mortar that hardens between the bricks of personal discouragement that make up the walls of the Eros prison of performance. Is it any wonder that religion and social interaction have become the two greatest bulwarks responsible for encasing us within its musty cellar?

11

The Rules of Disgust and Contamination Psychology

According to the rules of disgust and contamination psychology, Beck says any outside toxin such as a fly in the orange juice contaminates the juice for *all time* once the contact and uncleanness takes place leaving the juice hopeless of full and adequate redemption.

Studies have proven that no matter how many times the contaminated juice goes through an observed purification process, after the fluid has become ill-affected and the foul contaminate removed, people will still not drink it.

Beck begins his explanation of disgust and contamination psychology by recounting Paul Rozin's classic hypothetical: imagine spitting into a cup and then being asked to drink the contents of that cup. In nearly every instance, people will not drink the sully expulsion for fear of poisoning or repulsing the flesh-body.

Although we swallow our own saliva thousands of times a day, once it is banished from the body, disgust and contamination psychologically dictate it cannot be allowed back into the body envelope without initiating our natural gag reflex. This is how our brains are designed to protect the body from contaminants or harmful pollutants, foodstuffs, and toxins.

Because many religious groups view homosexuality, smoking, drinking, or sexual promiscuity through a purity metaphor, the psychology of this metaphor initiates the emotional and psychological gag reflex and therefore exposes the "impure" people to *emotional quarantine* from the in-group. This misplaced behavior is not very helpful or remedial as it ignores the divine authentic-*self* within all peoples.

Remember the Zacchaeus story we spoke of early on in this work and consider the words of Jesus when he spoke to Zacchaeus while he was on the road: "Salvation has come to your house today." Unfortunately many today misinterpret these words because they are not understood in the context of the culture.

In the Jewish mind, salvation had nothing to do with eternal life beyond our earth. Those Jews who were the receivers of this story or those who witnessed it viewed salvation as a deliverance from being an outcast or ruled by another controlling power such as Rome.

Salvation for the first-century Jew meant social validity, success, autonomy from subjugation, and intimate familial bonds. The Jewish concept of heaven was entirely different than what it has morphed into since the death of Jesus. They did not believe in hell as a place of torture for violation of purity ethics, but rather they believed in *Sheol* or the grave.

Most of their concepts were derived from Hebrew wisdom literature on these issues wherein it was believed the grave was simply the place of departed spirits—they didn't know what happened after death or where people actually went, just as we don't know.

> ". . . set apart among the dead, like the slain who lie in the grave (*Sheol*), whom you remember no more. They are cut off from your hand." –Psalm 88:5

These concepts have been broken down throughout millennia to mean something entirely different. Therefore, when Jesus spoke to the crowd in the Zacchaeus story he said, "For he too is *also* a son of Abraham . . ." meaning he is also a benefactor of the things you are benefactors of, seeing he is from the same lineage.

Regardless of the fact that he is a scoundrel, a cheat, and involved with organized crime, I see him as a son of Abraham (as he is) and therefore I am publicly restoring his dignity to the place it always should have been. Love breaks the power of bad behavior.

Zacchaeus' *salvation* did not come about because of any form of initiation, baptism, or ritual, but rather by an *awakening* to what he *already* was—a son of Abraham. His awakening was a "spontaneous receptivity" to the reality of who he *was* provoked by the invitation of Jesus to enter into an authentic and intimate meal.

This is exactly what happened to the Samaritan woman (we'll discuss in chapter twelve) *after* a spontaneous conversation with Jesus followed by an invitation to drink of what he calls the *water of life*. Jesus saw Zacchaeus as he *was* (in this case a son of Abraham, which was highly important for identification with *Yahweh*), not as he *did*.

Jesus also saw the allegedly adulterous woman the same way (Luke 7). The devout Jews saw Zacchaeus as a rule breaker and nothing else. Jesus spoke to Zacchaeus' authentic-self, not the behavior his flesh-body was engaged in.

This is what Christianity is supposed to do, only it appears it is worthwhile only *after* an initiation process called *salvation* or conversion. This is something Jesus NEVER did. In Jesus' world, salvation always is a constant we just have to be reminded of it.

Deliverance is a byproduct of believing one is worthy to receive it based upon one's knowledge of the authentic reality within the self. All Jesus did was point it out. Instead of seeing faith as something *brought* about through certain religious actions, beliefs, or homage, Jesus saw it as a preexisting reality (Luke 23:43)[1].

Thought Invader: When Jesus identified Zacchaeus as a son of Abraham, he immediately treated him like one.

In the mind of Jesus, no matter what Zacchaeus was engaged in as far as his actions went he was STILL a son of Abraham, something Zacchaeus likely was forced to forget by everyone else.

Jesus never focused on people's *doings*, but rather he focused on people's *beings*. He only pointed out actions to those who pointed out everyone else's although they were acting in the same way. Actions were always seen as an extension of who people were.

Unfortunately, expelling people from in-groups as the Jewish leaders were in the habit of doing (tax collectors were unable to vote among other things) in the same way one would reject their own spittle in a cup becomes the only reasonable cure for such violations of man-made rules attributed to a deity for affect.

Violations of sanctity and purity rules are thus nearly impossible barriers to break within certain social and religious groups. This psychology can readily be seen in the biblical Revelation of John

1) And he said to him, "Truly, I say to you, today you will be with me in Paradise."

when the writer claims that God "*vomits out of his mouth*" toxic behaviors in violation of common purity and sanctity rules. This assault on the authentic-self is downright scary if one believes it.

Many are taught in Christian circles that Jesus was the author of these letters in the Revelation, not knowing that this particular document almost didn't make it into the canon of scripture. Whether God actually does this is anybody's guess, but after observing Jesus' actions towards known violators of purity standards, it seems unlikely.

Examples of how Jesus responded to people such as in the infamous tale of the woman caught in adultery and Zacchaeus, I'd be inclined to chalk this up as John's (if he actually wrote the document—no one knows) personal wish.

John already was known for loathing the Samaritan community for simply being a product of those who formerly violated Jewish purity-breeding rules, seeing he begged Jesus to call down fire from the heavens and kill them all in the book of Luke:

> "As the time approached for him to be taken up to heaven, Jesus resolutely set out for Jerusalem. And he sent messengers on ahead, who went into a Samaritan village to get things ready for him; but the people there did not welcome him, because he was heading for Jerusalem.
>
> When the disciples James and John saw this, they asked, "*Lord, do you want us to call fire down from heaven to destroy them*?" But Jesus turned and rebuked them. Then he and his disciples went to another village." –Luke 9:51-56

The Old Testament is rife with purity violations and harsh consequences that follow based upon the suzerain/vassal treaty between the Hebrew God Yahweh and Israel as a community in Deuteronomy 28, which is solely based upon rewards and punishments as we mentioned earlier.

This is what emboldened the first-century Pharisaic group to walk on the other side of the road when approached by an oncoming sinner, tax collector, Samaritan, or a publican, to name a few known untouchables.

To have direct contact with such a one was to be morally contaminated by the filthiness. This was also true with lepers, outsiders, and menstruating women. According to Beck, psychologists call this action *magical thinking*. Magical thinking is when a person or social group believe a physical outside source or influence such as a homosexual, a tax collector or a whore, can have a causal effect on a moral or *internal* state of *being*—the safe-self.

This kind of thinking when adopted and acted upon can have grave implications on a person's *being* as it focuses all the attention on *doing* or *not doing* rather than *being*. According to the rules of magical thinking, violations can corrupt the internal state of being and turn the true-self's light into darkness.

This ability to turn off and on the light within the true-self creates a pandemic of performance-driven behaviors for serious followers of the faith and will create instability within the self.

I personally know a religious person who disallowed their children to enter the house of a Mormon neighbor for fear that their "sin" or uncleanness would somehow rub off on their children and affect their internal state of *being*. I have no words for this.

Jewish traditionalists and most Christian groups today believe that when something considered *holy* converges with the profane; the holy is besmirched and ruined from the *inside* out as in this Old Testament passage:

> Ask the priests, if a person carries consecrated meat in the fold of his garment and that fold touches some bread or stew, some wine, oil or other food, does it become consecrated? The priest answered "No."
>
> Then Haggai said, "If a person defiled by contact with a dead body touches one of these things, does it become defiled?" "Yes," the priests replied, "It becomes defiled."—Haggai 2:12-13

Nevertheless, the negative emotional impact produced by this philosophy will have an overpowering affect on the emotional and internal state of affairs within the violator, which in turn inadvertently produces the very same performance patterns their faith was destined to remove.

And because religious in-groups believe holiness is a state of being as in, "*be ye holy even as I am holy*," the internal state is subsequently damaged through the external contaminant, which may very well be another person. This is the formula for creating "us against them" issues between people groups thus fueling the social and culture wars of our modern day.

The results of these culture wars foster performance based lifestyles as each in-group tries to outperform the other through the keeping of behavioral rules and systems of rewards and punishments in their feeble attempts to please their cherished deities and those in direct competition for the graces and favor of the gods.

Was Jesus a Liberal?

Churches, synagogues, temples, and other gathering spots unfortunately become more or less places of performance in order to act out what we believe others expect in terms of behavior and acceptance solicitations. It's nearly impossible to see this from the inside, but once one leaves the social order along with its patterns and performance stratagem, things may become increasingly clear.

When it comes to the actions of Jesus, Beck points out that Jesus did not place purity and sanctity ideas *above* harm, care, and injustice like most diehard followers of Jesus do today. Clearly when Jesus said, "*I desire mercy, not sacrifice*," he aligned himself with the *Harm and Care* as well as the *Fairness and Reciprocity* foundations as opposed to the *Purity and Sanctity* foundation alone.

In other words, Jesus was not "disgusted" with people as many of his followers are today and thus placed himself closer to the Liberal position of fairness rather than Conservative position of purity. He never divided people into class or positions "closer" to God, that we know of.

According to most modern day scholars, Jesus was about as liberal as you could get based upon the current religious system of his day. This is why he touched *unclean* lepers and had lunch with those whom orthodox Jews considered to be *sinners* as well as prostitutes and weirdos.

He believed the *clean* was not defiled by the dirty, but rather it was the other way around. St. Paul, because of his roots in ancient Orthodox Judaism, believed bad external relationships would corrupt good internal character or *being* as many do today, but good decision-making isn't corrupted, it can only be influenced or abandoned. People thus willingly trade in their healthy decisions for bad decisions when they're convinced the *unhealthy* decisions carry more benefits after making them.

Thought Invader: You cannot corrupt the incorruptible authentic-self by external body actions or soul-mind thinking.

When Jesus told his tale about the sheep and the goats,[2] two distinct people types within the population of Israel, his story was again based upon the *Harm and Care* and the *Fairness and Reciprocity* foundations. Many make the mistake of believing this group is representative of the world at large, but this is a failure to understand the Jewish culture and of whom Jesus was speaking.

He didn't appeal to the *Purity and Sanctity* rules, which could include body sins, lying, stealing, adultery, or the like.

He didn't appeal to the foundation of *Authority and Respect*, which includes things such as civil violations, going faithfully to synagogue, or the *In-Group and Loyalty* platform, which encompasses things like missing church, joining the free masons, or attending a weekly bible study or not attending it.

Jesus was not *as* interested in what people believed as he was interested in what they *did*—this is something we could write a note to self about. When condemning the behavior of the Jews towards those outside their sect and the nonreligious, his emphasis was on fairness principles, hospitality, and moral people judgments like visiting people in prison or feeding the hungry.

Beck points out that Richard Shweder[3], a cultural anthropologist, after studying morals in diverse people groups found that despite a wide array of ways that these moral areas could be operationalized. There were only three main areas of ethics within society. According to Shweder, these ethical platforms consist of:

---

2) The sheep and goats analogy reflected Israelite behaviors toward the poor and disenfranchised. It was not a parable explaining Christians and non-Christians as used today.
3) Richard Allan Shweder (born 1945) is an American cultural anthropologist and a figure in cultural psychology. He is currently Harold H. Swift Distinguished Service Professor of Human Development in the Department of Comparative Human Development at the University of Chicago.

> **Community:** "Based on moral concepts such as duty, hierarchy, and interdependency, which is designed to help individuals achieve dignity by virtue of their role and position in a society."
> **Autonomy:** "Based on moral concepts such as harm, rights, and justice, which is designed to protect individuals in pursuit of the gratification of their wants."
> **Divinity:** "Based on moral concepts such as natural order, sacred order, sanctity, sin, and pollution, which is designed to maintain the integrity of the spiritual side of human nature."

In another controlled study according to psychwiki.com's notes on moral psychology and ethics, several professionals including Haidt and a few others mapped emotions onto Shweder's three ethics by asking students in the United States and Japan to look at moral situations and determine which emotional reactions, represented by pictures of facial expressions, would be appropriate.

There was general agreement that contempt was a natural reaction to violations of the community ethic, while anger was a natural reaction to violations of the autonomy ethic, and complete *disgust* was the natural reaction to violations of the divinity ethic. This was later confirmed by looking at the actual facial reactions of American students to these moral situations.

Thought Invader: The Bible is a compilation of manuscripts written mostly by Jews, to Jews, about Jews, and about their ideas surrounding the Jewish messiah.

It is this disgust and contamination psychology that has created the problems and conceptual actions with Christians and Muslims as well as a few other people groups. Because those outside these religious in-groups are considered *infidels* in the eyes of Muslims or *lost* in the eyes of Christians (these are the same today), they are thus contaminated and *unredeemed* and must be expelled (like the spittle example) from the earth along with anyone else *outside* the proverbial camp.

God will judge those on the outside; but as the Scriptures say,

"You must remove the evil person from among you"—1 Corinthians 5:13.

The third Reich also believed this way concerning blacks, the handicapped, and the Jews, as do many groups today within our own country. Christians may display this behavior by creating terms like pagans, unbelievers, secular, the world, sinners, and them.

Since the modern Christian church has its own version of insiders and outsiders, it psychologically and emotionally expels all those who are in violation of its preferred purity ethics, which are nestled nicely within its divinity ethic, to a yet future fiery torture chamber below the ground for trillions of years.

The powers and difficulties that stem from these religiously driven and psychologically established frameworks help create strong performance-based behaviors within these people groups, thus denying the blessed state of *divine being* we are all consciously and subconsciously pursuing.

All these false perceptions including their purity rules are simply shadows cast by a greater malevolent mindset—we are never good enough. Whether religious or otherwise, human beings are on a desperate search for significance. And when one is on this search for significance, one typically must believe everyone else is *lost* with them. The real divine authentic-self is where this search needs to begin *and* end. We need to begin believing we are good within our true selves and that if God truly made all things, he made them good.

Living in the Shadows

What about *you*? Are you living in the shadow of who you *wish* you were? What about the shadow of what you believe others *expect* of you? Is your real divine authentic-self simply not divine enough? Or are you like Zacchaeus and you have lost your compass and are beginning to believe you are corrupt to the core, so you might as well go no holds barred into debauchery.

These shadows are nothing more than dark places of performance initiated by the shadow-self. We all cast shadows and live in shadows. We cast shadows on others when we manipulate circumstances or align ourselves with external religious patterns and behaviors so others will see our best effort.

We cast shadows when we stealthily point out the perceived imperfections in others in our feeble attempt to feel better about ourselves in light of someone else's success or talent or maybe someone's unfortunate state.

We live in shadows when we allow the casting of others' shadows to dim our own personal light of being, or when we believe or accept the casting of a shadow in our personal space and live down to its false assumptions about our being. Every interaction becomes an opportunity to not measure up or down.

Admittedly, our society has developed classifications within its social order like the verticality ethic as if nature itself has not had ample opportunity to impose such perversion upon its people. I read a story once that touches upon this subject in a marvelous way; it nearly stopped my breathing when I read it. It was a story as only the late Brennan Manning could tell it.

Larry Malaney's Divine Moment

In the late 1960s, Brennan Manning[4] was a professor at a university in Ohio. He tells a vivid story about an Irish boy named Larry Malaney who attended the campus there in his astounding book, *The Furious Longing of God*. Not graced by society's standard of visual excellence, Manning says, Larry struggled to make friends and make grades, and had never been able to overcome the personal obstacles preventing his social or academic success.

Manning says Larry told him that every morning when he awoke, he would look himself in the mirror and spit at it. Manning had never in his entire life met a boy with such low self-esteem and self-hatred. Larry lived to hate himself.

According to Manning's astonishing narrative, Larry found himself home for Christmas that year in Providence Rhode Island. When his vacation had ended, his father rode the six o' clock bus with him out of town. Larry was going to catch another bus to the airport after his father and he disembarked the first bus.

They had ridden in silence as was the custom with that gen-

4) Richard Francis Xavier Manning, known as Brennan Manning (April 27, 1934 – April 12, 2013) was an American author, priest, and public speaker. He is best known for his bestselling book The Ragamuffin Gospel.

eration. As they walked without speaking, some men across the street started shouting terrible things to Larry like "Oink, oink, oink" and "Look at that fat pig!" "If that were my kid, I'd hide him in the basement," one construction worker yelled.

Manning said that in that moment, for the first time in Larry's life, his father reached out and embraced him, kissed him directly on the mouth, and said, "Larry, if your mother and I live to be two hundred years old, that wouldn't be long enough to thank God for the gift he gave us in you. I am so proud that you are my son."

Boom. His father's statement immediately broke through the walls of Larry's chest like the bolt cutters used by trauma surgeons in the ER, grabbed his heart in ruthless fashion, and aggressively massaged it to life.

The transformation that took place in Larry that year beat anything Manning had ever seen in any student up until that time. Not only did Larry get the girl, he also became president of one of the fraternities that year. And if that wasn't enough, he was the first student in the history of the university to graduate with a 4.2 grade point average.

On June 14, 1974, Larry Malaney was ordained a priest in the diocese of Providence, Rhode Island, and for the better part of his life was a dedicated missionary to South Africa where he loved the outcasts and cared for the poor.

What was it that happened to Larry? Before his father's kiss, Larry was simply surviving—he wasn't *being*. But after that kiss, something happened on the inside of Larry. A door was opened to his authentic-self that had been shut since his early childhood.

The shadows that had been constantly cast in his direction for so many years had built up a pile of worthlessness against the door to Larry's heart. But the loving kiss of his father in the public square melted it all away.

The contentment and personal satisfaction that followed catapulted Larry forward in a remarkable and dramatic fashion. Larry was enlightened. And that enlightenment translated into missions work for Larry—pleasure and fulfillment followed.

The love in his heart was so great that it spilled out onto

another continent for nearly twenty years through his selfless service to others. Larry was the epitome of living satisfaction—of the divine nature.

We don't all have a story like Larry, but many of us have a story to tell that may be similar to Larry's beginnings. Stories of pain and suffering in the shadows of others' lack of personal being have plagued many of us. The story of Larry Malaney reminds me of one of the most celebrated, award winning musicals to ever hit the modern stage: *Billy Elliot*.

Billy Elliot's Need to Be

It was also a movie (2000) written by Lee Hall and directed by Stephen Daldry. The film is set in fictional Everington during the 1984-85 UK miners' strike, and centers on the character of 11-year-old Billy Elliot, his love of dance and his hope to become a professional ballet dancer.

Billy lives with his angry widowed father (Jackie), and older brother (Tony), both angry coal miners out on strike, and also his invalid grandmother, who once aspired to be a professional dancer in Durham. The scenes are stomach pitting.

According to the story, Billy's mother died in December the previous year at age 38. The film depicts Billy's all to familiar struggles to be liked for who he *is* by his family and peers while also managing the death of his mother and the pitfalls of puberty.

Billy's father sends him to the gym to learn boxing like a man, but inwardly Billy dislikes the sport. While at the gym happens upon a ballet class that also uses the facility while their basement studio is temporarily being used as a soup kitchen for the striking miners.

Unknown to his father, Billy joins the ballet class with eager anticipation. When his father discovers this he verbally assaults him, ridicules him, and forbids him to take any more ballet because he is locked in the Eros prison of performance—the scene is gut wrenching.

But, passionate about dancing, Billy covertly continues lessons with the help of his dance teacher, Sandra Wilkinson. Mrs. Wilkinson believes in Billy when nobody else does.

She believes he's talented enough to study at the Royal Ballet School in London, but due to his brother's arrest during a skirmish between police and striking miners, Billy misses the secret audition.

Finally, Mrs. Wilkinson musters the boldness to tell Billy's father about the missed opportunity, but fearing that Billy will be considered to be gay, both his father and his brother are outraged and sickened at the prospect of Billy becoming a professional ballet dancer. They are unable to scale the walls of their personal prisons of social acceptance in a male mining town.

Over Christmas, Billy learns that his best friend, Michael, is gay. Although it appears Billy is not (it's hard to tell), he is humble and supportive of his friend. Later, his father catches him dancing in the gym and realizes through painful deliberation that his son is truly gifted. In a moment akin to "the fathers kiss" in the story of Larry Malaney; he will do whatever it takes to help Billy attain his dream—his father escapes the Eros prison in this emotional moment.

Because of the family's financial hardships, Mrs. Wilkinson tries to convince Billy's father to let her pay for the audition, but he replies, "*Billy is my son.*" This is the Larry Malaney moment. Billy's father has an epiphany and attempts to cross the picket line to pay for his sons trip to London, but Billy's older brother, still locked within the Eros prison blocks him.

Rather than let Billy's dream die, the miners and the neighborhood raise some money and the father pawns Billy's mother's jewelry to cover the cost and takes him to London to audition for the Royal Ballet School.

Though exceedingly nervous, Billy performs well, but he punches another boy in his frustration at the audition and the fear that he has ruined his chance of attaining his dream grips them all. He is sternly rebuked by the review board but when asked what it feels like when he is dancing, he describes it in a most passionate way using electricity as a metaphor.

Seemingly rejected, Billy returns home with his father. Sometime later, he receives the letter accepting him to the Royal Ballet School, and he leaves home to attend—this is the climax to the story and I found it to be extremely emotional.

The film's final scene is set fourteen years later (approximately 1999): the mature Billy takes the stage to perform the lead in *Matthew Bourne's Swan Lake*, as his proud father, his older brother Tony, and his friend Michael watch in the audience. This story is a wonderful picture of personal freedom derived from letting go of the perceived expectations of others.

Early Impressions

Similar to Billy Elliot, all our stories begin early—during the formative years as our worldviews are still in the developmental phase. We are taught to perform for our teachers, our parents, and our communities. We are encouraged to be something else, something supposedly *better* than we already are—smarter maybe or more socially acceptable. Of course not all of us have a poor formative phase, but many do.

Sit up straight—don't slouch. Why can't you get good grades like your sister? You should be a boxer and not a dancer. Raise your hand if you know the answer. Let me see your report card. If you feel called into the ministry come up front and stand with me here; the rest of you stay in your seats.

These aren't attempts by our elders to hurt or discourage us; on the contrary, many parents and teachers are simply trying to help. But little do they know of these shadows cast upon our person or the kinds of scars inadvertently produced when making comparisons or pointing out flaws. Even recognizing others many times by default creates nonrecognition in the rest.

Because of this adult to child early expectation, we try desperately in our immaturity to perform for parents, teachers, and our peers or for the affections of leaders, friends, and family. We are taught early to *apply* ourselves, to compete so others will take notice.

There's nothing wrong with competition, but for many it becomes intoxicating. This is when having to win defines us—or possibly in a few cases, destroys us. Although these behavioral dynamics are necessary for our survival within social groups, they also can at times create a performance-based mentality, a prison of performance if you will that ends up becoming the driving force for many years.

It's a new world today. Communities are not what they were thousands of years ago or even thirty years ago, and the things that define us as people and groups have changed dramatically—shoes, cars, cell phones, education, etc. These are the new affordable marks of definition between people and in-groups.

Am I socially acceptable? Is my hair the right color or do I need braces on my teeth? Are my clothes socially adequate? Am I too fat or too skinny? Do I have the newest phone? We have all secretly asked ourselves these questions. But how do we answer them? Inevitably, without a healthy in-look to start with or without the *father's kiss*, we will struggle to answer them correctly, or with only a shred of confidence.

12

The Power of Parenting, Personality, and the Self

The late Dr. Edwin Louis Cole[1], Author of the groundbreaking books *Maximized Manhood* and *Communication, Sex and Money*, used to stress nine attributes that should be adopted by fathers (and mothers, but this was a conference for men and fathers I attended in the 1980s) if they were going to raise emotionally healthy children.

These nine behaviors would function as a foundation for building strong children—children who would be less performance driven when they matured into adults. These factors would likely produce children who would be comfortable in their own skin regardless of its color—satisfied with who they were as a person.

As I understood Cole, the mother and father were to *share* the responsibility of assisting their children in world navigation and healthy decision-making. This process of rearing would ultimately diminish the *need* orientation characteristics that typically defined the young and create a healthier balance between wanting and needing within a child.

I've listed the nine word descriptors Cole came up with (Cole used the words without definition) and I have added my own definitions, as I believe they should be:

> Guide: Assisting children through potential difficulties in traveling through the formative years in an effort to en-

1) Edwin Louis Cole (September 10, 1922 – August 27, 2002), also known as Ed Cole, was the founder of the Christian Men's Network, a religious organization devoted to helping Christian men and fathers. He published many books and preached numerous sermons relating to men and religion.

sure they reach their destination.
Guard: Keeping children safe from harm or danger; carefully watching over them.
Govern: Exercising a directing or restraining influence over children in order to provide better outcomes through times of peer pressure or difficult decision-making.
Direct: To manage and supervise or to assist in directing the course of children.
Protect: To defend or guard from attack, invasion, loss, or insult.
Correct: To scold, rebuke, or teach in order to improve the effects of one's behavior on self and others.
Cherish: To hold and treat as dear or to care for tenderly or cling to fondly.
Nourish: To strengthen, build up or promote.
Admonish: To caution, advise or counsel against poor decision making.

Likely, children who have received a good healthy dose of all nine attributes during the formative years will have a better chance at emotional health and sustenance compared to those who lack at least three of the nine attributes. In other words, if a child receives these behaviors from either one or both parents, they will typically have a healthier in-look and display more confidence.

Of course this does not mean there aren't opportunities elsewhere to feel rejected and scorned such as the schoolyard as in my case, but the *safest* place is typically the *best* place to start. Many parents have fallen down on the job, but it's not too late to make amends. According to psychological theory, as long as *love* and *security* are provided, everything else can be fixed without major therapy.

Think of your own childhood. After careful examination of the nine descriptors, where do you come in? Bear in mind that these attributes are not to be excessive or overpowering. Correcting should not escalate into punishing, and guarding should not become micro managing. Balance is always the key to life.

Take a moment and reflect on how you felt when you were young and interacting with peers or when you were alone in light of these listed descriptors. Process your feelings now. After a few minutes, continue reading.

Disciplined Learning and the Self

Oftentimes we mistakenly define punishment as discipline. But this is an incorrect assumption. Punishment is payback whereas discipline in its rudimentary form is remedial. Discipline is *training* a child with the welfare of the child in mind, to act in accordance to the best interest of their true authentic-*self* and their current social group.

A parent might say, "*You made me look like an idiot in the store today. Go to your room and think about it for a while.*" This would fall under the punishment category because the best consequences of this action sit on the side of the parent and not the child. The parent may *feel* emancipated about being embarrassed in public, but the child ends up lacking the instruction necessary to avoid the misbehavior in the future—classic misplacement.

It's difficult to train children with them in mind and not yourself and your emotional need machine. Understand that discipline, which falls more in line with instruction, is supposed to *empower* children by placing them in a better position of *being* through a life lesson. Because the more a child's awareness is increased, the better equipped they will be for future challenges.

Parents who see their role as that of a teacher while considering children as *learners* are more apt to produce socially healthy citizens than parents who simply punish poor behavior out of inconvenience or forbid it without proper explanation.

The term "discipline" is derived from the word disciple, which means a *disciplined learner*. Therefore when children are disciplined (discipled) or more importantly, trained rather than punished, they are characteristically better equipped to navigate social groups, competitive environments, and life challenges with better clarity, courage, and contentment thus ensuring a better likelihood at *being* rather than *doing*.

Consequently the odds increase that children rather than performing for a parent or peer will in simple terms be a better-performing person in essence. Thus, better performance becomes a *result* rather than a goal as the child grows and develops their own sense of safe self-worth.

The environment we grow up in bears responsibility for many of the characteristics we display later in life. We call this the home-life. As a behavioral analyst and personality consultant, I have seen my share of behavioral profiles from all walks of life and routinely, when a child lacks descriptors such as the *cherish*, *nourish*, or *admonish* aspects from child development or the guarding and protecting units, developmental disorders tend to become more commonplace.

Performance and Behavioral Difference

One of the more familiar outcomes derived from a lack of parental affirmation is performance-based living. Similar to the outcome of religious dos and don'ts, an emotional hands-off approach from parents can produce the same thing—an insatiable need to perform.

There are four kinds of performers based upon Galen's Four Humours—the *doer*, the *feeler*, the *helper* and the *thinker*. I also refer to these temperaments as mad, glad, sad, and scared. Our performance behavior is largely associated with our temperament.

The Doer

The doer is a dominant, aggressive behavioral style fueled by the anger emotion. This person usually lacks tact and diplomacy and is self-sufficient. This is the *Choleric* style, sometimes known as the "driver" or the "dominant" and it's many times associated with the color red and is allied with the "mad" descriptor, which is representative of the *anger* emotion. Tied to the element of fire, an idea from the ancient Greeks, this color embodies the hot-tempered quick-fused person.

This person always takes the direct route and is entirely focused on the goal. The anger-based person is quick, determined, eager, and many times impersonal, but not on purpose. They are *external* processors usually concerned with completion through direct channels in very efficient ways as opposed to slower methodical approaches that cover many paths, thus becoming a time vampire.

Their ability to foster relationships can feel like washing their feet with their sox on—it simply escapes them—it feels weird. These are typically logic-based thinkers with an *active* rather than *passive* behavioral pattern focused on accomplishment, high risk, and excessive goal setting.

Thought Invader: When within the Eros prison, doers will perform through accomplishment.

Rather than being proactive, they stereotypically become reactive when *more* emotional and faced with problems and challenges. These dominant styles usually have a high need for problems and challenges in order to feel alive or worthy. And if they don't have current problems at hand, they will be sure to create some.

This is the child who hits and breaks things for no apparent reason. They often find themselves looking for trouble in order to feel at home. This can be known as the "Hell is Home" delusion. If it isn't hell, it isn't home. And we all know there's no place like home.

Their answer to most any problem is to get a bigger hammer. But when these performance-based, active styles have a strong limbic bent, they will tend towards need-oriented behaviors and relationships—this is the classic attention getter.

The differences between these two types are striking. The dominant pattern needs no one, but the emotional pattern needs everyone. If you are blessed with the combination, others may perceive you as being hyperactive, creative, spontaneous, or even autistic at times. There are many pluses to these styles, but when drenched in need, they can create increasing problems, creating more chaos and confusion than one might expect.

The Feeler

Need oriented relationships are far more drama-reactive based at their core. Individuals with a high *need* factor like the feeler doesn't necessarily *want* dramatic occurrences; they *need* them. This is what is known as *emotional stroking*.

Love me. Touch me. Hold me. Talk with me. Listen to me.

And when it's all said and done, it's never enough. The need to be liked, understood, to be important, interesting, listened to, and so on becomes paramount within these need-oriented feeler styles. Unfortunately the euphoric feelings produced, when on the receiving end of praise and strokes, lasts only a moment.

Thought Invader: When in the Eros prison, feelers will perform by entertaining.

Need-based children oftentimes become obsessed with this kind of attention. Classic *Attention Deficit Disorder* may be summed up this way: the need to *gain* attention becomes so great, they fail to *pay* attention. They are so busy stealing the show and spending the energy gained from public recognition, they have nothing left over to give to the attention of others or to potential important matters aside from a wounded-self.

They become chair of the look-at-me club and this position doesn't have term limits. This pattern is usually very chaotic and spontaneous. The innate need to *be* comfortable with one's self never gets satisfied because the excessive need creates emotional insatiability. They spend their days *doing* rather than being—performing for praise and strokes in order to fill the black hole of emotional need and self-acceptance.

Do you find yourself preoccupied with what others are thinking about you? Do you find yourself comparing your belongings and appearance with others such as your clothing or your weight? What about your occupation or your position?

Do you hear a little voice in your head that condemns you for not looking better or like so and so? This is a sign that you are discontented with who you are. There is no emotional rest in this place—it's a tiresome treadmill of endeavoring to be something or someone else.

This may come as a surprise, but a large percentage of persuaders, influencer's, and motivators are nothing more than professional need-machines. This might be the biggest secret in the world of motivational speaking. The fear of social rejection essentially empowers many motivators.

They in turn use this power to help others *not* feel rejected like they do. It's an amazing portrayal of the power of need. This is classic psychology. The minister who pounds others for the sin in their life is more or less trying to frighten it out of their own life.

Because these need-oriented styles need a steady diet of public praise and strokes, they will build on the potential in others and see the positive side of all the negative situations others face. The reason why they do this is because they receive public praise and strokes by diehard followers who are happy to return the favor.

This *need machine* can become a continuous cycle masked by enthusiasm, wit, and charm. It's really their best-kept secret. This is prevalent among ministers. Much of what is called *ministry* in Evangelical social groups today is nothing more than a personal and professional self-help program funded by parishioners'.

Unfortunately the *feeler* is no different than the *doer* when it comes to emotional need. The rules to the game are the same, but the feelers play on the other side of the board. The worth of the doer is wrapped up in their accomplishments while the worth of the feeler is fastened to the opinions of other people.

It's all the same in the end game, but the needs are met in different ways. Neither one simply rests in a state of *being*, but rather they actively pursue performances and accomplishments treating life as if it's a giant stage. Because these emotionally driven behaviors are so unreliable, they are more apt to bloom later in life—mid to late forties more or less. While the doers sledgehammer their way through life, the feeler dawns a blindfold and runs headlong into the woods at full speed.

Both create problems and challenges where there need not be any, thus prolonging reliable patterns and predictable living. It's much like purposefully skiing in an avalanche zone so you have the opportunity to dig out when the side of the mountain collapses on you.

This is the dilemma. When we are incapable of *being*, we end up in a position of *needing* in order to fill in the hole produced by our lack of being. And whether it is problems and challenges or needing to be the star of the show, both conditions can likely become a magnet for chaos, drama, and challenges.

The Helper

The third style is the *Phlegmatic* or the helper. This temperament was associated with the season of winter (wet and cold) and the element of water or rain. Helpers perform by helping. Phlegmatic types are very loyal, consistent, predictable, relaxed, and non-emotional. In other words, they are nearly impossible to read from an observable standpoint.

Their shy personality can often create resistance to change and is typically associated with a much lower sense of urgency and worth. The Phlegmatic temperament is always accompanied by patience and *steadiness* and is acquainted with *security* (safety).

The *Phlegmatic* person sometimes referred to, as the "steady" style is associated with green because they make things grow. The steady Phlegmatic are like glue, they hold things together and pace themselves patiently like a growing plant—predictable, reliable, relaxed and often sullen, which is where the *sad* descriptor comes into play.

They also act like fertilizer, many times assisting others in their own personal growth. The sad-based behaviors are also more private, protective, serene, introspective, and closed—they don't think out loud like the glad people do because it isn't safe. They rarely tell others where they actually stand on the issues and sometimes won't tell themselves. The helper style typically sees others as more important than themselves.

Thought Invader: When phlegmatic people are in the Eros prison they become overly concerned about the welfare of others at personal expense.

They become extreme helpers, experts at masking their feelings like nobody's business. Oftentimes the helper's need-machine is masked in virtue. Their excessive helping can be seen, as loyalty when in reality, is nothing more than an impulsive need to be needed.

It's harder to detect if a helper is within the Eros prison as their behavior is nearly always tied to good works and charity. Unfortunately this becomes the perfect veil for feelings of unimportance. For this reason, helpers rarely ever get the help they need when they need it.

The Thinker

The final of the four styles is the *Melancholic* temperament. This temperament is characterized by black bile and correlated with the season of fall (dry and cold). The melancholic is connected with the element earth (dirt), which may factor into the down-to-earth realistic style. This style is known to be perfectionist.

This person is often precise, cautious, neat, and exacting. They tend to be cold and aloof and are often (not always) preoccupied with the world's tragic and cruel condition. They are at times susceptible to depression and loneliness. The Melancholic temperament is always associated with being *conscientious* and acquainted with *information*.

The thinker requires information and may spend hours deciphering problems and challenges associated with getting to the bottom of difficult answers. These terms can also be misleading, but a careful analysis of each will undoubtedly assist you in understanding the *whys* and *hows* of each behavioral framework. We will look at the *doer*, the *feeler*, the *helper*, and the *thinker* in more depth in the following chapters.

Thought Invader: When the thinker is locked within the Eros prison, they display their performance through perfection.

We could say a lot more about the personality differences between people, but we cannot distract from the pull of the Eros prison. Are you in the Eros prison? Do you mask your self-doubt by exaggerated accomplishments or entertainment opportunities? Maybe you mask your need for attention by helping others.

Maybe you're smart and heady and your need machine functions by outsmarting those around you or correcting them when the opportunity presents itself. Regardless of how our personalities affect our need to perform, the performance prison continues to work its magic on the unsuspecting who believe they need to prove their worth to themselves and those around them.

Understanding what drives us, what motivates us, and what inspires and is deemed important to us is a vital first step in improving performance, satisfaction, and job alignment in any person's life.

When our proper desires (healthy desires not prompted by fear or insecurity) and our proper needs align with a safe authentic-self, we create harmony and collusion between who we are at the deepest level and that which we do with the four extensions of being, which are head, hands, heart, and mouth. These are the tools for building the world around us with the energy from the authentic-self.

13

Our Insatiable Need for a Satan

Many religions depend wholeheartedly on ancient manuscripts and some more modern writs for their rules for conduct and faith. Most Christians believe that everything written in the Christian Bible is actually *God* speaking and it is the measure of all other words spoken by mankind. This has been a belief for centuries. Since people have walked the earth, there have been followers and leaders within differing people groups.

No matter where you set foot in the world and no matter how remote you may be, you will find people following some idea made available by some person or persons. Whether it's written down or passed down verbally through story, people have a natural compulsion to follow.

In the next few chapters I want to discuss one of many ideas within the context of evangelicalism in America—the idea of the devil. I will reference Strong's Exhaustive Bible Concordance with Hebrew and Greek Lexicon when referencing terms.

The idea of a devil is what it is, but *why* is it at all? How did we come up with this idea and what has kept it going for so long? It's clear a lot of people don't really want a devil, but unfortunately the majority of people *need* one. I want to discuss this idea in relationship to the authentic-self as it battles with the shadow-self.

As we have already discussed, the authentic-self is our divine-self, our divine nature. The untouchable part of us that transcends the flesh-body and is responsible for hope, love, and intension. The shadow-self on the other hand is its nemesis. It's that shadow part of you that rises up when watching a video on Facebook depicting an innocent person being beaten or taken advantage of by another and wants to kill or harm them.

Like a simple car battery, we too are made up of both positive and negative charges. You cannot separate them; they can only be distinguished and regulated by reason-ability, knowledge, and will. Although the idea of a devil works in tandem with the yin-yang paradigm, which has been around for centuries, the myth may not be as harmless as one might think.

I'm going to depart for a bit from the teaching of the authentic-self and the Eros prison in order to fully establish where these ideas of Satan and sin come from.

The Satan myth has been a religious stronghold for a few thousand of years and has not been as much responsible as it has been supportive of the bizarre behaviors and mental reasonings of millions of dedicated followers.

The Eros prison by all accounts finds strong support through the mystical and spurious ideas put forth by the big three religions, and has been responsible for controlling large bodies of people throughout the world and keeping them in a form of solitary confinement. My hope is to set as many free from the distorted ideas and beliefs that bind us and hold us captive to performance, competition, and unnecessary compliance as much as possible.

I want to begin with the Bible. The Bible is believed to be a direct message from God to mankind on earth written down by men allegedly inspired and *controlled* by an unseen spirit-directed force. It is believed to be inerrant, perfect, and binding. Those who refuse its message and methods are believed by adherents to this holy book to be doomed to an eternity of immense torture and regret forever without end.

But is this really true? As soon as we believe we "know" what God says, the sooner we lock the door to the Eros prison and misplace the key. Most people will agree that we actually can't *know* anything about the ethereal. It remains elusive, subjective, and a matter of belief, hope, and opinion.

Nobody living can know anything concrete about the unknown—we can only believe, hope, and wonder. Granted, many believe their hopes are educated hopes, but still, these hopes are rooted in the ideas and beliefs of others that have gone before us. If we *believe* at all it's because we *choose* to believe.

Christians depend upon the shared Holy Bible while other religious groups have their own instruction manuals such as the Book of Mormon, the Vedas, the Bhagavad Gita, or the Koran. Some use the Apocrypha and others possibly the Avesta, a Zoroastrian holy text sometimes called the Zend.

No matter which group one subscribes to, their book will for all intents and purposes become the *only* sacred book. All other so-called sacred texts will be forced through behavior and reason to be an anathema—an abomination.

There also have been plenty of groups throughout the ages that have allegedly *experienced* the mysteries of life in a different respect and through a prism of logic and reason-ability. The difference oftentimes is the publicity, or perhaps the lack of publicity given to them.

Some of these philosophies may go against your present way of belief if you are a fundamentalist Christian or a dispensationalist,[1] but we need to realize that often what we assume to be correct is actually the fear of thinking otherwise.

I'm wrong on many occasions as is everyone, given enough hours in one day. But if one has a misconception of Satan, it can reflect negatively on so many other concepts (and it does) not only in the Bible, as you may already know, but also in life and in the lives of others you come into contact with.

What does the Bible really say about Satan? Does the Bible actually teach that Satan is a being that is responsible for all evil and earthly chaos, as we know it? Does the Bible really teach that there is an evil being that is so powerful that it can ruin God's entire creation and keep it in turmoil for millennia? To hear what is commonly preached in pulpits or on the television and the radio, you would certainly think so. Millions believe this is true.

Unfortunately, the belief is more an impulse: an excepted notion that comes with the package much like a child's toy in a cereal box. It is an idea not necessarily fully investigated, but rather automatically *believed* as it accompanies the whole Christian or Muslim package.

1) Dispensationalist or dispensationalism is an evangelical, futurist, biblical interpretation that understands God to have related to human beings in different ways under different biblical covenants in a series of "dispensations," or periods in history.

Like the child's toy in the cereal, it's usually tossed aside, misplaced, or consigned to a shelf while the cereal is consumed. Some are embarrassed by the idea, so it remains hidden away in the hope someone someday will uncover some hidden or lost text that confirms its absurdity.

Yet, I doubt that anyone who truly believes in a devil believes this being is all-powerful, all knowing, and omnipresent. Although many see this being as supposedly wreaking havoc on everyone all over the world at any given moment in space-time, it's not because they've given it ample thought.

Yet, millions simply accept all trials and obstacles to be from the hand of this malevolent creature. We see this behavioral pattern most often in the lives of devout Christians who are taught to avoid him (or it).

This way of thinking perpetuates and builds upon itself as it gives people something to blame, as if mankind is incapable of such evil on their own. But if we allow ourselves to look more closely at the Bible, man is completely capable of such evil and always has been. My goal in covering this topic is to help you understand the issues that arise within the shadow-self and why we alone are responsible for our choices, both good and bad.

In other words, the plausibility that every human being is capable of the worst atrocity is something we must embrace wholeheartedly and accept as true. This in no way is to say we advocate the harm of ourselves and others, but rather it is the first step in personal responsibility, the first and healthiest move towards wholeheartedness and unrivaled authenticity.

Human evil is unfortunately not the work of a supernatural being, but rather it is the ugly human-condition we are all forced to deal with. The decision to harm another person or animal rests solely with us alone, along with our morbid reasons for doing so. We all wrestle with understanding the extent of evil a person can invoke upon another, but this is not a reason to blame it on a supernatural entity or deceptive spirit influence.

I fully understand the need to find out why things are the way they are, and I understand why the ancients created ideas to explain it, but just as we now know that dirty rags do not create mice and bloodletting doesn't heal sickness, we must move on to more reasonable assumptions based on reason and not superstition.

In the following pages I'm going to do my best to decipher where these concepts originate within the Christian tradition, how they have been grossly misinterpreted, and what we can do to realign ourselves with a more sensible antidote to unhealthy human behaviors.

It's almost as if people have an *interpretation* blank check when it comes to the Bible as long as the idea of a devil or any other unreasonable assumption is promoted or believed. Take John chapter 10[2] for example; I have never heard John chapter 10 explained outside of the idea of the devil trying to steal from Christians, kill Christians, or destroy everything they have.

But unpardonably within the context of John chapter 10, there is no such idea whatsoever of a devil or anything supernatural. Most unfortunately, people for the most part spend more time understanding the instruction guide to their flat screen than they do the esoteric texts they are staking their life on. The context of the gospel of John's tenth chapter is the "shepherds of Israel" and their abusive power over the Hebrew people for generations.

But because it "preaches" well, meaning it motivates people to hate the devil and depend upon Jesus for sustenance while giving them hope for better circumstances, many ministers manipulate ideas in order to influence people into staying on board their boat.

This leaves individuals in a state of dependence rather than independence when it comes to navigating life, love, and work. We end up depending on the biblical strategies as outlined by leaders of particular sects for course plotting. Like the modern day therapist, it keeps us all coming back for more biblical formulas for fighting the devil and maintaining health, wealth, and wisdom strategies.

These strategies ultimately translate into competitive anecdotes within Christian in-groups and subgroups, leading to denominational divides. Groups such as "Spirit Life," which have capitalized on militant spiritual-warfare stratagems, have grown out of the boring conundrum created by blindly following the older formulas that have lost their luster.

---

2) "The thief comes only to steal and kill and destroy; I have come that they may have life, and have it to the full." John 10:10 NIV. This verse is always used to promote the greed and destructive power of the devil with evangelical movements. Its main use is fear based in an effort to promote Jesus' desire to make one wealthy.

Unfortunately in the end, it all ends up being the same prison food. Let's take a look at some of the inter-working of words and ideas within the hermeneutical malaise of Christendom and see if we can discover how the devil got his fame.

Loanwords

A loanword is a word taken from another language that is completely or partially letter for letter. In other words, it is a transliterated word. This is done when there is no equivalent word or name in the second language.

The problem is often times there is a corresponding word in the second language. This causes confusion especially when translators take the liberty of picking and choosing when to translate and when to transliterate, depending on their understanding of a given text.

Consequently, the very meaning of the loanword is changed. Though not always practical, for the most part a translator should translate and leave the interpretation to the reader, but rarely does this happen. Fortunately for faith, nobody really cares.

The word "Satan" is one of those loanwords. The word Satan, as translated using Strong's Exhaustive Concordance of the Bible #7854, is a Hebrew word meaning "adversary," or "accuser." I want to invite you to ask yourself, as we go along, whether or not it seems proper to assign the word Satan as a proper name at all, or should it be rendered as *adversary* or *accuser* each time it appears because it's a descriptive term, not a person.

If you've ever seen a copy of Robert Young's Literal Translation of the Holy Bible, you might notice that this translation never uses the word Satan, but rather it uses the term *adversary* in each and every occurrence. Sometimes it's capitalized and sometimes it's not, depending on the translator's (Young) own understanding of its use and context.

In the New American Standard Bible, you'll find the word Satan used 18 times. Surprisingly, the same word Satan appears 9 other times in the Hebrew text, but is translated "adversary" or "accuser" when used. Some examples of this inconsistency are Numbers 22:22; 1 Samuel 29:4; 2 Samuel 19:22; 1 Kings, 5:4, 11:14, 23, 25; and Psalm 109:6.

However, the English reader is entirely unaware that the same word "Satan" is used whether it's translated accuser, adversary, or Satan. Fortunately for religious leaders, most people simply read the Bible, but few ever study it through real analysis, contextual setting, or cultural background. This is known as the ABCs of context dependence. It's read with the same glasses everyone within the in-group is wearing, so nobody really notices.

Unfortunately, many people depend upon those whom they believe are "qualified" to interpret its meaning and never feel the need or the confidence to understand it for themselves. It's actually a taboo to come up with your own interpretive ideas, especially if they contradict the mainline. This is the reason why this approach ensures a weak Eros prison belief rather than a powerful personal discovery.

This is based upon hundreds of years of letting the "gifted" church leaders make the distinctions for the non-gifted church followers. Throughout history, most of the world has been illiterate. It's only been in the last several hundred years that people have been given access to the scriptures, and only in the past twenty years have people had unprecedented access through online venues. There is no longer any excuse to be in the dark about anything these days if you take the time to do your homework.

There is also another word for Satan (Strong's #7854) that is spelled the same except with one vowel sound different (according to the Masorets). This is the root from which #7854 comes. It is a verb meaning to *accuse* or to *oppose*, but it's also translated as a noun, *accuser* or *adversary*. Again it's never translated as "Satan," as if it's someone's title or proper name.

This is very telling. As I said, we need to understand whether this word is actually applied as a proper name for an evil archenemy of the Hebrew God or not. We simply cannot allow assumption, as assumption is life's *lowest* level of knowledge.

If it is a proper name, there would be little or no problem with the rendering *Satan* within Hebrew scripts. On the other hand, if it is not a proper name, the rendering should be changed and replaced with *adversary* or *accuser* once and for all to eliminate the confusion and maintain a reasonable consistent flow.

But as you can see, this would create a problem for those who have built a "devil empire" out of these translations that have kept people in check since the Roman church began capitalizing on it, beginning in the third century. For those who may not know, the ancient Hebrew language had only one case; in other words, there was no capitalization of single words to help us out.

We will take a look at the places where our English Bibles use the word Satan shortly, but I want to say a few words about the Greek word first. Remember, this is how we get to the bottom of things—it's work. It takes initiative, time, and thought—just as heart surgery does.

Without getting to the bottom of the sources for our beliefs, we are left to believe whatever we are told by a select few who influence everyone else all the way down. Every person deserves to know as much about something as they are able to know, especially seeing the tools at our disposal these days. Otherwise we are stuck with traditional mindsets designed to keep our ladders up against the wrong house.

The way we view our authentic-self is oftentimes distorted through our religious lens, leaving us groping in a fog of ambiguity. Depending upon traditional ideas that never change means we never change. If something isn't changing, it isn't living. If something isn't alive, it must be dead.

Even Jesus told the religious professors of his day: "Ye do error, not *knowing* the scriptures nor the power of God." Without someone like Jesus to straighten us out again, we are doomed to suffer the same human pattern of spiritual blindness as they did.

The corresponding biblical word in the Greek language is *satanos* (Strong's #4567), also a loanword from the Hebrew language. And surprisingly, Satan is found only one time in the Septuagint, the Greek Old Testament, typically abbreviated by the Roman letters, LXX, in 3 Kings 11:14 and 1 Kings 11:14 in English Bibles.

> "Then the Lord raised up an adversary (Hebrew word for satan) to Solomon, Hadad the Edomite; he was of the royal line in Edom."[3]

This is a wonderful example of how distorted biblical concepts can create wrong ideas. There is no mystery here as to what this

3) 1 Kings 11:14.

word means within the context of the Hebrew source material. The man known as Hadad the Edomite was an *adversary* or *enemy* of King Solomon.

If we would only make the decision to understand that *only* people are enemies of people, life would become less mysterious. Embracing concepts that include invisible devils or spiritual forces unknown to reality as culprits when trying to make sense of catastrophes and chaos can be very confusing and lead to the Eros prison of performance. I've seen these theatrical performances with my own eyes for many years within the church environment.

Another question worth asking and that rests comfortably within the context of the LXX (Septuagint) is what word do we find in place of the word *Satan*? It's no surprise we find *diabolos* (Strong's #1228), which is commonly translated as "devil." The word again literally *and* simply means "slanderer" or "false accuser."

It's that straightforward. Unfortunately scholars have taken the liberty to re-imagine, or you could say, *re-purpose* this loan-word and make it a title for an alleged arch evil-being in order to both make sense of the *darker* shadow side in all of us *and* keep the acceptable tradition resuscitated.

This begs the question: is this the proper thing to do with the text? I invite you to allow the renderings in the following passages of scripture to enlighten you further if you are willing to open your mind to the possibilities that await you. Wouldn't it sound rather humorous to render the word *diabolos* within these well-known passages as *devil* in these three examples?

> "Women must likewise be dignified, not malicious gossips (diabolos), but temperate, faithful in all things." –1 Timothy 3:11.

And again:

> ". . . unloving, irreconcilable, malicious gossips (diabolos), without self control, brutal haters of good . . ." –2 Timothy 3:3.

And again:

> "Older women likewise are to be reverent in their be-

havior, not malicious gossips (diabolos) nor enslaved to much wine, teaching what is good . . ." –Titus 2:3.

Moreover, you might be surprised to know that the title "the devil" is not used in the Hebrew Old Testament at all—ever. Not only that, but the King James Version of the Bible uses the word "devils" four times when referring to false gods to whom sacrifices had been given and not a supposed evil ethereal being.

I hope you can begin to understand how misleading these translations can be for both building upon, and perpetuating the idea of an arch evil-being called Satan or the devil. What have we done? We have assumed the devil is a real entity and therefore don't even bother with the literary facts lest they get in the way of our traditional ideology. This is not only dangerous, it's folly. It's madness.

Can we need something so powerfully that we dismiss reality in place of fantasy? Absolutely. And we will accompany these fantastic ideas with the corresponding behaviors to match. This is known as the *Consistency Rule*, one of the six rules to persuasion.

The *Consistency Rule* dictates we *act* in line with a belief that has been established through our words or our writing. As humans, we are more committed to what we "confess" with our mouths than we are to what we actually want to believe with our hearts.

This is why people are taught to *confess* Christ, and it's why there is so much weight behind *confessing* to a crime. Confessing can close the doors to the Eros prison and keep us locked inside if what we are confessing is not aligned with our best interest as people.

Ultimately, you must make up your own mind based upon your own diligent study, as I suggest everyone do, before concluding on matters of life and death. These are important issues, and in my opinion deserve more attention than they have been given.

Unfortunately, when someone disrupts years of traditional thinking within any religious framework, they become a target for ridicule much as the modern day "*truthers*" who question the government's role in current conspiracy theories such as the 9-11 attack on the twin towers in New York City.

Regardless of whatever evidence they may come up with, the ultimate destination will be a crazy person. Even in light of videography, personal testimony, or raw data, it won't matter for one minute. I personally don't have any interest in these findings at the moment, but either way, whatever the top brass believes needs to be the story, that rendering will stand as it does within the church.

During the dark ages, you were a witch if you disagreed with the current establishment regardless of any evidentiary difference. You will be jailed if you disagree with the Internal Revenue regardless, and you will be assigned to the insane if you disagree with a psychiatrist who benefits from your incarceration. Nothing has changed over thousands of years.

I hope we have learned by now not to base our understanding upon popular opinions or what the "authorities" claim as *truth*, as all of us are skewed in the direction of our hard-core beliefs, and we are all measurably flawed within our own systems of reason.

I won't ever tell anyone *what* to believe, but I will always present alternative ideas for us to consume as food for thought in order to make a much more informed decision on such important topics as these. You can join me if you desire freedom of thought.

Hath God Said?

Let's begin with Genesis. It's commonly claimed that the serpent (a common snake) in the garden myth was somehow literally or figuratively Satan or a *form* of Satan. I'm going to suggest it was neither. If the serpent analogy were to be taken literally in the story, it would seem that the serpent was the *cause* of Eve to disobey God's command as the idea of disobedience is believed to have originated with the serpent and not Eve. It would also imply that she was literally conversing with a snake, which apparently could verbally communicate with the couple.

As a thinking person, I must take issue with this story. The serpent's original question was "Hath God said?" In other words, *are you sure God is telling you the truth*? We don't need Satan in order to ask ourselves this question, any more than Eve did. The human brain reasons all by itself as a matter of instinctive protective measures in an effort to ensure its continued existence in an unpredictable world.

Most human beings will question everything they know nothing about such as a frozen pond or an unfamiliar piece of food.

Unless we have been taught to *not* question unreasonable concepts, we will do it as an *automatic* impulse for survival. Unfortunately, established authorities within all religious systems are all to eager to disallow objective reasoning when it comes to matters of belief.

If taken figuratively, the serpent metaphor may represent our capacity to reason thoughts and ideas through to a meaningful conclusion based upon our own chemical or natural desires to act contrarian. Our rebellious nature (an important part of who we are) is paramount for disallowing circumstances not in our favor. If the problems, challenges, and opportunities we face are misinterpreted, we may unwittingly rebel against a *good* thing.

If the garden story is representative of one's own internal shadow-voice of *temptation* (the voice of conscience or reason-ability or even lustful desires within the shadow-self), then the element of a separate deceiver is all but eliminated, which in my opinion removes the magic and mystery and makes the most reasonable sense.

We must remember that the shadow-self is *only* focused on the unsafe-self drenched in fear and need along with its desires and always at the expense of others. This is self-protectionism rooted in the Eros prison self-interest.

For example, in the case of Cain's sin against his brother Able (they were the offspring of the garden couple), a *separate* deceiver is not present in the story unless one infers it, only the element of sin, which is representative of nothing more than making the poorest choice available.

Choices which involve poor judgment that credits the self at the expense of others are typically made by and *for* the unsafe shadow-self. For instance, in the Cain and Able narrative the Hebrew God tells Cain:

> "Sin is crouching at the door and its desire is for you, but you must master it." –Genesis 4:7.

Observe how Cain's decision, although it had not been made yet, is referred to as *sin* and is termed "*it*." This is because *sin* or *it* is nothing more than the wrong choice in any given matter. In other words, like all of us, Cain was faced with a choice and was *compelled* to make a poor choice at that. This is referred to as the *sin* that was crouching at his door of opportunity.

Like Cain, every human being is faced with the same three separate yet distinct encounters on any given day: problems, challenges, and opportunities. Our continued response to these three perpetual dimensions determines our destiny.

Sin, within the Hebrew mind, was something that they believed *desired* to have them. Thus sin is seen as a separate entity. This was their way of making sense of our dualistic nature known to Eastern minds as the yin and the yang. I mentioned earlier that St. Paul believed this as well, but it bears repeating:

> "I have the desire to do what is good, but I cannot carry it out. For I do not do the good I want to do, but the evil I do not want to do—this I keep on doing. Now if I do what I do not want to do, it is no longer I who do it, *but it is sin living in me that does it.*" –Romans 7:19-20 (italics mine).

This happens to all of us, and it's not a devil that is responsible for it. We all feel it when it's about to overtake us—that inner battle between doing the right thing and the wrong thing when nobody's looking. We're all faced with these yin and yang choices every day.

We can make a good choice or we can make a poor choice. This is why good and bad or right and wrong are simply concepts rooted in the "decision-making pattern" within all peoples.

This was what Dr. Robert S. Hartman[4] (whom we mentioned earlier) spent his whole life theorizing. Rather than utilizing the story of Cain and Able, Hartman wrestled with the inhumane decision-making patterns of the Nazis.

The quest for a science of *value* originated with early Greek philosophers and then ultimately culminated in the work of Dr. Robert S. Hartman. Facing the inhumanity accompanying Hitler's rise to power in prewar Germany, Hartman envisioned a science which could categorize "good" as effectively as the Nazis categorize "evil."

---

4) Born January 27, 1910, Robert Schirokauer Hartman was a logician and philosopher. His primary field of study was scientific axiology or human decision theory, and he is known as its original theorist.

Dr. Hartman dedicated his life to the realization of this vision and, after years of research, created a new mathematical system which successfully orders the values of our everyday decisions and experiences. This has come to be known as *Human Decision Theory*, and the tool for measuring it is called the HVP.[5]

Choices

Our choices will always affect not only *our* best interest, but also the interests of humanity in general—the welfare of others to put it bluntly. In the Cain story, Cain was warned that he would be experiencing *both* the desire for his self *and* a desire for his brother, and was admonished to make the better choice when the time came. The entire context of this narrative reflects upon our fragile humanness and our propensity towards offense.

Cain made the wrong choice as the story goes because he was offended at God for looking poorly at what he produced with his own hands—his offering was not prepared according to the standard custom.

Rather than understanding the difference between the wrong article for the offering and *being* a bad person, his immaturity got the best of him. Rather than seeing his dilemma as an opportunity, he saw it as an *option* and chose the wrong one as many of do from time to time.

In other words, he brought a basketball to the football game. A basketball is not an option at a football game. It's an insult. It wouldn't be described as a *bad* ball in this instance, but rather we would consider it the *wrong* ball. Cain thought his sacrifice was bad instead of just wrong. He then believed himself to be *bad* (the foundation of *shame*) as the sacrifice was supposed to be his *best* effort.

Thusly he lived *down* to his personal lower expectation of self based upon his misunderstanding of the deity's remarks in the story. This yet again is another example of measuring down within the Eros prison. Cain's *performance* for God was a failure.

Thought Invader: The problem with religion is that it forces perfor-

5) The Hartman Value Profile (HVP) is an effective, proven methodology for the prediction of performance.

mance under the guise of obedience.

Now let's look at what the author of the Genesis narrative says in Genesis 6:5—"Then God saw that the wickedness of *man* was great on the earth, and that every intent of the thoughts of *his heart* was only evil continually."

That is a strong statement against mankind, allegedly by the Hebrew deity. But let's ask ourselves a question: do we see this deity blaming mankind or Satan? The deity was said to have destroyed the world with a flood of water because of *man's* evil nature, not because of a Satan figure and his supposed influence upon mankind at that time.

Even as far back as 600 BC, the authors of these stories knew the decision-making power of mankind was malevolent at times, and the capacity of mankind to do evil was unstoppable. The gods we invent within our own minds are really the only beings we believe capable of stopping human selfishness.

Although good and bad are present throughout nature as is light and darkness, north and south, and up and down, humans tend to attribute its origins to the gods. This is why we call well-behaved people "angels" and unscrupulous people "devils." Likewise even Jesus when speaking to his disciples about the one who would betray him said, "I have chosen twelve of you yet one of you is a *devil*."

If the Satan were the cause of all this evil, wouldn't it have made more sense for this deity to destroy the Satan and spare the creation? Looking at the barbarism of this deity who is believed to be able to wipe out most of the human race including those disassociated with the deity's demands such as small children, is it any wonder why the Hebrew tradition was in absolute terror of displeasing this angry deity who was subject to being "ticked off" at mankind?

This is exactly where the modern ideas of God using disastrous weather patterns to execute judgment against the gays or other people groups behaving outside the bounds of religious behaviorism come from. The Hebrew deity is viewed as a brat child, unpredictable and choleric. Wishing [he] never made man is tantamount to an emotional person yelling, "I wish I never married you!"

> "The LORD regretted that he had made human beings on the earth, and his heart was deeply troubled." – Genesis 6:6

These ideas are created in the minds of people. People fear God. People regret relationships. The Hebrew Scriptures consistently paint the deity as ruthless and demanding, jealous, enraged, and vengeful. These destructive traits are all part of its personality—"*Vengeance is mine saith the Lord, I will repay.*"[6]

Many people today, including *some* ministers will fall back on this part of the deity's profile when they don't feel their message is heard or considered important; they hide behind their big brother or their psychotic father while condemning the gays to hell.

It's obvious not all ministers are this way, but that's not what makes this so terrible. What makes this unnerving is that those who do have biblical grounds for their outrageous claims against humanity.

Ghastly plagues, death, destruction, floods, fire, all of it can be comparable to a crazy man who demands praise and devotion *or else*. This is the profile of the Hebrew deity that has influenced minds over millennia. And it's why people within the monotheistic Abrahamic faith circle (Judaism, Christianity, and Islam) are so rigid, narrow, and black-and-white in their behavior.

Although the Bahá'í Faith's teachings emphasize the spiritual unity of all mankind, it is still often times considered *Abrahamic* because of its monotheism.

These are *all* entryways into the Eros performance prison. If we perform for the deity, it will not harm us. Is it any wonder why these faiths are losing ground among those who read and study before investing their hearts and minds into any idea? Could this be why so many people are not attending services anymore?

Could this be why the concept of hell and sin has been largely dropped from the program at so many religious institutions today and reserved for member's class? People are simply evolving and outgrowing superstition and barbarism. This has not stopped the quest for the unknown; it has only stripped it of its severity and its punishments.

6) Hebrews 10:30.

The Bahá'í Faith believes all major religions have the same spiritual source and come from the same deity. They also stress the unity of all humanity, that all humans have been created *equal*, and that diversity of race and culture are seen as worthy of appreciation and acceptance.

Out of the "big three" Abrahamic faiths it is only Christianity which has retained the idea of a Satan and given him a broader stage. This is likely out of convenience, as it becomes the perfect answer to why things don't consistently work out for the good or why Jesus consistently fails to fix *all* our ills. Unfortunately, like the rest of the world, bad things happen to good people.

Unfortunately, the Satan figure over time has become nearly equal to or greater than the deity who allegedly created it. Nearly every negative or uncomfortable situation surrounding anyone with an evangelical mindset will be attributed to the *Enemy*. From adultery, divorce, to drug addiction, the enemy is a full-time warrior against the souls of the faithful both through manipulation and coercion.

But as the old saying goes, "*sh*t happens*." Could it be that people actually want to cheat on their mates? Could it be as simple as that? Does it have to be the devil's fault or some elusive deceiving spirit? How about stupid? What about mental illness? What about simply having a messed up childhood? Many people make poor decisions because their decision making capacity sucks.

Thought Invader: According to Occam's razor theory, among competing hypotheses the one with the fewest assumptions should be selected.

Other, more complicated solutions may ultimately prove correct, but—in the absence of certainty—the fewer assumptions that are made, the better. And nowhere else will you find *less* certainty that faith-based beliefs rooted in ancient texts.

The Hebrews were not accustomed to contributing disaster to the devil, as their wisdom literature will attest. God was the author of both good and evil as portrayed directly within the Job story. Job's life was ruined including the killing of his children and livestock.

"All his brothers and sisters and everyone who had

known him before came and ate with him in his house. They comforted and consoled him over *all the trouble the LORD had brought on him*, and each one gave him a piece of silver and a gold ring." –Job 42:11

Let's break this down even further. Say you were in charge of a group of children and you taught them properly, but the group of kids turned to evil and unpredictable ways because some malevolent bully down the street had influenced them negatively. Would you think it best to destroy the children or to destroy the evil bully who influenced them?

Surely by destroying the evil bully, you could remove the evil and straighten the children out again. But if you destroyed the children, what would be gained? The evil would still be within the bully to infect the next group of unsuspecting children.

However, (I recommend using your reasoning here) if the evil was a part of the children themselves, and there was no outside influence to thwart their action, the only way to rid the evil *within* the children would be to destroy the children. In the Genesis narrative, which did the God destroy? The devil serpent or the children the deity created? Correct! In the story, the deity destroyed the "children" with a flood.

However, the Hebrew God was said to have saved eight people (Noah and his family) with an ability to do evil all over again, and from them, the seed of evil lived on and grew, remaining with us today. It isn't long after the ark came to rest on Mt. Ararat that we see a drunken Noah, nudity, and lascivious behavior between Noah and one of his sons.

Let's look at Genesis 8:21:

"... I will never again curse the ground on account of man, for the intent of *man's heart* is evil from his youth . . ."

Here again mankind is accused of evil and a Satan is nowhere mentioned. This agrees with the philosophy of James the brother of Jesus in which he states in his epistle, chapter 1:14-15:

"But each is tempted when he is carried away and enticed by his own lust. When lust has conceived, it gives birth to sin; and when sin is accomplished, it brings forth death."

There was a perfect opportunity to set the blame on Satan, but James puts the blame again on *man's* evil nature as his God did in the former Genesis narrative he was very familiar with. I will set out to argue that there is no single devil-being (or demons) that tempt or trick us, but rather it is our own characteristic ability to reason, will, and choose wrongly.

These poor choices have translated into *evil* outcomes, and they have been labeled *demonic* and diabolical (from diabolos), a worthwhile scapegoat for our own poor decision-making prowess. People cheat on their mates simply because they want to have sex with another person.

Women are typically attracted to the emotional stroking and men are typically attracted to the act of sex itself without emotional attachments—in both cases, devil not included.

Unfortunately, the knee-jerk response to evil in the world among the religious in no longer a thoughtful process; it's become a reactive impulse based in ancient mythological rationalizations for poor human decision-making. You must remember it was the heart of *mankind* that the scriptures labeled as "desperately *wicked* above all else"[1] and not a devil or a devil's trickery or influence. Bottom line is people consistently do stupid things for no apparent reason.

The Slanderers of The Way

You may consider reading James 4:7 where it says: *"Resist the devil and he* [personal pronoun] *will flee from you."* But does this passage necessitate an arch evil-being? And if not, why is it in the *male* voice? Why is it a personal pronoun?

Think about this: getting rid of the loanword and translating *diabolos* as it should be instead of how we have allowed it. It should be rendered, "Resist the *slanderer* (or false accuser) and *he* will flee from you."

1) Jeremiah 17:9: "The human heart is the most deceitful of all things, and desperately wicked. The heart is deceitful above all things, and desperately wicked: who can know it?

In the time that James was writing, the Jews were most definitely the false accusers (hence the personal pronoun) of the brethren or those of *The Way*. They slandered the followers of Jesus unrelentingly. This again brings me to the whole theme of the Bible: God's covenant people (the Hebrews), their rebellion against him, and their subsequent salvation through an apocalypse.

The early followers of *The Way* were to resist the resistance, as it was believed that the apocalypse was upon them. The *opposition* was the orthodox Jew benefiting from the political and temple corruption much like congress does today. This can easily be related to that idea or a call to resist our *own* base urges and shadow-self that many times controls and then condemns us.

14

Satan and the Old Testament

Let's look at the places where *ha satan* has been translated as Satan in an attempt to again establish the inconsistencies that have disseminated this idea of a devil. The first place you will find it in this usage (in the Bible, NASB) is in 1 Chronicles 21:1 where it says, *"Satan rose up against Israel and caused David to take a census of the people of Israel."*

Are we forced to read this account with the notion that this demands a separate deceiver? Or was it purely and simply the fact that David became arrogant (ego-self) and self-absorbed as anyone would in such a position of authority? Does it make sense that he likely fell victim to his own desires and pride, as do we all?

Something interesting to note: this same story (the older version in Samuel) claims it was the Hebrew God who tempted the boy king to take the forbidden census, not Satan, but the later version changed it to a Satan. Could it be his own ego-self that both *tempted* and accused? Have we ever been tempted to take a shortcut or to self-promote in a fleeting moment of insecurity? Why does it have to be the devil's fault?

> Again the anger of the LORD burned against Israel, and He incited David against them, saying, "Go and take a census of Israel and Judah." –2 Sam. 24:1

According to the above verse, it appears the deity simply gets mad and like some thug on the school playground makes David pay for embarrassing him. These human behaviors are reminiscent and reflective of the minds that contrived them. People like to "get even," but I find it difficult to embrace the idea of such a *high* being stooping to such low levels.

These are far more suggestive of dishonorable behaviors reserved for soulish performers rather than a lofty deity. As adults, many of us grow out of behaviors such as these, but it would appear the deity did not.

The older version of this story is likely the more accurate, rendering this Chronicles passage (likely written *after* the Babylonian captivity) less reliable. The word Satan is also used three times in Zechariah 3:1-2. However, this is a *prophetic* vision and so taking it literally would not be considered sound exegesis of the scriptures.

The only other place where the word Satan is found in the Old Testament is in the first two chapters of the story of Job. Here it is used 14 times. In this particular text, Satan is portrayed as a *personal being* within a *celestial* courtroom of sorts as this curious drama unfolds.

Most scholars believe the book of Job is an elaborate parable, a literary invention dealing with the crude sufferings of mankind, and how mankind struggles to understand why the righteous suffer along with the unrighteous—we still have trouble with this today.

One person gets what we believe another person deserves. It's the question we all are forced to face when the eighty-nine-year-old woman with no family wins the twenty-million-dollar lottery and leaves it to her cats.

If this literary work *is* a parable, it by no means detracts from the value of the message any more than the parables that were spoken by Jesus. Parables are intended to make a point, not a proof. I must agree that this is worthy of debate. I'm also aware that Jesus himself mentions the story of Job, but why wouldn't he? The Hebrews would be exceedingly familiar with the story as well as the meaning behind it as it was typically quotable to most if not all Pharisees.

In an effort to uncover some glaring conflicts, if Satan is an evil being, how could he or it be in the *presence of God* as is portrayed in the Job narrative? I think about this often, especially since growing up within the "God cannot look upon sin" construct.

In the same light, how could he or it be in the presence of God along with Adam and Eve, who were said to be in God's *presence* in the Garden? Does that make sense? The scriptures are acutely clear that no one can look upon the face of God and live.

If sinful man cannot be in the presence of God according to Christian doctrine, how can the Satan, allegedly the greatest evil being of all time, be in the presence of Yahweh? It is stereotypically preached that God cannot look upon evil when attempting to persuade people to turn from it, but here it is apparently easily acceptable.

The Satan as an Angel

Many contend that Satan was originally an angel that subsequently lost his position in heaven because he wanted to be more important than God. This idea is taken mainly from two passages, Isaiah 14 and Ezekiel 28. It also pongs of the same old human-performance prison with all its competitive tones. Both positions are erroneous conclusions, bereft of any reason.

Reading the passages plainly eliminates these silly conclusions from "God's Word" and leaves them on earth where they likely came from. These misinterpretations are also a much *later* development as early commentaries resist this notion. Let's look first at Isaiah chapter 14.[2]

By reading *selected* parts of this prophecy against Babylon, one cannot even force the conclusion that it might infer a devil or malevolent being as it has been described by modern ministers.

How *he* had fallen from the "heavenly place" is nothing more than descriptive language describing the lofty king and his memorable demise. But let's not start in the middle of the text; instead, proper exegesis requires that we understand the context first.

Babylon lay in a vast and fertile plain watered by the Euphrates, which flowed through the city. Its walls are described as 60 miles in circumference, 300 feet high, and 75 feet wide (Jeremiah 51:44). A deep trench ran parallel with the walls. In each of the four sides were 25 brazen gates from which roads crossed to the opposite gates.

On the resulting squares, countless houses and gardens were made. Nebuchadnezzar's palace was in an enclosure six miles in circumference. Within this were also "the hanging gardens," an

2) Isaiah 14 is typically known for its elaborate description of the early life history of Lucifer. In reality, it is a description of the lament or taunt by the prophet concerning the death of the king of Babylon.

immense artificial mound 400 feet high, sustained by archers upon arches, terraced off for trees and flowers, the water for which was drawn from the river by machinery concealed in the mound.

The city did not remain the capital of the world for long under the reign of Nebuchadnezzar's grandson Nabonnidus, the Belshazzar of the Scriptures. It was besieged and taken by Cyrus, the king of Persia.

The accounts of Greek historians harmonize here with that of the Bible: Cyrus made his successful assault on a night when the whole city, relying on the strength of its walls, had given themselves up to the riot and debauchery of a grand public festival, and the king and his nobles were reveling at a splendid entertainment.

Cyrus had previously caused a canal which ran west of the city, and carried off the superfluous water of the Euphrates into the lake of Nitocris, to be cleared out, in order to turn the river into it; by these means, the river was rendered so shallow that his soldiers were able to penetrate along its bed into the city.[3]

The book of Daniel also records the story of the great fall of the king. The writer first describes the fall of Nebuchadnezzar before he describes the eminent destruction of his son, Nabonnidus:

> "Your Majesty, the Most High God gave your father Nebuchadnezzar sovereignty and greatness and glory and splendor. Because of the high position he gave him, all the nations and peoples of every language dreaded and feared him.
>
> "Those the king wanted to put to death, he put to death; those he wanted to spare, he spared; those he wanted to promote, he promoted; and those he wanted to humble, he humbled. But when his heart became arrogant and hardened with pride, he was deposed from his royal throne and stripped of his glory.
>
> "He was driven away from people and given the mind of an animal; he lived with the wild donkeys and ate grass like the ox; and his body was drenched with the dew of

3) Biblos.com.

> heaven, until he acknowledged that the Most High God is sovereign over all kingdoms on earth and sets over them anyone he wishes.
>
> "But you, Belshazzar, his son, have not humbled yourself, though you knew all this. Instead, you have set yourself up against the Lord of heaven. You had the goblets from his temple brought to you, and you and your nobles, your wives and your concubines drank wine from them.
>
> "You praised the gods of silver and gold, of bronze, iron, wood and stone, which cannot see or hear or understand. But you did not honor the God who holds in his hand your life and all your ways. Therefore he sent the hand that wrote the inscription." –Daniel 5:19-24

This is the original story of the mysterious hand that wrote on the castle wall the inscription "*Mene Mene Tekel Parsin*"; the inscription that was queerly written and that prophesied the king's destruction. This is where we get the saying, "The handwriting is already on the wall." The inscription ends with "*Your kingdom is divided and given to the Medes and the Persians.*" This is the man the prophet Isaiah speaks to in his infamous lament.

Thought Invader: All meaning within ancient writing is context dependent.

The prophecy begins with chapter 13 verse 1 and states that it's an oracle—a lament equivalent to a funeral dirge regarding the ancient city of *Babylon* and the fowl king. The writer goes on telling of cataclysmic destruction, which was typical for prophetic language concerning the destruction of a city or nation.

In verse 17, God says he will use the Medes to destroy them. Verse 19 again tells us the subject is Babylon and that they will be destroyed like the cities Sodom and Gomorrah. This is simple warfare between tribes and nations.

The discourse continues into chapter 14 and verse 4 identifies the subject as the king of Babylon. Again, verse 22 identifies the subject as the city of Babylon. Isaiah 13:1 through 14:23 must be read as a whole not in pieces. After you finish reading through 14:23, you must contrast it with Daniel 5:18-30, and compare the language.

It is strikingly similar, and both are speaking of the arrogance of the king of Babylon. Even the NIV Study Bible concludes this, although they didn't back when I taught this in 1993 as far as I could tell.

Much of the error surrounding a Satan figure stems from 14:12 and the King James Version: *"How art thou fallen from heaven, O Lucifer, son of the morning."* First, the term Lucifer is merely the Latin translation of the Hebrew word helel (Strong's #1966), meaning daystar, star of the morning, or shining one. Isaiah 14:12 of the King James Version is thus the *only* place it can be found in the entire Bible.

It comes from the root word halal (Strong's #1984), meaning to be boastful—arrogant. This has wrongly been taken as the formal and proper name for Satan. This is because of the preconceived idea that the text is speaking of Satan and his alleged fall from heaven. There is no text for this inference. The idea can only be interjected on purpose. These desperate attempts at creating a devil are not only shocking, they're brazen!

Next, the word translated "heaven" is not *shamayim* (Strong's #8064), the normal Hebrew word for heaven or *sky*. The word here is *maal* (Strong's #4605), and it merely means above or upwards. With this in mind it is easy to see that the text is saying that the king of Babylon, the morning star, has exalted himself, not to a literal heaven, but simply *above* other people, and the Hebrew God destroyed him as a result. The devil is *not* the subject here; the Babylonian king *is* the subject.

The term morning star is a figure of speech only meaning brightness that is short lived because it is swallowed up by day, as is Venus in the morning. *In other words, the bigger they are, the harder they fall.* The taunt against the Babylonian king was that he was a *shooting* star not a *shining* star like King David.

All these attempts at establishing a devil are nothing more than grasping at straws in order to make sense of the human conundrum—to understand why we have both pure and impure thoughts—to understand how both fresh and salt water can flow from the same stream. These are simply metaphors that reflect the human condition—the battle that wages between the authentic and soul-self.

With my heart I desire to do the right things, but my head will make attempts to talk me out of it. With my heart I long to do what is right, but many times my head will desire revenge. This is the dualistic nature of the human being. Biblical stories and metaphors are designed to reveal this truth.

Ezekiel 28 is a similar misconception. Verses 2 and 12 plainly address the subject as the *human* leader of the ancient city of Tyre. But let's back up and get the context again. Chapter 25 tells of God's judgment on Ammon, Moab, Edom, and Philistia. These are all natural cities on earth during the time this funeral dirge was written. The next judgment pronounced is that of the city of Tyre. Chapters 26, 27 and 28:1-19 are also dealing with the natural city Tyre.

After this we have judgments on both Sidon and Egypt. Why would an account of the fall of Satan be wedged in between all these lamenting woes on natural cities? Such would not fit the context or make any sense at all. But this is what people do; in an attempt to make sense of what we cannot allow ourselves to believe, we will force-feed an idea until the in-group swallows it whole.

A king represents his nation, and so this prophecy is not only against the king, but also the nation as a whole. Chapter 26:2, 3, 4, 7, and 15 show the subject to be Tyre. In chapter 27, verses 2, 3, 4, 8, and 32 all reveal the subject to be Tyre as well. Then chapter 28 seems to be directed to the *king* of Tyre.

Because of the lofty language used, it is commonly thought that the text must refer to the devil, even though the text plainly says it is the human king of Tyre. But once an idea is cemented in tradition, it is very difficult if not impossible to get rid of it.

Verse 28:13 in particular causes difficulty: *"You were in Eden, the garden of God."* One instantly thinks this could only be Satan the serpent which hung around the tree containing the forbidden fruit, as the serpent was present in the Garden of Eden according to the myth. Fortunately, Eden is another loanword meaning delight. The LXX (Septuagint) says: *"You were in the delight of the paradise of God."* In other words, "You had it made!"

In order to demonstrate for you how terrible these interpretations have been throughout the years, I will present you with two verses from the book of Ezekiel. One is from the original King James translation of the Bible from the year 1611, the other from the New International Version from the early 1980s. First, the King James Version:

> "Thou hast been in Eden the garden of God; every precious stone *was* thy covering, the sardius, topaz, and the diamond, the beryl, the onyx, and the jasper, the sapphire, the emerald, and the carbuncle, and gold: the workmanship of thy tabrets and of thy pipes was prepared in thee in the day that thou wast created." –Ezekiel 28:13

Now, the New International Version of the same verse:

> "You were in Eden, the garden of God; every precious stone adorned you: carnelian, chrysolite and emerald, topaz, onyx and jasper, lapis lazuli, turquoise and beryl. Your settings and mountings were made of gold; on the day you were created they were prepared."

The idea that Satan was an angel responsible for the music in heaven comes from the phrase "*the workmanship of thy tabrets and of thy pipes was prepared in thee in the day that thou wast created.*" This is believed to mean the archangel had musical pipes built into his throat. Not only was the serpent able to deceive, he was able to sing as well according to the tremendously shallow interpretation involving the *King James* English literary expression.

We have already challenged the idea that the serpent or snake in the Garden story refers to Satan (at least the common misconception of Satan). We are also told that the text is "God's Word" and cannot contradict itself. The text says it's the king of Tyre, so what does the phrase "You were in Eden, the garden of God" actually mean?

It is figurative just as it is in the Genesis account. Tyre was a righteous city and believed to have found great favor with the gods (it was a trade route and very prosperous), but when the king became highly elated as a result of his wealth, it was believed that the gods destroyed it.

Whenever cities in ancient times fell to attack, it was believed to be an act of the celestial gods of either the attacking party or of the benefactor of the attack. This holds true today for mystical thinkers. Many Christians today believe the hurricane Katrina was an act of God cleaning up the polluted city.

This rendering of the texts is again an Eros interpretation. A convoluted attempt to decipher mere ancient riddles associated with wars, kings, and competitive tribes on the earth. If this were an *actual* account of the fall of Satan from heaven, wouldn't the text simply say so? Why all the mystery? Verses 2 and 9 both say, "You are a *man* and not a god." Was Satan a man? Certainly not traditionally.

Many theologians disagree with this verse. Rather than accepting it at face value, they shrink back to inferring it to be the Satan, but only to line up with theological traditions hard to be overcome for fear of being ostracized by those in need of a devil.

When scripture is metaphorical, people call it literal; when it is literal, people call it metaphorical. Is it any wonder why religion hasn't worked in ten thousand years? When we're taught to ignore reality and to settle for myths instead, we're never able to deal with the real issues we all face. The answers to the troubles we face, much like the scriptures, are left within the Eros prison of imagination and fable.

Returning to the Ezekiel text, it speaks of how Tyre gained riches and wisdom through trade. Again, how could this refer to Satan? What does Satan, an alleged spirit being from the ether, need with gold, silver, and precious stones? These are only earthly elements and would contain no value for an ethereal being. Power is essentially a desire of people (traditionally speaking, based upon the Isaiah lament against Babylon and its king).

People desire riches, as they are difficult to come by and thus have been coveted dating back thousands of years. From Ezekiel 28:12 to the end of the chapter, we see highly figurative and symbolic language. It's poetic and emblematic in nature. Is there really any sound literary reason to insert *Satan* as the subject here?

It goes against the very context of the entire prophecy. In Ezekiel 28:2 and 12, the deity tells Ezekiel to communicate this to the human king of Tyre. Now, suppose for a moment that the subject *is* Satan. How is the prophet Ezekiel supposed to deliver a message to Satan, a nonhuman entity? Why must we force Satan into the context when the text itself tells us time and time again that the subject is the city or region of Tyre and its human king?

It makes no literary sense that Satan (a proper celestial being) butted in on God's creation and deceived Adam and Eve in a garden. If this were the case, God could have removed Satan from the picture, but did not. If God created Satan or evil for a purpose, it would have been part the God plan all along and should be welcomed. No one or no thing should foil an omnipotent God's plan, seeing that the created is subject to its creator.

You may say, "God is righteous and cannot create evil." The fact is there is plenty of evil in the creation, and if you say God did not create evil, then you are forced to say that God created something that was imperfect and somehow *became* evil. Either way, it boils down to God's work if there is a God that works.

The Hebrew God would have foreknown this, and therefore, it cannot be considered as brought on by a force outside of the deity's control. It would have to be relegated to an *oversight* on God's part. I know you may not see this the way I do, but let's not let that interfere with our pursuit of the possibilities.

The Bible does admit the Hebrew God created evil. Proverbs 16:4 states:

> "The Lord has made everything for its own purpose, even the wicked for the day of evil."

Also, Isaiah 45:7 states:

> "The one forming light and creating darkness, causing well being and creating calamity; I am the Lord who does all these."

Salvation for the Hebrews, therefore, could not logically be a plan to counter a Satan they did not believe in. The Hebrew God would have to be in control of *all* the creation. Is God a creator of evil, as these verses seem to reveal? Does God actually create wicked people such as pharaoh as the scriptures teach?

These all are questions humans from every corner of the world ask themselves. Unfortunately, there are no ironclad answers so we are left to reason it out ourselves. It is part of the human dilemma. We want to know why we are here and for what purpose. The Bible is one explanation of this, but not the *only* one.

Science has its own ideas and so do various other philosophical platforms. When one makes the Bible the *absolute* book of answers to all questions on earth, then one limits their discussions to only those who believe it. We cannot forget that it was people who wrote the Bible—people with personalities, agendas, mental disorders, biases, and the like. To believe the book was written by God is preposterous, but necessary for those who's lives are marked and made meaningful by their identification with the Hebrew deity.

Many characters in the Bible are murderers, liars, deceivers, manipulators, conflict avoiders, fornicators, you name it—humans. We cannot eliminate these important human ingredients when reading it. Make no mistake, the Bible is a very important literary work containing timeless principles for life, love, and happiness.

I have read the Bible more often than any other book I own (likely about 15,000 hours). It takes tens of years to get past preconceived notions; not everybody is able to do it. Most won't.

Therefore, based upon the exegetical evidence within the Bible itself we can safely conclude that in the Old Testament nothing is *revealed* concerning the devil at all. Any orthodox Jew will tell you this. They don't believe in Satan proper. This begs the question, what then is *the* adversary? Is it in reference to an evil being or a malevolent spirit or angel? You might or might not be surprised that the answer is none of the above.

The adversary is simply anything that sits in opposition to something. It is also, more simply put, the inherent ability to choose *wrongly* within mankind itself. The adversary is the wrong choice: the choice that sits in opposition to the choice that *should* be made—that's it. Unfortunately, no bells and whistles attached.

The evidence, however, is in favor of the free will decision-making power within mankind, rather than an evil being that influences us to be stupid. Although this idea is opposed to the traditional answer, which insists Satan is the "supreme" evil being of trickery and negative influence, it is the most sensible one.

From what we have seen, tradition seems to be correct in understanding that the terms Satan and diabolos are interchangeable. They are both in reference to an accuser or anyone or anything that accuses another and they are clear that they do not infer an invisible winged angel with a bad attitude towards humanity.

15

Satan and the New Testament

What does the New Testament say about a Satan? Does the New Testament shed new light on the subject or does it continue to muddy up the waters through errors in human judgment and Eros ideas? The first place we encounter the term Satan in the New Testament is Matthew 4 and its parallel Mark 1:13 where "*Jesus was led into the wilderness by the Spirit.*" He was said to have fasted for forty days and then was *approached* by the "tempter."

Reflecting back on the story of Eve and the tempting serpent in the Garden, we are forced to ask ourselves again, is this truly a separate deceiver, or again, is it the voice of temptation working on the humanity of Jesus? Surprisingly, many early church fathers relate the garden myth with the first sexual experience.

John also recorded in his gospel that Christ said, "Ye are of your father the devil, and the lusts of your father ye will do. He was a murderer from the beginning, and abode not in the truth, because there is no truth in him," John8:44. Advocates of the "serpent-seed doctrine"[1] have interpreted these verses to imply that the New Testament writers believed that Cain, the first murderer, was indeed the serpent's seed or offspring.

They believe Eve had an adulterous affair with the serpent and produced Cain. Here again, are we to take this literally or figuratively? If you believe Jesus was God (somehow a fully divine

1) The Serpent Seed idea appears in a 9th-century book called Pirke De-Rabbi Eliezer. In his book, Cain: Son of the Serpent, David Max Eichhorn, traces the idea back to early Jewish Midrashic texts and identifies many rabbis who taught that Cain was the son of the union between the serpent figure and Eve.

unearthly celestial being with skin) as opposed to a human being having the *divine nature* in him as we all do, then you will claim it was the *deity* of Jesus that disallowed him to succumb to the temptation.

But if not, is it possible that Jesus simply said "no" to his natural desires to let his fame go to his head? Have you said no to stupid before? I have. Was Jesus really a "perfect" human devoid of all normal humanness? That would be crazy talk to most thinking people. It wouldn't be fair either.

The scripture does say, *"Jesus was tempted in all points as we are yet without sin."* In other words, according to tradition, he had the opportunity to miss the mark, but apparently didn't. According to the Bible he always aimed for the decision making bulls eye and apparently hit it 100% of the time.

Was Jesus actually speaking with the devil as Mel Gibson portrayed in his film *The Passion*? Was Jesus truly without blemish or is this a convenient way to look at a much-needed ideal we can follow that withstands the pressure of the ego and shadow-self? I believe this is the answer. We *need* Jesus not to fail. We need somebody to do things perfectly—an example to promote hope and keep us encouraged.

Jesus is the ideal man. In a world full of womanizers, users, liars, cheats, and self-centered bullies he's our champion. He fights the devil and celestial crime like Super Man. He stands for truth, justice, and the celestial way. This also goes for the Buddha, Joel Osteen, Santa Clause, and any other human or figure of our imagination that can stand up to misguided scrutiny.

When Jesus told his disciples he must go to Jerusalem and suffer many things, be killed, and rise up on the third day, Peter rebuked Jesus saying, "May it never be." Astonishingly, Jesus' reply was:

> "Get behind me Satan! You are a stumbling block to me; for you are not setting your mind on God's interests, but man's." – Matthew 12:22, 23

Was Peter *the* Satan? It's reasonable to suspect Peter was *not* actually Satan, but rather he was playing the part of an adversary or a *ha-satan* in the same way Hadad the Edomite was an *ad-*

versary or *enemy* to King Solomon? Peter was "accusing" Jesus of being wrong in his interpretation of future events.

He was pushing for a different course of action than the *spirit* within Jesus' authentic-self had intended. Peter could not let go of his Super Man and allow him to be human and die.

In the gospel of Mark 4:15 when Jesus explains the parable of the sower, he says, "Immediately after the *logos* has been sown in them, Satan, the adversary takes it away." The soil in this parable was representative of the authentic-self (the heart—*kardia*) and the *logos* was the message of good will.

Who was the adversary that incessantly struggled to strip away the words of Jesus from those who were in line to accept them? The devil? Or was it simply those local leaders who were opposed to the message of Jesus?

The Orthodox Jews who were against *The Way* are a perfect candidate for this. When the seventy had returned from their mission to the local Jews (warning them of the coming wrath or apocalypse), Jesus said:

> "I was watching Satan fall like Lighting from heaven" –Luke 10:18.

Jesus was seeing the great opposition of the Jews fail in its attempt to prevail against his message. This was also nothing more than a "pep" talk for disgruntled disciples in need of more enthusiasm during a very dark time in history much like church is today. Church today is a pep talk that allows people to go out Monday through Sunday and keep fighting for their constricted idea of truth, justice, and the celestial way. This is what every tribe does.

Many take this passage to mean that Satan fell from his place in heaven (outer space) where God allegedly lives (we have already established that there is no biblical evidence for Satan falling from the sky). In the first place, Satan would have had no place in heaven to begin with.

Second, the statement isn't saying that Satan was falling from heaven, but rather, the "adversary" to the early members of *The Way* was falling or *failing* in its mission against *The Way* in the same manner that lightning falls from heaven. It's a metaphor.

Early followers of Jesus believed all adversarial plans against

God's ultimate eschatological plan were indeed failing as was also believed by St. Paul (1 Cor. 2). It was a figure of speech. In other words, the Gospel [the Way] was gaining ground over pockets of Judaism while the seventy were out proclaiming it despite the fierce opposition by the ruling party.

> "The God of peace will soon crush Satan (the adversary) under your feet." –Romans 16:20

The Roman letter is likely about 30 years out from Jesus' initial commission (known as the Great Commission) to evangelize Jerusalem before the coming apocalypse. This proves the Jewish adversaries of those disciples eager to fulfill the Great Commission were still withstanding their cause.

But the followers of The Way would take comfort in the words of Jesus that the "gates of *hades* would not stand against the *called out ones*." Those who were called out of the coming destruction upon Jerusalem and its temple state.

Notwithstanding when Jesus said, "I saw the adversary fall to the ground like lightning," this had to be the *adversary*, the ruling Jews who were persecuting and trying to interfere with the growth and development of the "Way of the Nazarene."

In verses 17-19 leading up to the above reference, St. Paul is telling the brethren to watch out for "*those who cause dissension and teach falsely*." "These *men* are slaves of their own appetites, smooth talkers who *deceive* the unsuspecting," he says. These men were the deceivers or the "great deceiver" singular much like America is the Great Satan according to Islam. Nothing has changed.

St. Paul wanted them to be wise in that which was good and to steer clear of evil behavior. For this reason his words were within the context of "smooth talkers and deceivers" as he conveys to them the idea that God "will *soon* crush their adversary (the ruling Jews) beneath their own feet." Does this fit within the context of the Jews who were wreaking havoc on the early Jesus followers? This actually makes the most sense of all.

Not only that, but we have historical documentation that supports they *were crushed* shortly after by the Roman army under the Roman general, Titus and scattered throughout the Middle East in 70 AD. This can be found within the works of Flavius Josephus[2] in *The Wars of the Jews*.

In regards to marital duties and obligations surrounding sexuality in 1 Corinthians 7:5, we find Satan again as the *tempter*. But again, is this an outside influence, or is it the evil, lustful, shadow-self?

> "Stop depriving one another, except by agreement for a time, so that you may devote yourselves to prayer, and come together again so that the *Satan* will not tempt you because of your lack of self control." –1 Corinthians 7:5

Remember what James the brother of Jesus said? "But each one is tempted when he is carried away and enticed by his OWN lusts *and enticed*" or *tempted* (James 1:14). Was James mistaken or was James aware of the shadow-self and its relentless desire for self and body pleasures?

I do not believe he was mistaken at all if he actually wrote this letter. Whoever wrote the letter was being quite clear with their words of admonition. Watch out because you will be "self-diluted if you don't pay attention." Unfortunately, taking way the mystery and mastery of Satan will be hard for some and impossible for most because he has become their much needed scapegoat.

We need to stop and think each time we see the word Satan in the Bible and ask ourselves, is the context speaking of our *own* voice of temptation within the shadow-self as James points out, or is it speaking of a literal adversary or accuser, such as the Jews.

The third and most unlikely choice is a supernatural monster—unfortunately it remains the most popular among evangelicals.

Many would rather blame the devil every time we act inconsistent with our authentic-self supported by the divine nature and listen to our shadow-self supported by the soul-mind. Without the devil peoples actions would be thrust into question more readily by their peers.

---

2) Titus Flavius Josephus (/dʒoʊˈsiːfəs/; 37 – c. 100), born Joseph ben Matityahu (Hebrew: יוסף בן מתתיהו, Yosef ben Matityahu), was a first-century Romano-Jewish scholar, historian and hagiographer, who was born in Jerusalem—then part of Roman Judea—to a father of priestly descent and a mother who claimed royal ancestry.

Temptation comes by being drawn away by our own personal desires according to both the Bible *and* reason. Therefore, I would conclude that every time temptation or a "tempter" is mentioned, it is referring to our own desires, our own ability to make very poor choices all by ourselves, and our own fight for survival many times at the expense of others.

Although this inner struggle has been metaphorically personified throughout the ages, the truth remains clear to all of us who have experienced the flesh-body's pull. We all desire to do what is contrary to sound judgment and have to balance our primal reason with informed responsibility.

This is the only way the term "responsibility" can have any meaning at all. If we have Satan as our scapegoat on whom we can blame evil or intent, where do we draw the line? In other words, do we blame it all on Satan or the God who made him? If we do, does that remove and shift the responsibility from us to it? Except for the fact that we allegedly carried out Satan's prompting, the origins of evil no longer rests with us alone.

This would mean people do not devise evil; we merely carry out what the instigator prompts us to do. We can't forget what we read earlier, that *mankind* is the deviser of evil, not a ha-satan. Or do we blame only the really heinous acts we commit on the devil?

As I asked earlier, where do we draw the line? What was it that hindered St. Paul from going to see the Thessalonians in 1 Thessalonians 2:18? "*We wanted very much to come to you, and I, Paul, tried again and again, but Satan prevented us.*"

Was it Satan the evil mystical being that somehow mysteriously put up an invisible roadblock, or was the adversary the Jews—St. Paul's well-known and main opposition?

In 1 Timothy 1:20 we read:

> "Among them are Hymenaeus and Alexander, whom I have handed over to Satan [literally, the adversary], so that they may be taught not to blaspheme."

St. Paul says these were among those who were "shipwrecked" in regard to their faith. If St. Paul had turned them over to *Satan the unemployed music director from heaven with a grudge*, how would that have taught them not to blaspheme unless this being is able to torture people and make them cry uncle?

However, if St. Paul had handed them over to the real adversary, in other words his physical adversary the Jews (think Taliban), you can bet they would have been taught a lesson on blasphemy. A good stoning would make them take notice, as was their tradition. This would be equivalent to handing them over to the Taliban today for a lesson on desertion of the faith—they would get the death penalty.

And what is meant by the term synagogue of Satan used in John's Revelation 2:9 and 3:9? The text tells us in both places that they are those that call themselves Jews and "are not." I rather doubt that it was Gentiles working for a celestial Satan and only pretending to be Jews. I would see it as regular people, Israelites, those who were teaching against the way of the Nazarene, the true Jews of these two passages.

These were Jews who belonged to St. Paul's "spiritual Israel"—the remnants as he called them. So there were two groups of Jews, the synagogue of Satan (the adversary) who were Jews outwardly, and the Jews who were Jews inwardly, the remnant St. Paul speaks of who followed Jesus' teaching (Romans 2).

St. Paul believed in two Jew types. Inward and outward. Those he called circumcised in the "heart" (the *kardia*) and those he called circumcised in the "flesh" (the body). He believed outward Jews to be posers and inward Jews to be the *real* children of Abraham—children of *faith*.

> "A person is not a Jew who is one only outwardly, nor is circumcision merely outward and physical. No, a person is a Jew who is one inwardly; and circumcision is circumcision of the heart, by the Spirit, not by the written code. Such a person's praise is not from other people, but from God." –Romans 2:28-29

It does seem to be true that the idea of a Satan has evolved much with the passage of time. The Old Testament idea of Satan is less defined if not all together absent, than the version we see in the New Testament. Demonology is all but absent in the Old Testament, yet it is found quite regularly in the New Testament, especially in the Gospels. Why did this type of thinking develop and where did it come from?

Does it have its roots in Babylon? Much societal and tribal corruption began there, as most scholars believe. After all, the first concept of dueling entities was a Zoroastrian concept from Babylon where the Jews were intermingling for a few generations and where many of the scriptures were penned.

Before that, the Job version of Satan worked "with" God and not *against* him. The two were in it together testing the patience and loyalty of Job. Whatever evil happened to Job was either directly or indirectly a product of the mind of Yahweh and *not* a devil.

Like the Pharisees who were responsible for corrupting the Law of Moses beyond measure, making it out to be something it was not (although minor corruptions were there from its founding), could it be that the same kind of growth in ideas changed the concept of Satan and demons, bringing them to be one of central thought and importance in the first century? I believe the answer is available to those who are looking for it.

Cosmic and Moral Dualism

Zoroastrianism is considered the first dualistic religion. In Zoroastrianism, the creator Ahura Mazda is all good, and no evil originates from him unlike the Hebrew Yahweh who embodied both good and evil at the same time. Thus, in Zoroastrianism good and evil have two distinct sources, with evil (*druj*) trying to destroy the creation of Mazda (*asha*) similar to the idea of the modern devil, and good trying to sustain it.

Cosmic dualism refers to the enduring battle between Good (Ahura Mazda) and Evil (Angra Mainyu) within the universe. This is very akin to the ideas that developed later such as the ha-satan taking the place of God in the Old Testament after the Zoroastrian influence.

It is important to understand that Angra Mainyu is not God's equal opposite; rather that Angra Mainyu is believed to be the injurious energy that opposes God's creative energy. This creative energy is called *Spenta Mainyu*. It is believed that God created a pure world through his creative energy, which Angra Mainyu continues to attack, making it impure. Like the modern Satan, aging, sickness, famine, natural disasters, death, and so on are attributed to the anti-energy that opposes the created order.

With *Cosmic Dualism* we have the mirror affect, life and death, day and night, good and evil—yin and yang. One can never be understood without the other. Life is a mixture of these two opposing forces in unending collaboration, yet in opposition.

Like Cosmic Dualism, *Moral dualism* refers to the opposition of good and evil in the mind of mankind. God's gift to man was free will; therefore man has the choice to follow the way of Evil (*druj*—deceit) or the way of Righteousness (*asha*—truth).

As in Christianity, the path of Evil always leads to misery and ultimately Hell. The path of Righteousness leads to peace and everlasting joy in Heaven. As with cosmic dualism, we have the polarity of happiness and sadness, truth and deception, and so on but with an emphasis on choice. These are the exact concepts that ultimately emerged through the teachings of Jesus and many others.

This choice is central as it determines whether we are the helper of Ahura Mazda or the helper of Angra Mainyu. This whole concept mirrors the teachings of Jesus in regards to the two-kingdom concept—the kingdom of God and the kingdom of darkness.

When all of mankind chooses the light over the darkness, evil will definitively be defeated and Paradise on earth will be fully apprehended. This also mirrors the teachings of St. Paul: "*...the creation itself will be liberated from its bondage to decay and brought into the freedom and glory of the children of God*" –Romans 8:20.

In practice, modern Zoroastrianism is nearly identical to the Christian perspective. It teaches that Mankind is ultimately *good* and that this goodness will finally triumph over evil. This could be easily understood as a rehabilitation of the faith's earliest form of dualism.

Beelzebul

Another idea to consider is whether or not the first-century people really believed in Satan. They obviously believed in demons, assigning things they did not understand to be brought about by demons such as epilepsy and Hanson's disease as in early Zoroastrianism. But do we have a single verse were the Jews brought up a Satan?

Not that I know of. Interestingly enough, the term Satan is only used by Jesus and the apostles. Why didn't the Jews ever use the term? Could it be because they did not feel comfortable using a term that was applied to them by Jesus and the apostles? Was Jesus' and the apostles' using of the term purely figurative? The Jews were not into using figurative language like Jesus and the apostles were.

The Jews for sure accuse Jesus of casting out demons by Beelzebul, ruler of the demons (Matthew 12:22-29), but Beelzebul is not Satan. Beelzebul, or Baalz-zebub was the God of Ekron and the name refers to "lord of the flies." Jesus only makes the comparison of Satan casting out Satan to show them the futility in arguing that Beelzebul could cast out members of his own party. He is not equating Satan with Beelzebul at all.

We owe it to ourselves to keep these ideas in mind when reading an ancient text such as the Bible. It may clear up a lot of problems elsewhere. Today most religious groups view Satan as the great evil being responsible for everything that goes wrong within the cosmos and within ourselves. That will never change in my lifetime, and maybe that's okay or is it?

What's more, it will never be proven wrong because there's no concrete evidence—religions secret sauce. However, the idea that Satan was an angel that fell from his place in heaven can be proven false, simply by the absence of facts to support it. This idea is the product of superstitions developed in the minds of people—taking verses out of context and creating their own versions.

The ideas that have been passed down through the ages such as Hebrew traditions and Zoroastrianism have, like splinters, lodged themselves within the minds of men thus perpetuating the Eros prison of performance and the need to have a safe-self.

Rather than simply celebrating our authentic divine nature and embracing the wins and losses we experience along the way while rejecting those that harm, we have embraced man's ancient attempts to please the gods as rigid antidotes designed to rid ourselves of the unsafe-self thus creating the Eros prison of perpetual performance.

16

The Power of Self-Worth

By now you may realize we all have an authentic-self, but each self isn't worth the same amount in the eyes of the beholder. The question still remains as to whether there is there a way to measure it—fortunately there is. The best way to measure yourself is to measure your behavior. Your *reactions* and *actions* speak louder than your words.

The field of behavioral science is interesting in that behavior is not only predictable, but also it's tantamount to reading an MRI report in order to establish physiological issues. Observing behavior is what many behavioral scientists do for a living, and they're really good at it.

As a behaviorist, I study people and personality difference. Over the last ten years, I have discovered some really unique patterns in human behavior. These patterns emerge in different types of people and for different reasons, but the behavior itself is telling.

It tells us what others think about themselves—what they believe about their divine authentic-self. I want to look at four different instances, and then I want you to determine your *own* reactions to them.

Unexpected Challenges

What is a challenge? It's something that by its very nature or character serves as a *call* to battle, contest, or a special effort. But what if this call is avoided at all costs? What if when we feel a summons to some special effort or battle with another person, situation, or cause (a conflict or struggle), we decide to opt out almost immediately? What would this say about us?

Many find unexpected challenges simply too difficult to maneuver. If they are emotionally unprepared, they may disqualify themselves straight away. I too find myself at times avoiding certain conflicts, and when I do, inevitably it coincides with self-worth. Some call this *throwing the fight.*

In other words, you decide you cannot win and therefore opt out in order to save face. Why do we believe we can't win? Why do we believe any attempt would be a wasted effort? Why would anyone give up before actually trying? But many do. This is a sign. It's a sign that your brain has already decided your fate. It's a sign that you do not believe you have what it takes to answer the call to action.

Challenges come in many forms, from asking for a raise to fighting on the front lines in real warfare. But the responses can be the same. What I mean is, asking for a raise can *feel like* the front lines for many people emotionally speaking—even if you deserve one. Allowing your authentic-self to pervade your mind is a key to overcoming feelings of insufficiency.

This can also be a sign of low self-worth, when our limbic system *only* says flight and rarely says fight. For many, this is life as usual. This is a *trust* issue. It's an inability to trust the true-self for fear it isn't enough. Similar to a statement like, "I trust you will show up, therefore I will show up too," if we don't trust our authentic selves, we likely won't show up for the challenge regardless of what it is.

Part of this problem is that some of us are *surprised* by the amount of effort it takes to meet a challenge. For those who are usually up for problems and challenges, they *expect* it to be difficult. They don't see difficulty as bad, but rather they see it as an *opportunity* for growth and excitement—fun even.

Rather than feel like you failed and therefore you are bad, think: *well, that didn't work out; maybe next time.* Our results are rarely if ever a reflection of us as a person, and they are never the results of our authentic-self. They simply reflect our ability, which is a *part* from who we are. It may also reflect where our soul-self is at—our mind.

When we are happy with *who we are*, it's easier to be okay with whatever we *can or cannot do* as that person. Look at challenges as opportunities for growth and development, rather than opportunities to fail. When we change the way we see things, the things we see change.

Unexpected Roadblocks

Roadblocks represent an action or condition that obstructs progress toward an objective. If I want something, it may be fair to say that I will have to overcome a roadblock or two in order to get it—especially if it is worth something.

This is what character development is all about. It's what makes great stories. A story is a character that wants something and has to overcome great odds in order to achieve it. Think Luke Skywalker in *Star Wars*. It's what makes a story a story worth watching.

What is hypothetically the greatest story ever told? Possibly the story of the Christ child. According to the story, he wanted this world of people (primarily the Jews—his *own*) to expand their Christ consciousness and had to overcome the greatest of conflicts in order to make it happen—the grave.

We are all living a story. But our story might not be a good one. I submit that one of the most common reasons why most people leave their mates and the reason why many youth run away from home is because they are in a bad story, and they want another one. If your life is predictable, boring, void of crisis, and not worth minimal risks, you may not be living a good story.

To be true, the characteristics of a story are interesting because it requires what we are typically against in order for the story to be good. We don't want or like crisis—we either avoid it or respond poorly in its wake.

The word Crisis in Hebrew is *mash-ber*, a word also used for birthing-stool, a seat upon which a woman in ancient times would give birth to a new life. Crisis will either crush you or create a new you, but it will never encourage you. The prophet Isaiah said concerning the nation of Israel:

> "We, too, writhe in agony, but nothing comes of our suffering. We have not given salvation to the earth, nor brought life into the world." –Is. 26:18

They were like a woman with child, writhing in the pains both labor and delivery, yet the only outcome produced by their cruel sufferings was wind as I mentioned elsewhere. They were unable to capitalize on the crisis. This is why they could not benefit from a great story. Whether falling to hunger and death in the wilderness or by the sword, their never-ending story was never good.

Thought Invader: The general rules to story are that the characters in the story do not want to change their circumstances until forced.

This is what is known as an "inciting incident." It's the "event' that forces the story or forces an individual into story. In his book, *A Million Miles in a Thousand Years*, Donald Miller points this out in fascinating ways. Without inciting incidents, we will not create a good story. Even Luke Skywalker needed an inciting incident, the death of his family, to thrust him into the story before becoming a Jedi Knight.

In the book of Joshua, a hooker named Rahab is thrust into the story through an inciting incident. The saving of her brothers and sisters at the personal risk of her life thrusts her into another story. The story she was living was a bad story filled with pain and prostitution. Her act of courage did more than save her future (because she didn't have one); it created a future that would have formally not been believed possible.

After the inciting incident, Rahab is married to an Israelite named Salmon, whose son was Boaz, the husband of Ruth the Moabite, whose son was Obed, whose son was Jesse, whose son was David, Israel's greatest king.

Thought Invader: You cannot have a testimony without a test, and you cannot change your world without first changing your soul-mind.

The courage of a pagan prostitute changed the world, as we know it. In the first book of Samuel in the Old Testament, David is living a boring story acting as a gofer for his father and brothers.[1] He is thrust into crisis through the inciting incident of Goliath from Gath and enters the story of his life. David goes from obscurity to maturity through a series of events, creating crisis after crisis and story after story.

His response to these incidents defines him. We are forced to think about our own stories as we read these narratives, and we are

1) 1 Samuel 17

confronted with our own avoidance. Be encouraged to enter your own inciting incidents in full regalia knowing that the greatest opportunities for greater stories await your response in a delicately balanced equation of both risk and reward. But what if I give up easily?

Thought Invader: We give up because we believe we cannot achieve whatever it is we need.

What do most people do when faced with a roadblock when driving? We look for the signs that detour us in another direction, in hopes of finding the intended destination another way. It's the same in life. Sometimes the phone is temporarily disconnected, so we have to write a letter.

But if I believe what I want is something I do not deserve, my effort will stop. If my effort is too quick to quit, it's usually a sign that I don't believe I deserve the outcome. If you suffer from this scenario, I suggest you rethink a few things.

Ask yourself why you don't deserve that raise if we can use this imagery. If your answer is *because I just don't*, then you need to realize that it isn't true. If it's because you are not good at that particular job, ask yourself what *am* I good at? Find a job doing what you excel at and the sky's the limit. Unfortunately self-pity always agrees with us, but we cannot allow ourselves to agree with *it*.

Always do your best because when you do, you deserve the best. If I don't try, I cannot expect a result. If I bring a basketball to a football game, is the basketball a bad ball? Of course not. It's not a *bad* ball; it's the *wrong* ball. If we can find the initiative to get the *right* ball, our game will be worth playing.

Unexpected Criticism

Criticism is the act of passing judgment as to the merits of anything. Nobody likes criticism, but some people are crippled by it. It's difficult to maintain confidence with low self-worth without distorting the world. We can distort reality by blaming and denying or defensively or aggressively rebelling against setbacks or the people we *believe* may be responsible for them.

This has become such a common problem that companies have had to redefine the term "employee evaluations" and call them *growth opportunities* in an effort to minimize the emotional damage it causes some people.

People with low self-worth unfortunately will only gravitate towards activities that *confirm* their abilities as opposed to activities that will *expand* them.

Thought Invader: Growth is never immediate; it's progressive.

The lower our self-worth, the more immediate our results need to be. So instead of learning through trials and errors, some are halted by them. This inability to move forward because of what we believe about our ability can be crippling.

I remember speaking at an event many years ago. It stands out in my mind because of what happened afterwards. My then mentor came to me and said, "*You're a good speaker, but I want to make you a great one.*" I was thrilled at the opportunity. But it could have gone another way if I had low self-worth. I could have heard, "*you suck*" if I allowed myself to.

Don't believe your performance is a *reflection* of your intelligence or motives. When I was eighteen, I worked on an assembly line. I screwed it up so terribly that they had to shut down the entire plant for an entire day. The only reason I wasn't fired is because they wanted me to fix it all.

I felt terrible, but I didn't believe I was stupid. One year later, I was the best person to date that ever did that particular job. What formerly took me six hours now took seven minutes. I almost made as much money as my father, and I was just out of high school. I later quit to move onto better things.

Unexpected Success in Other People

Some people are threatened by others' success. Favorable or prosperous outcomes in others can be daunting in light of our own. For many imprisoned within the Eros prison, watching someone else succeed can kill motivation. In other words, if you are successful then I am not.

This happens to a lot of people. They cannot rejoice in someone's prosperity, so they criticize it instead. "*Typical rich white guy*" or "*She's always had things handed to her*" or "*It must be nice!*" These slogans are indisputable signs of insecurity and a failed belief in the authentic-self.

I remember a friend who received a very large inheritance after his parents sold their business for over two hundred million dollars. One of the perks was a brand new car every three years of his choosing. I'll never forget the day he pulled up with his new Suburban in 1994.

An acquaintance walked by and in a sigh of disdain and sarcasm said, "*Must be nice.*" I remember thinking about what he said and the reaction I might have had if I was the fortunate one in this story. "It is nice," I probably would have said. I then congratulated my friend and said, "Good for you! *You deserve it.*"

Learn to rejoice in other people's success.

Think of what it would actually *feel* like if it were you. Imagine how happy you would be and how you would feel as others shared your joy. Then be glad it's them by showing it through your actions. Let your soul rejoice!

Thought Invader: It's difficult to be happy for others when we are sad about ourselves.

I see others' success as a sign that I could succeed just as well. I'm inspired by it. It stands as proof that we all have a chance in this life so we should always aim for it. The true-self rejoices in other people's achievements, it doesn't feel threatened by them.

Report Cards

Self-esteem is a system of *self-rating* that we participate in each day both consciously and unconsciously. We give our true selves a report card every time we test ourselves in this area whether we know this or not. But what does this report card say?

I never feared bringing home a report card when I was young. Times have changed—I mean report cards have changed. But when I was young, report cards were a dreaded dilemma. An "A" or a "B" was good, but "D's" and "F's" were extremely bad. I was not school material. In fact, I was awful at school, taking tests that is.

I remember having to take my tests alone in the library stockroom so I could pay enough attention to pass. Eventually, I was placed in a "special" class above the library on the balcony for a few hours a day with the children with special needs because the teachers thought I was mildly retarded.

My mother was the report card reader in our home. But she didn't read it like most parents. She didn't pay all that much attention to the letter grade, but more importantly she would look for effort. If there were a letter "S" in the effort column, she would speak to me about it.

"S" stood for satisfactory and that wasn't acceptable. If I had a "D" in the grade point column and an "E" (excellent) in the effort column, then I got an "A" at home. I believe this is why I try so hard. My effort column is always trying to produce the "E" as opposed to the "S."

This I believe is primarily the reason for my continued success in life. Although I do not sport a degree of any kind in higher education, I have an "A" in life. I do my best every time I put my hand to something. Whether it's taking care of my car, putting together a website, helping a person navigate their life circumstance, or studying a subject, I go all out. Sure, I have problems like everyone else, but they don't cripple me.

I'm still a "C" student when it comes to taking written tests, but I'm an "A" student when it comes to life, people, and work. This is what matters. Life is not a series of written tests; it's a series of opportunities to fail miserably or succeed wholeheartedly at life and love by embracing our authentic-self.

Thought Invader: Your greatest hurt in life will probably involve a person or a social group.

Whether it is family, community, church, or work, our greatest pains begin and end with people. And how we navigate this maze will more than likely determine our successes and failures in life. Statistics claim it is rare that people quit their job—they usually quit their boss. The same goes for marriage.

Understanding people will be the most important endeavor you ever undertake. Understanding ourselves is even more important. Why people think the way they do, what cultural and ideological differences they have, religion and social in-grouping, all of it.

I've spent the last thirty years in the people business, in one form or another, and one thing is clear—they are all the same. We all have needs that are dying to be met.

Thought Invader: Unmet emotional needs create problems. It takes courage to find out what those emotional needs are.

Think about it. You are a boss. You've gone through nine people in the last eight years in a position subordinate to you and for whatever reason, none of them works out. Ask yourself what the one common denominator is within this series of equations describing your efforts with a number of employees over the eight years.

You are. If this is you, *you* are the one common thread throughout all these people equations, but because your eyes are only looking outward, you only see the people you let go or who quit under your command. Odds are good you are the problem because you are the only consistent person within every people group.

It takes an "A" in the effort column to figure this out—the amount of effort you put into self-discovery, self-love, and the amount of effort you put into desiring the right answers.

Thought Invader: People with self-awareness have a better chance at personal success than those with little to no awareness.

But if you are unable to admit fault because it becomes another failed attempt at life, you will place the blame in a more suitable place—on someone else.

Authentology

Authentology is what I call the study of the true divine-self in authentic ways. It's the ability to look at yourself authentically and deal with it ruthlessly and swiftly without personal remorse or fear of being a "bad" person.

Some of our greatest challenges come from a failure to see ourselves as we really are. This is why many of us judge others based upon their actions, but we judge ourselves based upon our intentions—in other words, we get an "F" in the self-discovery class.

If you've ever read the Holy Scriptures, they address this concept well. The author of the epistle of James tells the reader that he or she must look into what he calls the "perfect law of liberty," meaning the Law of Moses in this instance, as if it were a mirror.

The one who goes away from his or her reflection forgetting what they saw will not succeed, "but whosoever looks therein and goes away not forgetting what they saw will be blessed in everything they do."

Thought Invader: Jesus' teaching was always according to a pattern and based upon a principle.

The scriptures can be very helpful for uncovering and discovering why we do the things we do. Like an old cow, we must be able to eat the hay and leave the sticks behind. This goes for all kinds of wisdom literature.

What about us? What do we see in our minds when we think about ourselves? More importantly, what do we believe about what we see? Seeing is believing for most of us. If we see inability, lack of courage, lack of talent, etc., we will lack all these things. But what if we choose to see something else? What if we see uniqueness, potential, and opportunity? And what if we believe it?

This is one of the reasons why many religious affiliations are successful in numbers, many in the billions. These religious in-groups bring a better definition to an otherwise undefined self. If I believe I'm a failure and you tell me that your God says I'm not, then I may enquire further of this mystery. Yes! This is a good thing as long as it doesn't grow into something terribly arrogant and harmful.

Pluses and Minuses

Uncover, discover, and recover. This is always the process. We must uncover ourselves in brutal fashion as if we're looking for gold. It will feel like having the bed sheets ripped off you while lying naked, out of shape, and unprotected on the bed.

Thought Invader: Discover all the wonderful and not so wonderful things about yourself and embrace them both.

We are comparable to a car battery. You cannot remove the negative post and expect the vehicle to still function. Removing the negative will not make the car function *better*. We all have minuses and pluses just like a battery.

Recover your self-worth through the process of appreciating

your uniqueness and applying yourself where you have the most pluses. *Recognize* (not despise) the minuses and only use them when necessary.

Susan Boyle, a singer who discovered her uniqueness on *Britain's Got Talent* several years ago, was faced with many minuses. When she had the courage to share one of her best gifts, one of several *hidden* "pluses" with the world, it changed her life and many others' forever. Her CD sales broke the existing sales records on Amazon at that time.

Don't Allow Your Minuses to Bury Your Pluses

Know you are important and special in the universe. Do not rate your internal worth by others' opinions or religious standards, but rather by the uniqueness of your authentic-self. You are the only human with the fingerprints you possess in the universe. This means you are unique, and it's a proven fact. Focus on who you are and not on what you can do.

When we do this, *what we do* emerges in fantastic ways. I went from sitting in a class of special-needs children and failing simple math to working with CEOs and entrepreneurs around the world for several reasons. For one, my mother said I could do anything, and I dared to believe it. And second, I simply learned to love my true authentic-self.

17

The Shame Game

Before I settled in for more writing this morning, I took a walk. It was an awesome walk, as I could smell the many breakfasts cooking throughout the neighborhood under clear blue skies on a fall morning. My walk took me down the street past a little country church. Outside the church was the all familiar church sign and marquee for onlookers to see in hopes of luring them in. This is what the sign said: "*God wants full custody, not weekend visits.*"

What am I to think of this statement? And what person knows what God wants for me better than I? And what does full custody look like? Is full custody spending an inordinate amount of time with this church's activity list? The problem with this kind of propaganda is that it's insulting. This is meant to *shame* people into doubting their time management with God, as if there is such a thing.

You don't have to be doing religious activities to be in touch with God or to be a spiritual person. This kind of rhetoric is only spoken from within the Eros prison. Free people don't care what you do with your time. It's sad that so many have to spend their time wondering what you are doing with yours. This too is meaningless.

"*I am what I am.*" Those are the words of St. Paul. What I like about this statement is its finality. After a life of murder, brutality, prejudice, and abusive power, St. Paul (formerly Saul of Tarsus) had an about face and for reasons that might shock you.

Formerly a persecutor and murderer of the people of *The Way* (followers of Jesus), this dominant influencer was now their greatest supporter. But how do you move forward from such a horrific past with this kind of peace and fervor?

> "No, dear brothers and sisters, I have not achieved it, but I focus on this one thing: Forgetting the past and looking forward to what lies ahead." –Philippians 3:13

St. Paul focused on one thing—just one. He looked forward. But how could he do this without being haunted by his past? He knew his true-self was not defined by what he did; it was defined by what it was.

Looking Back

St. Paul's secret sauce involved the simple act of looking forward and not behind—but how did he do it? Jesus of Nazareth taught this same principle.

> "But Jesus told him, 'Anyone who puts a hand to the plow and then *looks back* is not fit for the Kingdom of God.'" –Luke 9:62

What is it with looking back? Is it really all that bad? Initially I wouldn't think so, but upon further investigation the results of doing so can be a problem. There's nothing more final than something that is finished. It's like sending an email and then wishing you hadn't just seconds after clicking the send button—it's too late.

But the past defines us. It's the only solid evidence that we are here. "I went to school there" or "That's me in that photo; I used to weigh forty pounds less." The past is nothing but evidence; it's not a definition. Your present is where you are now, and the future is where you will be. Focus on the now and then tomorrow will be now tomorrow.

I Was What I Was

The problem with a poor past is that when we focus on it we can only implore certain emotions—emotions not on our side.

Regret | Guilt | Shame | Remorse | Sadness

These emotions are associated with what we *did* and what we cannot change. Even our present condition looks through the eyes of the past, as we are a product of every decision we made before this present moment. The past can be haunting and debilitating for some. But what did Jesus of Nazareth mean when he said one was not fit for the Kingdom? The context was discipleship and living the life of Christ Consciousness.

Many traveling teachers of the first century had followers. They would leave their station in life and follow the teacher and many never went back to their former lives. To follow the "Master" was to let go of what defines you. This was important to Jesus.

Thought Invader: To follow Jesus is to no longer live for selfish desires rooted in your past.

Your identity was to be swallowed up by his. This means we no longer live after our natural human desires, but rather for the will of the divine untouched-self—God. This *Death That Counts* must encompass our PAST, PRESENT, and FUTURE.

Jesus didn't believe people were defined by what they did, but rather by who they were. I understand that he said people would be known by their fruits, but this was concerning the religious who claimed one thing and lived another. This was bothersome to the hyper religious who defined themselves by their religious activities, popularity, group-worth, and *self*-worth.

Jesus and the Wishing Well

This is why Jesus was able to love and live with any person who was willing to allow themselves to be defined by a new standard. In the case of the *Samaritan woman* at the well in John 4, we see one of the most amazing dialogues within any ancient text. It demonstrates how Jesus saw ordinary people. In the story, Jesus sits down by a well and asks a woman if she would fetch him a drink.

> "The woman was surprised, for Jews refuse to have anything to do with Samaritans. She said to Jesus, "You are a Jew, and I am a Samaritan woman. Why are you asking me for a drink?"

Jesus lived in the now and therefore was unable to recognize her past even though he was familiar with it. Nor did he recognize her heritage, a product of former interbreeding with other nations that produced the Samaritans. His simple asking for a drink redefined who she was, but she didn't see it—not yet.

The simple fact that he would engage and initiate a conversation with a woman let alone a Samaritan woman redefined who she was and canceled all she ever did. As the story unfolds Jesus begins to speak about the water of life and the new life she could live and then asks her to fetch her husband so he also can accept this water of life.

The water of life is similar to the light we spoke of earlier. It's the cleansing flow that washes and reminds us about our true-self in the love of God and our divine nature. Her reply is stunning:

> "I have no husband."

What Jesus says next is awe-inspiring. He lets her in on a secret. He modestly allows her to understand that he already knows everything she has ever done, but there's a catch—he doesn't care. His conversation with her is living *proof* that what she believes about herself is *her* problem and not his.

Her past has defined her present condition resulting in her poor decision-making. I would imagine that as Jesus spoke with her she was in constant reminiscence of her heritage, her Samaritan scar.

Similar to a scarlet letter, her entire village was in social quarantine by the Jews. I imagine she wished at the well it wasn't so. Samaritan's lived in continuous shame. They were avoided by the Jewish people and were considered scum by the religious and the pious Jews.

> "Jesus said, "You're right! You don't have a husband—for you have had five husbands, and you aren't even married to the man you're living with now. You certainly spoke the truth!"

Jesus seemingly adds insult to injury when he claims she goes through husbands like laundry—a sign of her dysfunctional life and the poor images of her unsafe-self. Shame, guilt, and regret—

all of it was now uncovered at the well. This is when something very amazing happens.

> Just then his disciples came back. They were shocked to find him talking to a woman, but none of them had the nerve to ask, "What do you want with her?" or "Why are you talking to her?"
>
> The woman left her water jar beside the well and ran back to the village, telling everyone, "Come and see a man who told me everything I ever did! Could he possibly be the Messiah?"
>
> So the people came streaming from the village to see him. –John 4:27-28

This statement by the woman, "*Come and see a man who told me everything I did*," is one of the most unusual passages in the New Testament. She couldn't have been proud of her past, nor could she make great claims to her present, yet she was excited to allow everyone else's past to be exposed just like hers was.

Why? Why would she be up for this uncovering? Because when Jesus exposed it, he also *expunged* it.

Thought Invader: Jesus' process was always three fold; Uncover, Discover, Recover.

Jesus didn't make her say a prayer or ask her to join his religious organization. He didn't ask her for money or sell her a book or turn her into a Christian. He sat by a well and had a simple conversation with one of the most hated people of the first century and in that moment loved her true authentic-self.

Her shame was likely so deep that she had lost all self-respect. But in that moment something wonderful happened. She ceased to see herself for *what she did* and adopted Jesus' view of her true authentic- and *now* safe-self. She was thus letting go of her own distorted view of self.

> Many Samaritans from the village believed in Jesus because the woman had said, "He told me everything I

> ever did!" When they came out to see him, they begged him to stay in their village.
>
> So he stayed for two days, long enough for many more to hear his message and believe. Then they said to the woman, "Now we believe, not just because of what you told us, but because we have heard him ourselves. Now we know that he is indeed the Savior of the world." –John 4:39-42

Many Samaritans believed the words of Jesus. His message of love and acceptance of the self permeated the entire village. Knowing that Jesus knew "*everything she ever did*" and that he was *still* interested in her in spite of her failures saved her from her unsafe soul-self's misinterpretation likely spawned by her shadow-self.

Her past was gone—wiped clean. She was no longer a Samaritan woman; she was her authentic safe-self, loved by God along with everyone else in the isolated village that dared believe it was possible.

Jesus and the Treatment of Women

Like everything else in the scriptures, how Jesus connected with women is based upon a particular principle and always according to a similar pattern and value. Throughout the New Testament, Jesus' actions and reactions to the feminine are constant and noteworthy.

Thought Invader: Jesus was great at making people feel safe.

The "woman at the well" scenario we just looked at exposes Jesus' view of women and his most fascinating approach to connecting with this "Samaritan woman." To be clear, the most common view as to the origin of the Samaritans is that they were a mongrel breed equivalent to dogs who developed as a result of intermarriages between earlier Hebrews of the northern kingdom of Israel and the Assyrian settlers in Israel following the captivity of the northern kingdom in 722-21 B.C. (cf. Ezra 4:2, 9, 10).

Samaritans were so repulsive to first-century Jews that they would go around Samaria rather than through it when traveling to locals on the other side of Samaria. This is equivalent to traveling from Boston to New York, but avoiding Rhode Island because Canadians lived there. Second, the Samaritan in question was a "woman."

The Jewish attitude toward women was less than ideal—it was barbaric. While the Old Testament afforded great dignity to womanhood (cf. Proverbs 31:10) in some instances, the Hebrews over the years had imbibed many of the corrupt convoluted attitudes of other cultures that were far less civilized. Those who fully live out of their authentic-self do not treat people poorly.

> "Many a Jewish man started the day with a prayer to God expressing thanks that he was not a Gentile, a slave, or a woman."

A Hebrew man did not talk with a woman in the street—not even with his mother, sister, daughter, or wife if you can believe that (cf. Lightfoot 1979, 286-287).

According to the most liberal view of the Hebrew Deuteronomy 24:1 divorce rule, a Hebrew husband could divorce his wife if she was found simply "familiarly talking with men" (Edersheim 1957, 157).

William Barclay tells of a segment of the Pharisees known as the "bleeding and bruised" Pharisees; when they saw a woman approaching, they would close their eyes, henceforth, they were running into things constantly and bruising themselves (1956, 142-143).

As ridiculous as this sounds, it is nonetheless a darker side to history. Women were tantamount to cattle within these shame-based cultures as many are today in the Middle East, especially those of Muslim origin. In some places, it's an honor to kill your own wife today (Known as an honor killing) if they shame your family through sanctity/purity violations or contamination ethics.

Jesus on the other hand, did not view women in this way. I find it fascinating how many autonomous-driven women believe Jesus to be oppressive and abusive to women. Frankly, Christianity in its seed form before the apostle Paul redefined it (according to the teachings of Jesus) is the most fortunate event and catalyst for freedom and equality women have likely ever known.

Granted, many men have been sexist and shameful in their treatment of women since this time and much of this treatment has been justified with the scriptures using the apostle Paul's "sacred sequence" reasoning.

The first-century Hebrew as well as other shame-based cultures was notorious for treating women poorly. The cultural retardation among these shame-based cultures still thrives today in the Middle East and other places. It's up to us to redirect our own prejudices by allowing our authentic-self to permeate everything we do.

Thought Invader: Religion always has a way of sorting, distorting, and then reporting the shadow sides of humanity.

Jesus interacted with women throughout his tenure upon earth in a manner most jaw dropping for the first-century man and Jew. Although modern fundamentalism has embraced ancient Hebrew patriarchal notions, Jesus *never* did.

That being said, the historicity of patriarchal communities and early Christian sects and communities were definite proponents of female bias and disdain for centuries, but this is *post*-Jesus and his gang of twelve.

Jesus' behavior toward women, even when viewed through the traditional lens of the Gospel texts, is nonetheless extraordinary. Jesus welcomed women into his inner circle of discipleship as Luke points out in his eighth chapter:

> "After this he journeyed through towns and villages preaching and proclaiming the good news of the kingdom of God. The Twelve accompanied him, and also some women . . . Mary called the Magdalene, . . . Joanna, the wife of Herod's steward Chuza, Susanna, and many others who were assisting them out of their means." –Luke 8:1-5

These women were actually supporting Jesus' mission out of their own sustenance. Women were not named in ancient texts unless they had social distinction or were associated with a man of renown. Some scholars believe the implication in this text (Luke

8) is that well-to-do Jewish women actually underwrote Jesus' entire mission.

Jesus welcomed female disciples into his entourage without respect of persons to learn the ways of God and Christ consciousness and He taught them side by side with the male disciples and never once apologized for it.

This was highly unusual seeing that Jewish men did not customarily speak in public to women outside their family relationship circle, much less travel around the countryside with them in tow.

The story of Martha and Mary is demonstrative of Jesus' open acceptance of both sexes. Luke shows us Mary at Jesus' feet. Not a few scholars' interpretation of this event is that Mary has taken the place traditionally reserved for male rabbinical students.

Martha, when the rules of the current patriarchal social system are opposed, protests in response to it expecting Jesus to agree with her—boy is she surprised. Amazingly, Jesus commends Mary's thirst to gain more knowledge and consciousness about God and corrects Martha:

> "It is Mary who has chosen the better part; it is not to be taken from her." –Luke 10:38-42

This was a cultural shift and a major turn of events, which is why Martha was so surprised.

Throughout the Gospels, we see Jesus challenge deep-rooted patriarchal, psychological boundaries, and socio-societal, and tribal assumptions such as "only women shoulder the burden of sexual sin" and purity violations and that "Samaritan and Canaanite women are to be rejected and disregarded as people" or that "prodigal sons are to be disclaimed and cut off forever from inheritances." But when it comes to Jesus, men are challenged to own their own malicious collaboration in adulterous and sexual situations.

The Samaritan woman we spoke of becomes a missioned presenter bringing her whole village to a knowledge and affirmation of Jesus, the one who "told me everything I had ever done," while the Canaanite woman's ferocious love for her daughter succeeds in widening Jesus' own understanding of whom the Good News is meant to envelop and change. Thus Jesus turns the whole societal view of women completely on its head.

It was customary for Jesus to tip these sacred cows, as his mission was to reform current Judaism and not save the earth as people think. When the Jewish disciples asked Jesus' opinion on "who sinned that caused this man to be born blind, him or his parents?" In John's ninth chapter, Jesus shocks them with his reply: "neither."

This must have been highly confusing as every first-century Jew believed bodily abnormality to be a result of the "sin" of your own purity violations or the "sin" of parental inheritance *through* proxy violations. Jesus utterly demolishes this traditional mindset with one word.

Some of the most outlandish actions of Jesus towards women are in the resurrection accounts, for it is on the testimony of women that the declaration of the supposed resurrection completely rests. My goal is not to argue the resurrection story, but rather reflect on the behaviors of the women surrounding the story as they paint a picture of Jesus' actions.

All four Gospels show Mary Magdalene (who allegedly sported seven devils or *personality differences*), Joanna, Mary the Mother of James and Joses, Salome, and the other women disciples openly escorting Jesus to his execution, anointing and burying his body, viewing an empty tomb, and experiencing first his alleged risen self.

To be clear, only one person prior to the death of Jesus actually understood his eminent death and that one person was a woman—nobody else was intuitive enough or emotionally intelligent enough to figure it out. Many biblical scholars regard the message of his subsequent resurrection was first given to a woman as one of the most convincing evidences for the historicity of the resurrection account in all literature.

If you are one to believe in a resurrection, had these manuscripts been fabricated by overenthusiastic males, scholars believe they would not have involved the testimony of mere women in a society that rejected their legal standing and viewed them as second-class citizens at best and subhuman stumped dumb dogs at worst. The point is that Jesus' treatment of women was so clear that it followed him through his story after his death.

Jesus overthrows many centuries of Jewish law and custom

during his three-year kingdom rampage. He consistently treated women and men as equals while hair lipping the whole of Jewish traditional bias against them. He violated numerous Old Testament regulations, purity rules, sanctity rites, and in-group/loyalty ethics, which specified gender inequality, not gender equality.

He refused to follow the behavioral rules established by the three main Jewish religious groups of the day: the Essenes, Pharisees and Sadducees, but openly violated them whenever He had the chance.

Jesus completely and intentionally ignored ritual impurity laws as seen in Mark 5:25-34. Mark unmistakably describes Jesus' cure of a woman who suffered from menstrual bleeding for twelve years. This is highly unusual as these women were seen as "unclean" as a dead body when on their monthly cycle because of purity violations and the contamination psychology it created among Jewish men.

In Judean society, it was a major transgression for a man to talk to a woman other than his wife or children as in many Muslim-driven societies today. He talked to foreign women such as the Samaritan girl in John 4:7 to 5:30 and engaged with her willingly, to her astonishment.

Although Jesus describes non-Jews as "dogs," (the current slang for Gentile women) he was more than willing to talk to them whether they were male or female. He also cures a foreign woman's daughter of "demon-possession" to everyone's astonishment. He also willingly taught "women students" when Jewish tradition at the time was to not allow women to be taught at all—period.

Rabbi Eliezer (an unfortunate male, lost within the Eros prison) writes in the first century:

> "Rather should the words of the Torah be burned than entrusted to a woman. Whoever teaches his daughter the Torah is like one who teaches her obscenity."

As wacko as this sounds, many today still believe this; yet within these shame-based religious societies they are far more tolerated than Christian societies as a rule. Jesus overthrew centuries of traditional bias in relationship to the oppression of women, but most secularists are willingly ignorant of this fact for fear of agreeing with the Christian influence or the religious right.

Jesus also told parallel male/female stories as in Luke, where the author of the Gospel of Luke and of Acts shows many parallel episodes, one relating to a woman, the other to a man without prejudice.

The facts are in and Jesus blows away Jewish and Christian oppression of women and models the role of a true spiritual gentleman when it comes to the equality of the sexes. His most infamous example was when the Jewish men threw the adulterous woman at his feet in lawful smug defiance of everything just. Jesus' response was not only unexpected, it was grizzly.

His appeal to the ethical foundations of "harm and care" as well as "fairness and reciprocity" as opposed to the religious foundation of "purity/sanctity" disemboweled the religious mindset of the current community. This turn of events fueled a hatred for him thus accelerating a thirst for his imminent death by crucifixion.

The Jesus pattern and principle in regards to women was the same as Paul's when making appeals to Christianity; there is neither male nor female when it comes to Christ consciousness and the self. All are *one* in Christ consciousness. Any wall of partition that would lay claim to a greater position between men and women is utterly demolished in Christ consciousness leaving no excuse for this kind of treatment.

Those who continue to hold to a patriarchal view of women within the marriage covenant are still stuck in the Jewish muck of tradition and unhealthy prejudice, and are not possessors of the equality exemplified by the life and spiritual teachings of the anointed one. The role of man and woman before the so-called awakening to full consciousness (good and evil) in the Garden myth is full-unadulterated equality.

It's only after full consciousness and the resulting choices that followed that women are "subject" to a man's ideas or authority in Judaism and Torah thought (Genesis was most likely written during the 6th century BCE during the Babylonian captivity).

Consider the scriptural descriptions of St. Paul in his Corinthian letter:

> "But I want you to understand that Christ is the head

> of every man, and the man is the head of a woman, and God is the head of Christ." –1 Cor. 11:3

These ideas although Jewish in root have an explanation far greater than simply being in charge. In the Jewish and Christian culture when the Bible was written, there was a concept called "Federal Headship" (Christian Apologetics & Research Ministry).

This means that the male is the one who represents his descendants and not the female. Proof of this can be found in the seventh chapter of a Hebrew letter found in the New Testament of the Bible:

> "And in this case mortal men receive tithes, but in that case one receives them, of whom it is witnessed that he lives on. And, so to speak, through Abraham even Levi, who received tithes, paid tithes, for he was still *in the loins* of his father when Melchizedeck met him." –Hebrews 7:8-10

According to Jewish thought, Levi paid law tithes while still in the loins of his father Abraham as a descendant of Abraham. How could this happen? By substitution. Since Abraham, his distant "father" through the ancestral bloodline represented him—he becomes the same as him. This is what the Jews believed.

We also see the concept of Hebrew Federal Headship in the garden-awakening myth. It was Eve who first awakened, but according to the Pauline scriptures the poor choices that followed entered the world through Adam and not through Eve. Romans five says:

> "Therefore, just as through one *man* sin entered into the world, and death through sin, and so death spread to all mankind, because all sinned." –Rom. 5:12

This is because Adam was representative of all humanity together. When Adam failed to choose wisely, Jewish teaching believes all people (both men and women) failed with him because we were in his loins (ancestral bloodline) just as Levi was in the loins of his father Abraham. This is why it says, "in Adam all die" in 1 Cor. 15:22 according to Judean theology.

Also, Romans 5:15 says:

> "For if by the transgression of the one [Adam] the many died, much more did the grace of God and the gift by the grace of the one Man, Jesus Christ, abound to the many."

And in Acts 17:26-28:

> "And hath made of *one blood* all nations of men for to dwell on all the face of the earth, and hath determined the times before appointed, and the bounds of their habitation; that they should seek the Lord, if haply they might feel after him, and find him, though he be not far from every one of us: for in him we live, and move, and have our being; as certain also of your own poets have said, for we are also his *offspring.*"

Now concerning woman, notice what it says in the Genesis narrative:

> "For this cause a man shall leave his father and his mother, and shall cleave to his wife; and they shall become one flesh."

Sacred Sequence

When a man and woman enter the Hebrew blood-covenant of marriage, they become one flesh according to their tradition. There is a unity between them. But, it is the man who is the head of the family representationally in Hebrew culture, which is why it says that the man is the head of the woman in the Corinthian letter. This has nothing to do with being the boss and everything to do with what the Hebrews believed to be the *created order* of things.

You may think that this was cultural, but Paul makes it clear in his beliefs that the headship idea is related directly to the created order and not rank of importance:

> "For man did not come from woman, but woman from

> man; neither was man created for woman, but woman for man. For this reason, and because of the angels (God only knows what this means), the woman ought to have a sign of authority on her head."–1 Corinthians 11:8-10

According to the Hebrews, there is order in all things. All headship represents is the order of a created sequence; one comes before two, three before four, and not the other way around. God is the head of Christ because Christ is the Son and not the Father according to later Trinitarian thought and theology that emerges in the fourth century AD.

When Eve allegedly disobeyed in the Genesis account, God never went to Eve to discuss it; he is pictured addressing Adam because Adam was trained first and should have known better. Likewise if your department goes sideways at work, the blame usually rests with the department *head* and not the subordinates; everyone understands this even if the subordinates are much smarter than the leader. It's all about position and the order of things, not more, better, more important, or more substantial.

The psychology of the verticality ethic suggests that first is better or that first is higher, but this is based upon the psychology of body design. The brain is higher than the feet thus the brain is better than the feet. This psychology encompasses everything people create including after-death theology, which has heaven as higher and hell as lower or in the earth below.

Conclusion: Jesus is clear that all people are to be treated with equal action and we should not be a respecter of persons above another. Claiming that there is "clergy" and "laity" is just as ignorant as claiming men to be better than women. In Christ consciousness, we are all on the same playing field although our job descriptions and degrees of responsibility may vary.

Thought Invader: Jesus was a destroyer of prejudice, prowess, and pride.

All in all, the mistreatment of anyone is more a sign of insecurity driven by the shadow-self as opposed to a teaching of Jesus. What about us? What do we regret doing? What have we done to others in reference to many of these ideas? It can all be changed.

If you're like me I'm going to assume you have done plenty of things you regret. I was what I was, but now, I am what I am. Like you, I am worth the entire world and my authentic-self is safe, which allows admittance to failure or missing the mark in our attempt at being acceptable to the gods.

The spirit of Jesus' message of love and acceptance still permeates this world, sitting at the well of everyone's life. It converses with us in full knowledge of our past dealing with people and simply asks if we would like a drink from the water of life.

Water represents refreshing and cleansing especially when the story unfolds in the heart of the desert. Many of our pasts are a desert wasteland of regret. But Jesus offered more than water; he offered the Samaritan woman the water of life—*living water.*

The spirit of Jesus turns Dead Seas into Jordan Rivers. When we suffer from our past decisions, we *thirst* for something more. We thirst to be refreshed—changed or authenticated. But our minds and thoughts (our soul-self) disallow it.

> "Come, all you who are thirsty, come to the waters; and you who have no money, come, buy and eat! Come, buy wine and milk without money and without cost." – Isaiah 55:1

When we drink of the *living water* offered by Jesus' authentic-self we never thirst again. We live in *constant content*—in Christ Consciousness. Only when your past is allowed to be swallowed up by the present reality of the safe-self is there hope for what is ahead.

Only then does your past cease to define you. Only then can we dare to believe in our new definition of self as defined by God's spirit within us.

Ever-presence

Living in the present moment is what Jesus tried to convey. When asked who was sending them to the officials, Jesus answered, "*Tell them I Am sent you.*" This was how Jesus saw himself—pastless. "Take no thought for your life," he said. "What you shall eat, drink, or put on." In Christ Consciousness, we live fearless lives filled with hope and anticipation without regret.

Jesus lived in the present moment every moment. He did not see himself as "I was" or "I will be," but rather "*I am.*" Remember, focusing on the past only brings guilt, shame, and regret. Focusing on the future with your past in tow creates feelings of fear and anxiety of repeating it. We must focus on who we are right now in this moment as redefined by the same spirit.

God loves people as they are, not as they should be. While sitting at the well of our own lives we can now embrace our past as part of our story and anticipate a hopeful future based upon the *NEW* definition of our true selves by the spirit of Jesus who says we are loved and cherished as people.

When we see ourselves through the eyes of God, we live better lives. And when we see others as through the eyes of God—through our authentic-self, we treat them better.

18

Our Preoccupation with Shadows

Is there an experience with God that transcends religion and religious experience? People seem to have a God vacuum; they develop concepts (mostly tradition based) outside of personal reality and natural experience all over this world whether Orthodox Jew, Muslim, Catholic Christian, Hindu, Protestants, etc. Billions of people do this because it's part of the human makeup.

Although this is not proof of a god, it certainly proves people need to do it. Appeasing an angry God or trying to please a difficult God is a unanimous fundamental mindset across all religions around the world, and there's no shortage of ancient texts within all religions to support this phenomenon.

There's also no short supply of people who are entangled in adultery, fornication, hypocrisy, marital dysfunction, substance abuse (both legal and illegal), sins of omission, family dysfunction, divorce, incest, pride, religion, unhappiness, etc., within these religious communities across the boards—including the modern Christian church.

Everything breakable has been and *is being* broken. Of course the more rules people make, the more rules people break. But this has reached an epidemic level—towards unsustainability. Listening to pastors and ministers talking about themselves and their congregations including the difficulties in maneuvering all these dysfunctional ties is heart stopping.

Could it be that human beings are just being human beings as they have been for millennia? Are ministers fighting against the tide of the sea of "normal-sea" when proclaiming God requires holiness and a life free from sin? We can all look closely at our own families and see this trend that is, and has always been, taking place within the sea of humanity.

The guilt, the shame, the sham, the hypocrisy (this means acting or role playing) is overwhelming within modern Christian communities, and there is no sign of it ever stopping, especially if we look into the past. This has been this way all throughout history—it appears to be unstoppable.

As far back as history goes, there are rules made by leaders of people (the Moses story comes to mind), and then there are the people lining up to break them in droves. In the story of Moses, he is allegedly receiving laws by the finger of God out of the sky on a mountain while hordes of people within his community are engaged in all kinds of debauchery while he communes with the deity. A typical scenario encompassing human nature at its finest.

Have We Created This Conundrum Ourselves?

When I was in a seminary they called this phenomenon "*the avalanche of sin.*" My professors described how this behavior cycles throughout history with all peoples. As one who lives in constant observation, I'm beginning to wonder if we created this avalanche ourselves. I call it the "*wet paint*" conundrum. As soon as we place a wet paint sign on a newly painted fence, people are auto-possessed to touch it by *nature*.

But it goes much deeper than this. We are curious creatures of habit. We have inquiring minds and complex emotions that we have been trying to curb since the beginning of time. We have been trying desperately to not be human. We are dualistic beings capable of both the profound and the profane—both heroism and the horrific. This dilemma has been the subject of relentless pursuits since the beginning of time.

As far back as Ancient Sumer, Acadia, Egypt, and many others thousands of years ago, we have been creating incantations, formulas, rules, laws, blood sacrifices, and the like in order to please the angry deity bent on destroying us for our natural albeit darker shadow-driven behaviors. After all, God is said to have already wiped out the earth and everyone on it once.

And there are countless modern-day believers who believe he must do it again with fire and brimstone from the sky, and sadly, many can't wait. I saw a bumper sticker a few years ago that read, "*Jesus is coming back and boy is he pissed.*" This is unfortunate for all of us as perfection is not a part of being human. We have solved this dilemma though—one only has to *believe*. That was easy.

Mantras

A well-known incantation or mantra used by Joel Osteen every week with his tens of thousands of worshipers chanting it along with him is a great example of how we continue to program our brains against its humanness:

> "This is my Bible. I am what it says I am, I have what it says I have, I can do what it says I can do. Today, I will be taught with the Word of God. I boldly confess; my mind is alert. My heart is receptive; I will never be the same.
>
> I am about to receive the incorruptible, indestructible, ever-living seed of the Word of God. I will never be the same, never, never, never; I will never be the same, in Jesus' name. –Amen"

This mantra is great if you're a Christian as you tell yourself every week that you are no longer a human being seeing that you made peace with your shadow-self. We know this because among the thousands who either show up or tune in every week are still human beings with problems and challenges that sentences will not cure.

The rate of divorce, drug abuse, and every other statistic is the same within the social group he addresses every week. I appreciate Joel and believe he is doing a wonderful job, but this is typical of us humans trying to align ourselves with what we "*believe*" God wants us to be in order to be received and liked by him.

But unfortunately, we create for ourselves expectations that fall outside of the human blueprint. And the avalanche of evil continues in spite of our mantras. This comes down to one interesting scenario—the Jesus phenomenon.

According to Christian thought, Jesus was sent to earth to protect the human race against the rage of his father because of the dark side within us known by many as *sin*. He is supposed to be the "mediator" between God and mankind—the buffer to keep us all still breathing, seeing we are so off-putting.

The Mighty Terrible God

Another mantra I have heard in the last ten years frequently is the "*God is good all the time*" mantra. A leader will say this to a corporate audience, and they will in unison reply "*And all the time, God is good*" in response. This is known as *behavioral stamping*. If we say something long enough in repetitive sequence it becomes real to us as a social group.

This keeps our minds focused on how *good* God is regardless of all the creepy stories about his fury unleashed throughout the Bible. After all, it's the Hebrew God that invented genocide, and it is the people of God who were the first ISIS when they pillaged and utterly destroyed every man woman and child in the ancient city of Jericho.

This enigmatic phenomenon also takes place in the New Testament when the Holy Spirit murders Ananias and Sephira for telling a lie. When the Holy Spirit executes a young couple in the Bible because they lied to an apostle about the sale of some land, it's a scary thing. Repeating "*God is good*" week in and week out can be a very therapeutic exercise in light of these stories.

For this reason, the modern concept of being a "God fearing" man or woman has an automatic expectation attributed to it. Anyone who claims to be God fearing traditionally will be expected to act in a particular way. Being in terror of God's wrath, they will be less apt to steal, kill, hate, or commit any other moral infraction that would negatively affect another person.

I was taught in the seminary that to fear God was "*the wholesome dread of displeasing our father*," but this may not be entirely accurate. Even Jesus was said to have said to the Jews, "Don't fear man who can kill the body, but fear him who can toss both body and soul into hell!" Now that's a terrifying statement. It's interesting to note that the Jews didn't even believe in a hell. This statement comes into perspective when read in context.

Tornados, floods, hurricanes, and other natural disasters are routinely attributed to the "angry God" who hates homosexual sin, Liberal agendas, and the like. Ministers such as Pat Robertson and others claim God's vengeance on America when these horrible effects take place within nature globally. This all ties into the need to appease the angry God scenario we have created over millennia.

We pray that storms will not come against us and pray them in another direction only to kill other innocents on the other side of town—bummer. This fascination with our shadows has been the main cause for this type of hysteria.

The Old Testament is rife with these terrorizing terms such as in Deuteronomy chapter 10 where God is called "terrible." Newer translations say awesome, but the word comes from awful, to be feared or to be in awe of. The scriptures claim that *scarcely* will any righteous enter therein, so where does this leave the *ungodly* and the *sinner*? Creepy stuff.

Fear is an excellent motivator, which is why hell and the devil are exceptional motivators. When the writers of these texts saw God as one who deals in rewards and punishments, it's no wonder they feared him. A preoccupation with the shadows in all of us perpetuates a wounded-self.

All these Judeo-Christian influences have had a big impact on our society as a whole. From famous sermons like "Sinners in the hands of an angry God" to modern hell-messages, all have had virtually *no* impact on society at all—we're still human and we still wrestle with that which we don't want to admit we think of doing.

Are we getting this right? Moreover, many today will never mention hell in a message (Like Joel Osteen) as they have witnessed the zero impact this has on human behavior. Most modern entrepreneurial preachers today simply motivate and teach people how to get ahead in regards to life, people, and personal and business finances seeing that the hell idea is out of date for most Americans and fails to curb our behavior.

The reason for the decline in hell and terror preaching is because it doesn't work emotionally or behaviorally. People give up too easily when they feel incapable of pleasing such a beast. This is why only 20% give more than 5% of their money to the church.

When 10% becomes some spiritual requirement, if folks can't

come up with the loot, they tend to not give anything at all for fear of being what the Revelation[1] calls *lukewarm*.

Behaviorally, people will tend to give *nothing* if they can't give *everything* they believe they are *supposed* to give. This fits nicely when they believe God requires they be either hot or cold according to the John the Revelator's idea of the divine.

They figure: why try? Ministers are figuring this out and are moving away from the terrorism of the Bible and are now focusing in on God's good side, love, mercy, relationships, financial freedom, and the like. But even this is no match for human behavior it seems.

Is there an answer to this human *sin* dilemma? Well sure, but religion won't buy it. If we leave the idea of reward and punishment, people will run wild in the streets right? I don't understand why we *must* make it our business what anyone does. Is it true that without God people are brute beasts?

It's interesting that many brute beasts tend to be *with* God, but *under construction* as they see it. The fact is this: human beings make great and terrible mistakes, and spirituality doesn't fix it—it apparently allows it.

Getting the Hell Out

The sin dilemma is what keeps the seats filled, at least it did up until about twenty or thirty years ago. People feared going to hell, so they went to church to appease the God who kills the unholy. This was my experience in the 1970s.

I became a Christian several times per week for years for fear of Jesus coming through the clouds with a big sword and hacking me to death as the prophet Samuel did to King Agag—"*and Samuel hacked Agag into pieces before the Lord in Gilgal.*"[2]

We would have what was called "watch night" services on New Years—we would sing songs through the night in fear with tears waiting for Christ to return and remove us from this trash heap. As a child this worked against me, as I never believed I was

1 "So, because you are lukewarm--neither hot nor cold--I am about to spit you out of my mouth." Revelation 3:16

2) 1 Samuel 15:33.

a good enough person.

This unhealthy focus on our inability has killed us. Much of what religion focuses on is who we are not, not who we are. Healthy people do not have a need for the devil. Only those focused on their failures and the shadows within need a devil to blame it on.

Nowadays we hear the promise of financial freedom, relationship health, body health, and business development. We have Christian health workshops, exercise class, yoga, debt-free classes, and the like. It's a new day! Notice how things have changed! I don't have *all* the answers; I hardly have some, but I am closely watching these trends as the culture moves forward into our future and our minds continue to evolve.

I remain skeptical that these cultural and religious antics will produce better living people. For sure it creates greater awareness, but this simply sends people back to the confessional, shaking in their boots. We are what we are, and as long as there are self-appointed people who set themselves up as masters of the roadmap to spiritual freedom, there will be masses of people in line to do whatever it takes to be welcomed on board.

My hope is that we will all believe we are loved and appreciated by God for what we are and not what we should be. Free yourself from the Eros prison of religion and focus your attention on the good in you. Does this mean we never endeavor to become better when we realize we fall short? Absolutely not. It means we don't make changes because we're scared to death of what will happen if we don't.

19

Living Without Wax

The history of the phrase "without wax" is an interesting one. "Without wax" stems from two Latin words; *sin* (without) and *ceras* (wax) and was often said to be the origin of the English word *sincerity*. The story went something like this. The phrase first became widespread during the height of Roman and Greek artistry when sculpture first became a popular artistic medium.

When a sculpture had a defect, artists would fill in the whittle mark with colored wax to match the marble or stone so the deformity would go unnoticed—genius.

Wax was said to serve as a cover-up, masking these imperfections on what was most likely substandard pottery. An arguably perfect or superior piece of work was therefore "*without wax*" because it was void of the need to cover its imperfections—it was considered already perfect regardless of its actual *perceived* perfection. Pottery and sculptures were even said to be stamped with the phrase "without wax" (sin ceras) as proof of authenticity much like signing a letter with the word *sincerely* today.

This is how we should live—without wax—without trying to make ourselves appear different from what we actually are. Many are tempted to appear unauthentic for fear of the opinion of others, similar to a counterfeit sculpture. Super heroes are not those who have super powers, but rather they are those who have recovered their own power to be real—authentic, and without pretense. This is courage.

Sincerity is living when we live out of the authentic-self with all our flaws in full view. Modern artisans are now taking advantage of flawed pottery by filling its cracks with gold glaze [Fig. 1]. This makes each piece unique and authentic bringing joy to thousands who enjoy their flawed beauty. Living this way is paramount for relationship building and continuance. Masking our true selves in an effort to gain the love and respect of others is a faulty self.

Unfortunately words like honor, honesty, integrity, and truth no longer represent the realities of the larger part of our current culture as many are involved in life-scale cover-ups.

Figure 1. Cracked clay bowl with gold glaze.

My invitation to you is this: free yourself from the Eros prison of performance! Allow yourself to breathe the free air of authentic living. This is the open life! This is the life of freedom and contentment we all desire but many fail to fully realize.

Seven Steps to Freedom

Step one: Accept vulnerability. Imagine being free to be yourself without the masks of pretense and perceived perfection. This is vulnerability and it begins with being faithful to the self—truthful with yourself. When we are honest with ourselves being truthful with others follows. Being truthful is easy. It's when we say how we feel without fear of not being liked or feeling like we failed. Personal truthfulness is a win for everyone.

Jesus said, "He who has bathed needs only to wash his feet, but is *completely* clean; and you are clean, but not all of you." When we are honest with ourselves we are clean. To live out of our authentic selves is to be bathed—naked and unashamed. Many live cloaked lives—cloaked in religious clothing or performance-driven behaviors that do not reflect the authentic-self.

Step two: Be real. Like Margery's velveteen rabbit, we must seek those who have spent years in the nursery being content with who they are, rather than spending our energy trying to live up to false ideals and posers who want to frame our world to fit their own distorted ideas about who we are or should be. Being real is authentic and flawed.

"Generally, by the time you are Real, most of your hair has been loved off, and your eyes drop out and you get loose in the joints and very shabby. But these things don't matter at all, because once you are Real you can't be ugly, except to people who don't understand."

Step three: Spend your time with those who *understand* not those who don't. Those who understand love you for who you are and not for what they want you to become. Like Zacchaeus we must spend time having dinner with Jesus and not the religious Pharisees.

Having dinner with Jesus means we spend our time with those we want to emulate not those who live to manipulate. Read about those who have discovered the freedom that comes from living authentically. Those who understand are those who will walk with you through your darkest hour.

Step four: Subdue your shadow-self. Your shadow-self is contrarian. It desires everything not healthy for your spirit and flesh-body. Learn to live out of your authentic-self and deny the voice that cries from inside the prison for performance and self-acceptance at the expense of your true-self.

Set your soul-mind on "things above" and not the things of the earth. The earthly things are competitive, performance-based and cliché- and clique-driven like religion and in-grouping. They exalt certain others as special and deny the ordinary.

Step five: Live in balance between your intuition and your intelligence. Master your heart moves. Heart moves are made through intuitive impulses that come from a more secure authentic-self. Over time your insights will be trusted. This doesn't mean you neglect intelligence; it means you balance your intelligence with your intuitive movements within the self.

Allow your intuition to take precedence without removing your intellectual authorities. Our intuitive self and our intelligent mind should be functionally obeyed when whatever one is warranted. Move between them with cautious optimism and balanced judgment.

Step six: Live for *inspiration* rather than *validation*. Validation creates a false sense of self whereas inspiration motivates the self. Act out of your inward inspired moments rather than waiting to be validated by some unrealistic external circumstance. Inspiration comes from within not from without.

Learn the difference between inspiration and motivation. When we live out of inspiration our destinies are received, but when we live out of motivation our destinies are achieved. This is why many are chasing their dreams and never catch them. Your dreams chase you. If we can slow down enough to allow them to catch up we will be able to receive them with open arms.

Step seven: Live in the present. Jesus lived in the present and so should we. He was "I Am." Who are you? Are you something that will develop later on in the future? Or are you precious right now? Live your life moment by moment, second by second.

Enjoy the present and ignore the past. Realize the past does not define you. It only helps design you. Design is not definition any more than our results are tied to recognition. Conflicts over immediate, long-term, and minor goals may lead to questioning the purpose of your design, which is why we must live within the moment and not in the future. Embrace the design that is and whatever will be will be.

This book has been a personal invitation. It's an invitation to free yourself from everything that once defined you. It's an invitation to attend your own funeral—the funeral of your own self-image. Accept the love of God and embrace your weakest self. Allow your perceptions to change and escape the Eros prison of performance, and live the life you were always meant to live.

20

What Do We Do Now?

We have come a long way since we started. And what have we learned? We have learned that we are simple people with complex lives and emotions. We have learned that living within the Eros prison produces competitive frameworks that play heavily on the fields of faith and religion. Faith and religion are more or less culprits when it comes to sustaining our exaggerated need to be loved and accepted.

We have learned that the Judeo-Christian model begins with "*all people* are fundamentally *broken*" and without following and embracing the fundamentals of Christianity including, but not limited to, a belief in a devil, a belief in hell, and a belief in a coming apocalypse, one will die and go to hell where they will endure a torturous and never-ending cruel death.

People feel worthless enough as it is. We feel helpless and unloved. We compete for affections and we criticize other people out of fear of not measuring up ourselves. We measure down and create lower standards easier to reach.

We create in-groups, out-groups, and loyalties in an effort to bolster our personal worth. We gain titles and positions of power to look more presentable to others while religion fosters the same attributes masked as "authority."

We associate more or less with similar styles and value streams. We perform in hopes of praise and strokes so we can keep going. We have realized that religion and faith no longer *cure* the ills of mankind, but rather promote it, only with a new face. Coming to faith for many is simply a change of scenery—every dysfunction remains the same while sporting a new suit. People don't change; they just look like it.

Within religious frameworks we typically blame the devil for everything wrong in our lives and we credit God when things turn out well. Few believe they made a great decision while others languish in the pain of failure—again.

We have become human-*doings* rather than human *beings*. Many capitalize on their strengths while despising their weakness—a prison favorite. Energies are only gotten so we can perform better at work, in church, or in the bedroom. We are insatiable need machines.

It's time to stop. It's time to get off this moving train and take a look around you. Where are you? Where did you expect to be at this moment in life? Are you there? Can we find ourselves amidst all the commotion? What are we to do?

I suggest you rethink some things—important things you may have formally felt unchangeable or off limits. What do you believe? Why do you believe it? And is it contributing to or is it taking from your life? It takes courage to be free. Remember, courage is not the absence of fear, but rather the absence of the ego-self.

When I was a child, there was a commercial on television that promoted Eggo Waffles. They used to say: let go my Eggo (*leh-go ma-eggo*). It's what we must do. Let go of our egos. Self-importance and all the rest of it: performance initiatives designed to get God to like us or those in our social circle.

Embrace yourself—your authentic-self. Reject the voice of the shadow-self within you and the manipulating attitudes of your soul-mind in need of over-importance or to fit in.

We must seek the wisdom of the skin horse and remember the velveteen rabbit's story of courage and vulnerability. We must make a decision that lasts a lifetime, but the decision has to be yours and *for* you. Decision-making will open some doors and close others. Part of moving into your destiny will come from making important and *hard* decisions.

Decisions create finality where uncertainty once ruled. James the brother of Jesus said, "Do not waver, for a person with divided loyalty is as unsettled as a wave of the sea that is blown and tossed by the wind." This is why many live unsettled lives—they can't decide what to do or they fear others who will respond to their decisions poorly.

Forces outside of themselves determine their outcomes. Like

the waves driven by the moon or the wind, their destinies lay in the hands of some unknown fate, force, or foe. Their doors are like unmarked graves.

Those who live out of their authentic selves take responsibility for their decisions as well as the assignment that creates them. Decision finality is the vehicle that moves them forward. When one situation receives the stamp of finality, it opens the door of opportunity for another, and so on.

The Hebrews would have never entered Canaan if they first hadn't closed the door on Egypt. Simply put, decision-making is the act of closing doors so others may open, more than it's about opening doors so others may close.

Many people leave doors open. They have a fall back plan in case things don't go quite as well as they expect. And because of this they remain indecisive—without finality. They will never move forward. Instead of seizing opportunity, they spend all their time sizing it up. Eighty-five percent of mainline churchgoers are either in serious deterioration or in a coma because they cannot let go of what isn't working.

We need an effective strategy for entering into our destinies. It's going to take risk and opportunity hunting in order to pull it off. We can't hang back yearning for the status quo or hunker in the bunker of fear and insecurity. We must hack a path. Like King David, we must trust in our instincts and act on our impulses. Only the brazen drop giants. We need a fundamental reinvention of what we have been calling "God."

We need more people who kick in the front door with a shotgun and less who sneak in the back window with a jackknife, when it comes to changing the way we do things. Our times demand it. Can you be that person?

Revolutionizing our Thinking

If we are to escape the Eros prison, we must be revolutionary. Radically innovative—outside the parameters of long-established norms. We must understand that the purposes for which we were created never change even though the assignments leading up to them always do—we cannot be deterred from the path full of opposition.

Daniel Pink says most people want autonomy, mastery, and purpose, but few ever find these ingredients without fighting for them. Revolutionaries like to be given the freedom to do their own thing, on their own terms without self-appointed hierarchies to dictate the modes operandi.

I saw a great movie once called *The Emperor's Club* starring Kevin Kline as Mr. William Hundert. He was a schoolteacher at an all-boys' school for smart affluent kids. At the beginning of the year when the kids came into the classroom for the first time, he would choose one of them to read a plaque above the door. This is what it said:

> "I am Shutruk Nahunte, King of Anshand and Sussa, Sovereign of the land of Elam. I destroyed Sippar, took the stele of Niran-Sin, and brought it back to Elam, where I erected it as an offering to my god." –Shutruk Nahunte, 1158 B.C.

According to Mr. Hundert's life lesson, this is a direct quote from a virtually unknown king who speaks of his conquests, but speaks nothing about the benefits of them. He is unknown in history because according to Hundert "great ambition and conquest without contribution is *without* significance."

He wasn't a revolutionary because he didn't make any significant change to history. He didn't contribute. Part of living the revolutionary life is contributing to it.

Many are just consumers—takers, void of bringing new things to bear or making any lasting difference to another person's life. Like Shutruk Nahunte, they destroy and take things without leaving anything better or of real consequence behind. They compete and claw for significance at the expense of everything around them.

I love the word, contribution. It comes from the word tributary—when a stream or a river flows into another river. Like when Jesus stood up during a feast and cried with a loud voice, "Out of your belly will flow streams of *living* water . . ."[1] Jesus was speaking of being a contributor to society rather than one who sucks up all its resources for themselves or one who competes with it. He was

---

1) John 7:38-39

talking about being a giver instead of being a taker.

Acting like the river pictured in the peculiar book of Ezekiel in the Old Testament of the Bible is the trait of a revolutionary. In chapter 47, there's a river flowing out of a temple. It flows all the way to the Dead Sea. And when it gets there it makes "everything alive." It's a revolutionary river because it makes a dramatic change to everything it touches.

What do you come in contact with every day? Is it changed because you touched it, or is it worse off than before you arrived because you viewed it from within the prison of performance?

There are two kingdoms at work in the cosmos. Like in the movie Star Wars—the kingdom of freedom and the kingdom of prison. And you are living in one or the other because there are only two. It takes real innovation in order to help people navigate the journey between these two places. People are trying to transition their way out of the Eros prison of performance, but most don't know how or have lost the address.

Many are just making transactions instead of transitions. They make an exchange, but they don't go anywhere. Our job as a revolutionary is to help people get from there to here as simply and beautifully as possible. It takes free people to free people.

People in prison cannot let other people out of prison. Go ahead, step outside of yourself. Free yourself because nobody else is going to do it for you. Becoming free is like becoming real. It takes time, but you must begin somewhere. I imagine the talk of freedom between the skin horse and the rabbit would look something like this:

"It doesn't happen all at once," said the Skin Horse. "You become. It takes a long time, but patience sustains it. That's why it doesn't happen often to people who break easily, or have sharp edges, or who fear displeasing the gods or those who guard them.

"Generally, by the time you are Real, most of your relationships have changed, and those you once competed with are no longer around. But these things don't matter at all, because once you are Real you can't be bad, except to people who don't understand."

"I suppose you are real?" said the Rabbit. And then he wished he had not said it, for he thought the Skin Horse might be sensitive. But the Skin Horse only smiled.

About Steven Sisler

Steve is a behavioral profiler and lead Behavioral Analyst at The Behavioral Resource Group. His behavioral consultation involves personality difference, leadership strategy, cultural difference, spiritual growth, and temperament strategy.

Working with clients in more than 18 nations, Steve gathers behavioral and attitudinal information on individuals within corporate and personal settings and develops strategies for effective leadership, teamwork, and entrepreneurial success.

Steve's clients have come to know him as their "go to" source for behavioral and attitudinal issues within the framework of business, family, and career intentions. His work is unconventional, his approach is practical, and his outcomes are unbelievable while he remains somewhat fashionable.

Steve has shared the platform with top speakers such as Guy Kawasaki, Kimbal Musk, Steve Sims, Dan Martel, Ben Greenfield, and David Asprey.

Steve makes normative judgments and brings thought provoking insights to the three ethical platforms within our society. The Community Ethic, The Autonomy Ethic, and The Divinity Ethic all have strong implications when challenged with ideological frameworks outside of those accepted within larger people groups.

Steve has lectured at The Vineyard Leadership Institute; Mastermind Talks, Toronto, Canada; The EMP Group at M.I.T. Boston; EOs Global Leadership Conference in Athens, Greece; EO Sydney, Perth, Adelaid, Melbourne, Brisbane, Australia; EO Auckland, New Zealand; and Hero Switzerland, as well as a myriad of dot COMs throughout the United States and the world at large.

Steve lectures on subjects such as Communication, The Emotional Framework, The Power of Imperfection, Post-Modern Influence, Attitudes & Values, Spiritual Difference, Leadership & Self-Understanding, Behavioral Language, Personality Difference, and the Maven Way of Management.

You may connect with Steve using: stevesisler.org

Made in the USA
San Bernardino, CA
21 March 2015